homemade soda

homemade
soda

Andrew Schloss

Storey Publishing

The mission of Storey Publishing is to serve our customers by
publishing practical information that encourages
personal independence in harmony with the environment.

Edited by Margaret Sutherland and Shauna Toh
Art direction and book design by Alethea Morrison
Text production by Jennifer Jepson Smith

Photography by © Aran Goyoaga, except for © George Marks/Getty Images, page 3
Photo styling by Aran Goyoaga
Illustrations by Alison Kolesar

Indexed by Christine R. Lindemer, Boston Road Communications

Storey Publishing
210 MASS MoCA Way
North Adams, MA 01247
www.storey.com

Printed in China by Toppan Leefung Printing Ltd.
10 9 8 7 6 5 4 3 2 1

LIBRARY OF CONGRESS CATALOGING-IN-PUBLICATION DATA

Schloss, Andrew, 1951–
  Homemade soda / by Andrew Schloss.
      p. cm.
  Includes index.
  ISBN 978-1-60342-796-8 (pbk. : alk. paper)
  1. Carbonated beverages. 2. Cookbooks. I. Title.
TP630.S35 2011
641.8'75—dc22
                              2010051171

contents

acknowledgments

Building a book is a huge project and though authors get most of the credit, it would be delusional to think that the name on the cover is solely responsible.

Two years ago my agent, Lisa Ekus, called to ask if I would be interested in writing a book on homemade sodas. Hesitant at first (the subject originally seemed esoteric to me), I began researching fermentation (amazing subject), bottling (in my kitchen?), and the history of fizz. The seduction didn't take long and, working with Margaret Sutherland, Storey's cookbook acquisitions editor, we quickly began to grasp exactly what a comprehensive, user-friendly book on an "esoteric" subject might look like. Then the real work began — a year of experimenting, concocting, writing, tasting, and cleaning up exploded soda bottles.

Since then I have tasted terrible swills and beautiful, subtle herbal blends. I learned how to nurse a speck of yeast into a bottle of silky bubbles and I was exposed to a score of new ingredients and flavors. But when the hubbub subsided and the pages were all filled I wondered, as I often do, "Do I really have a book here?" Fortunately for me, Storey hired a brilliant, hardworking and easy-to-work-with project editor, Shauna Toh, who along with Nancy Ringer, the copy editor, helped organize the jumble I sent them into something that reads very much like a comprehensive text.

Meanwhile Alethea Morrison, the creative director at Storey, was taking the same manuscript and transforming it into beautiful pages. It wasn't until I saw her work that I knew we had something. What a wonderful surprise the day the first pages arrived!

Lastly an acknowledgment of sacrifice: while writing this book our kitchen was transformed into a carbonation laboratory, as bottle sanitizing took precedence over counter space, so I give an apology to my wife, Karen Shain Schloss, for taking over her life with countless concoctions that burp, fizz, and go pop in the night.

to my dad,
a real soda jerk

Introduction

SWEET, COLD & BUBBLING

✦✦✦✦✦✦✦✦✦✦✦✦✦✦✦✦✦✦✦✦✦✦✦✦✦✦✦✦✦✦✦✦✦✦

Next to oxygen, we need nothing more than we need drink. Plain water is the perfect thirst quencher, yet we have been seeking ways to improve its palatability since the first human took her first sip. Thirst must be fulfilled to sustain life, but once we have satisfied our essential needs, our sensual desire for flavor, color, and invigoration takes over, spurring us to transform plain water into more elaborate beverages whenever we get the chance.

✦✦✦✦✦✦✦✦✦✦✦✦✦✦✦✦✦✦✦✦✦✦✦✦✦✦✦✦✦✦✦✦✦✦

Soda pops are incredibly diverse, but three threads connect all of them: they are all sweet, they are all consumed cold, and they are all carbonated. And now we live in a culture where thirst-quenching has become big business. Sodas, beers, juices, coffees, teas, flavored waters, energy drinks, and sports beverages compete for our potable dollars. But you can stir up homemade sodas that match any of them with better nutrition, with less sugar, and for a fraction of the cost. It can be as simple as mixing a flavorful base into still or sparkling water in your own kitchen.

Sips from the Past

We have no record of the very first human-enhanced beverages, but they were most likely herbal teas or other infusions brewed for medicinal effect, such as the tea North American natives boiled from the roots of sarsaparilla to take as a cough remedy. Historically, people have tended to prefer their beverages hot or cold rather than tepid, a preference that we must presume lies deep in the collective unconscious. Fresh water is naturally susceptible to microbial infestation, and lukewarm water is a natural breeding ground for bacteria, viruses, and parasites. Humans must have learned early on that boiling water made it safe to drink, but what about cold drinks? Chilling does not make contaminated water safer to drink, but naturally cold flowing water is far less likely to contain a harmful amount of contaminants than lukewarm standing water, which is probably why cold running water, particularly bubbling icy cold water, suggests the very essence of purity and refreshment.

The most primal source of bubbly drinks would have been naturally carbonated waters from underground mineral springs. Ancient civilizations believed that bathing in these geologically effervescent waters had healthful and medicinal value, and over the centuries, "taking the cure" at mineral spring baths became a standard health regimen. Starting in the late 1700s, drinking naturally sparkling mineral water was prescribed for its therapeutic benefit, and by 1810, a method for mass producing "soda water"— made by mixing still water with sodium bicarbonate and acid to create carbon dioxide bubbles, in imitation of naturally sparkling mineral water — had been given a U.S. patent. Soda fountains producing flavored carbonated waters became commonplace in pharmacies during the nineteenth century, dispensing bubbling remedies for the cure of headaches, hangovers, and nervous afflictions.

However, since geologically carbonated water is relatively rare and the mechanical soda carbonation process came on the scene late in the game, early imbibers experienced effervescence most often as a by-product of fermentation. Fermentation occurs naturally when wild yeasts (microorganisms floating freely in the air) find a source of sugar on which to feed. Given enough food and water, yeasts digest sugar and produce alcohol and carbon dioxide, resulting in a sparkling beverage.

Since yeasts are everywhere, the first effervescent beverages probably developed accidentally. Fresh sweet fruit juices can ferment readily upon a short exposure to air. Fresh apple cider, for example, ferments so quickly that before the advent of pasteurization and refrigeration its transformation to hard cider was just a matter of hours. When early American colonists spoke of "cider," then, they were referring to an effervescent alcoholic beverage. (Its alcoholic content was mostly a non-issue, however. Before the proliferation of the temperance movement in the late nineteenth and early twentieth centuries, few distinctions were drawn between non-alcoholic and mildly alcoholic beverages.)

Because most of the sugar in a fermented juice is consumed by the yeast, brewers commonly added honey or date syrup after fermentation to replenish sweetness, creating an association between sweetness and thirst-quenching that remains today. In the nineteenth century an explosion in the availability of sugar transformed medicinal soda water into dozens of sweetened root- and bark-based soft drinks, including root beer, birch beer, and ginger ale.

Making Bubbles
Methods of Effervescence

Why carbonate drinks? No one has yet proven that carbonation has health benefits, but one contemporary theory looks toward the sensation of carbonation itself for a euphoric effect. We don't experience carbonation as bubbles. Bubbles bounce. They swell and yield, and when they burst they explode with a whisper. But carbonation feels more like a rapid succession of irritating pinpricks in the mouth. It's slightly painful but also invigorating. The same can be said of eating chile peppers, which has been shown to release pain-relieving endorphins into the blood, resulting in an afterglow of well-being and pleasure. Does drinking a carbonated beverage produce the same effect? It could explain why we experience carbonated beverages as more refreshing than still ones.

There are three methods of carbonating liquid: geological carbonation, fermentation, and carbon dioxide infusion.

//////////////////////

Soft Drink Time Line

1772	1798	1807
Joseph Priestley publishes a method for artificially carbonating water.	The term *soda water* is used to sell natural sparkling water from "soda fountains," an early name for mineral springs.	Benjamin Silliman, a chemistry professor at Yale University, bottles and sells water carbonated with carbonic gas.

Geological Carbonation

Geological carbonation predates man-made methods by millions of millennia. Carbonated water occurs naturally in underground springs, when gases produced by microorganisms get trapped in stone-locked reservoirs of water. Because the underground water is held in contact with stone on all sides, it becomes infused with soluble minerals, which gives spring water most of its health benefits, and its nickname, "mineral water." In the United States, the FDA allows any water that is drawn from a geologically and physically protected underground water source and contains 250 parts per million of total dissolved solids (minerals) to be sold as mineral water, either still or sparkling.

The innate carbonation of naturally sparkling mineral water can be very subtle or obvious, depending on the amount of gas dissolved in the water. Carbon dioxide liquefies readily, but its solubility increases as water gets colder, which means that sparkling mineral water taken from warmer springs tends to be less effervescent, with larger, weaker bubbles, while water taken from colder springs can be wildly bubbly and sharper on the tongue.

Fermentation

People have been making wine, beer, mead, and other fermented beverages for more than five thousand years, but we didn't truly understand the process until the 1850s, when Louis Pasteur linked the conversion of sugar into alcohol to the life cycle of yeasts. Yeasts are a group of microscopic single-celled fungi so small that twenty thousand of them could fit in the space of this period. There are hundreds of different species, but humankind has latched on to one in particular, *Saccharomyces cerevisiae* ("brewer's sugar fungus"), that is useful for both baking and brewing. For most of history brewers and bakers maintained their particular yeast strains by saving a piece of dough from a batch of bread, or skimming the yeasty surface foam from a vat of brewing beer, to "start" the next batch, but now manufacturers cultivate special strains of yeasts for specific purposes. Although any yeast can be used for making soda, the one commonly used for fermenting champagne (*Saccharomyces bayanus*), sold as champagne or wine yeast, yields the cleanest-tasting (least "yeasty") fermented soft drinks. (See page 20 for more on choosing a yeast.)

1809	1810	1812	1819
Soda water is sweetened and flavored with gingerroot to make "ginger pop" (a.k.a. ginger beer, ginger champagne, or ginger ale).	The first U.S. patent is issued for the manufacture of imitation sparkling mineral waters (soda water).	British poet Robert Southey refers to a new word, *pop*, deriving from the sound made when a cork is drawn from a bottle of soda.	The first U.S. patent for a soda fountain is granted to Samuel Fahnestock.

Yeasts metabolize sugar for energy and produce alcohol and carbon dioxide gas in the process. Winemakers allow that carbon dioxide to escape, leaving behind the alcohol. Soda makers, however, trap the CO_2 gas and stop the fermentation before a significant amount of alcohol accumulates. The carbonation resulting from yeast has a silken and soft quality, with a network of bubbles so fine that they often take the form of foam rather than self-contained bubbles.

The concentration of alcohol in fermented beverages can range from a fraction of a percent to about 12 percent. At that point the level of alcohol will kill most yeast, so if you want a stronger alcoholic beverage you have to concentrate the alcohol content, usually through distillation. Typically wines are 5 to 12 percent alcohol, and beer is around 6 percent (although some ales are made to 9 percent). A highly distilled liquor like vodka is usually around 40 percent alcohol, though it can range up to 96 percent. In contrast, soft drinks' alcohol content is less than 0.5 percent.

Carbon Dioxide Infusion

Sources of naturally carbonated water are limited, and carbonating beverages through fermentation can yield inconsistent results. In 1772, Englishman Joseph Priestley published a pamphlet, *Directions for Impregnating Water with Fixed Air*, describing a process of infusing carbon dioxide into still water by dripping sulfuric acid onto chalk and capturing the resulting gases in a bowl of agitated water. Priestley erroneously proposed the process to Captain James Cook as a means of curing scurvy aboard ship for his second voyage to the South Seas. Priestley never exploited the commercial potential of his discovery, but others did. Ányos Jedlik, a Hungarian inventor, opened a bottled carbonated water factory in Europe in the 1830s and began selling carbonated water on a large scale. And about 25 years earlier, in 1807, Benjamin Silliman, a professor of chemistry at Yale University, carbonated water under pressure and started bottling and selling carbonated water locally in New Haven, Connecticut.

In commercial soda production, carbon dioxide is forced into filtered water at about 120 psi (pounds per square inch). This makes artificially carbonated water far more effervescent than water that is naturally carbonated through geologic happenstance or fermentation, and because the bubbles are under more

1824	1825	1829	1835
Patent issued for Ayer's Sarsaparilla (which was nothing more than a sweetened sarsaparilla beverage) as a blood-purifying medicine.	The first commercial soda fountain opens in a Philadelphia apothecary.	The soda siphon is invented in France by Deleuze and Dutillet, two Parisian jewelers. They name their invention the "siphon champenois."	The first bottled man-made soda water is sold in the United States.

pressure, they become wildly active upon release. Artificially carbonated liquids can be painful to consume directly upon being opened, which is why most of us have learned to wait a few seconds before downing a soft drink right out of the bottle. Transferring the soda into a glass releases a good percentage of the carbonation, making it easier to drink. Because carbon dioxide is more soluble at lower temperatures, icing sodas preserves their effervescence. (This is also why warm soda is more likely to bubble over when poured — more carbon dioxide is released from the liquid.)

Flavoring

When carbon dioxide is forced into water, a small amount of carbonic acid forms, giving carbonated water a brighter, cleaner flavor than that of still water. That slight acidity is one reason that mineral waters, which tend toward alkalinity, taste better when bubbly than when still.

The natural acidity of carbonated water is a benefit to flavored sodas. Like salt, acid sourness expands our sense of taste, which is why tart foods and beverages taste clean and fresh. Acids also have the ability to break down the molecular structure of other ingredients, thereby releasing flavor molecules into the nose and elevating the perception of all the aromatics in a beverage.

The various flavors of sodas come from brewed flavor bases. To make a flavor base, you simply simmer or steep aromatic ingredients in water, infusing the water with their flavor. Once the flavor base is fully infused, you sweeten it, dilute it to the desired strength with water, and carbonate it. Voilà! Soda. (See page 18 for more about flavoring ingredients.)

Sweeteners

Sweetness is a universally appealing flavor. Our first food, mother's milk, is sweet, and the taste of sweetness suggests to us a quick and easy source of energy. For most of human history, sugar from fruits and vegetables has offered an efficient way to get a lot of calories while expending minimal effort. Sugar dissolved in water is the most efficient form of energy, and it could be that some of the stimulation we feel from sodas is the promise of an energy boost.

I use a variety of liquid sweeteners in home soda making, including simple syrup, agave syrup, honey, and molasses. (See page 15 for more about sweeteners.)

1845	**1854**	**1855**	**1858**
Poland Spring Water begins to be bottled in Maine.	Vanilla-flavored cream soda is introduced.	Prohibition laws are adopted by Delaware, Indiana, Iowa, Michigan, New Hampshire, and New York.	J. Schweppes and Co. of London introduces tonic water as an improved quinine water.

High-Fructose Corn Syrup

ALTHOUGH SUCROSE (TABLE SUGAR) WAS THE MOST COMMON SWEETENER for the first soft drinks, high-fructose corn syrup took its place in most commercial soda production starting in the mid-1980s.

Sugar syrups are used to sweeten beverages because they do not readily form crystals. Although syrups can be made from almost any vegetable, the most common source in the United States is corn. Corn syrup is made by heating cornstarch with acid, which breaks the starch into simple sugars. Regular corn syrup is 14 percent glucose, 11 percent maltose, 20 percent water, and 55 percent starch, making corn syrup about 40 percent as sweet as sugar. In the 1960s, researchers discovered that adding an enzyme to corn syrup converted much of its glucose to fructose, which is much sweeter. The high-fructose corn syrup used most often in beverage fabrication is 55 percent fructose, making it about one and a half times sweeter than sugar. Because it is relatively inexpensive and supersweet, with a flavor similar to that of sugar, high-fructose corn syrup has become a popular cost-effective sweetener for many processed foods, and it has transformed the soft drink industry.

The industry's switch from sugar to high-fructose corn syrup was largely a matter of cost. In the United States massive subsidies for corn growing ($56 billion in the last decade) have kept the price of corn sweeteners low, and import tariffs have kept the price of cane sugar high. And though high-fructose corn syrup is frequently blamed for the epidemic of obesity in industrialized countries, it does *not* have more calories than regular table sugar. The association between high-fructose corn syrup and obesity may be a simple fact of overconsumption — we're eating a lot of sugar these days, and most of it tends to be high-fructose corn syrup.

Making sodas at home is an excellent way to reduce your consumption of high-fructose corn syrup, and to moderate your sugar intake in general: you brew only what you'll drink, and you can adjust the sweetness of the brew to your own taste.

1874
The first ice cream soda is sold at the semi-centennial celebration of the Franklin Institute in Philadelphia.

1876
Charles E. Hires introduces bottled herb tea in Philadelphia, made from various roots and herbs; by 1880 he changes the name to "root beer" and advertises it as the "National Temperance Drink." In the same year, Moxie soda, a soft drink made from gentian root, is introduced under the name Moxie Nerve Food in Lowell, Massachusetts.

1881
Imperial Inca Cola is made from extracts of kola nut and coca leaf.

continued on page 10

1916
Coca-Cola adopts its distinctive curvilinear bottle shape.

1915
Chemist Neil Callen Ward invents Orange Crush in Los Angeles.

1910
Coca-Cola is exported to England.

1907
Gas-powered trucks replace horse-drawn carriages as delivery vehicles for bottled Pepsi-Cola. Sales increase and the company opens forty bottling plants.

1902
Bradham founds the Pepsi-Cola Company. The trademark is registered the following year.

1904
Pepsi-Cola becomes a bottled beverage. ❖ Poland Spring is declared the best spring water at the Louisiana Purchase Exposition in St. Louis.

1905
Claude Hatcher opens Union Bottling Works in Columbus, Georgia to package Royal Crown Ginger Ale and other sodas he'd begun brewing in the basement of his family's grocery.

1898
Caleb Bradham, a pharmacist in New Bern, North Carolina, starts marketing his own cola formula under the name Brad's Drink. In the same year, Perrier bottled water is introduced.

1893
The Coca-Cola trademark is registered. ❖ Hires Root Beer is introduced in bottles, but advertising promotes the advantages of brewing at home from Hires concentrate.

1892
The crown bottle cap is invented. The cap keeps carbon dioxide from escaping bottles of soda pop, allowing it to be enjoyed at home, rather than at soda fountains.

1890
Canada Dry Ginger Ale starts production in a small Toronto plant opened by pharmacist John J. McLaughlin.

1885
Charles Aderton, the fountain man at Morrison's Old Corner Drug Store in Waco, Texas, develops the formula for Dr Pepper.

1886
Dr. John S. Pemberton creates a cola and sells it at Jacob's Pharmacy in Atlanta, Georgia, as a cure for hangovers and headaches. His bookkeeper, Frank Robinson, names it Coca-Cola.

1887
Asa Candler, another Atlanta pharmacist, buys the rights for Coca-Cola syrup for $2,300 and repositions it as refreshment rather than medicine. By 1890 it is the most popular soda fountain drink in the United States.

1919
The American Bottlers of Carbonated Beverages, predecessor of the modern-day American Beverage Association, forms.

1920
The Eighteenth Amendment to the U.S. Constitution initiates Prohibition, banning the manufacture, transportation, and sale of alcoholic beverages. Sales of soft drinks skyrocket.

1923
Hom-Paks, six-pack cardboard cartons for bottled soft drinks, are created.

1929
The Howdy Company debuts its new drink, Bib-Label Lithiated Lemon-Lime Soda, which will later become 7UP.

1962
The pull-ring tab for aluminum cans is introduced. ❖ RC Cola's Diet Rite, a no-calorie soda sweetened with saccharin, is introduced nationwide.

1957
The first aluminum cans are used for packaging soda. Until this time 95 percent of sodas had been sold in returnable bottles, which were typically used up to 50 times each.

1952
Kirsch Beverages of Brooklyn introduces No-Cal ginger ale, a sugar-free, saccharin-sweetened, no-calorie soda marketed locally to diabetics.

1963
Coca-Cola introduces Tab, sweetened with saccharin, to compete with Diet Rite.

1964
Pepsi-Cola introduces Mountain Dew, a soda with a pronounced citrus flavor and more caffeine and calories than either Coke or Pepsi.

1965
Diet Pepsi is introduced (a renaming of Patio Diet Cola, launched in 1963). ❖ The resealable bottle cap is invented.

1966
The American Bottlers of Carbonated Beverages, formed in 1919, renamed themselves the National Soft Drink Association.

2009
Full-sugar versions of Coke, Pepsi, and Mountain Dew, without any high-fructose corn syrup, are launched.

2007
Coca-Cola introduces a "healthy" cola by fortifying Diet Coke with B vitamins, magnesium, and zinc, selling it as Diet Coke Plus.

2005
Coca-Cola launches Coca-Cola Zero, sweetened with aspartame and acesulfame potassium.

1985
Coca-Cola introduces a sweeter version of its cola, called New Coke. The traditional beverage is reintroduced as Coca-Cola Classic.

1933

Ratification of the Twenty-First Amendment to the U.S. Constitution repeals Prohibition.

1936

A Spanish pharmacist introduces an orange soda he calls Naranjina ("small orange") at the Marseilles Trade Fair. Leon Beton buys the formula, renames it Orangina, and introduces the product in his home country of Algeria, where it is a huge hit.

1939

Pepsi-Cola challenges Coke with the jingle "Nickel, Nickel," which became a hit: Pepsi-Cola hits the spot. / Twelve full ounces, / That's a lot. / Twice as much, for a nickel, too, / Pepsi-Cola is the drink for you.

1950

Pepsi reduces the sugar content of its cola and repositions itself as "the light refreshment."

1945

Coke becomes a registered trademark.

1942

The United States enters World War II and imposes a sugar ration on U.S. soda companies, limiting use to 50 percent of the amount used the previous year.

1941

Coca-Cola is officially sold as Coke for the first time.

1970

Plastic bottles are used to package soft drinks.

1974

The stay-on pull tab for aluminum cans is invented.

1975

Pepsi launches the Pepsi Challenge marketing campaign against Coke.

1976

Perrier water is introduced in the United States.

1984

All the sugar in Coke and Pepsi is replaced with high-fructose corn syrup.

1982

Coca-Cola releases Diet Coke to the marketplace and, due to the link between saccharin and cancer, curtails Tab production.

1980

Reacting to high sugar prices and low corn prices, Coke and Pepsi replace half the sugar in their products with high-fructose corn syrup.

1979

Coca-Cola introduces Mello Yello to compete with Mountain Dew.

PART

1

Getting Started

*W*e are all used to the instant gratification of store-bought sodas, and you may have the impression that making sodas at home is overly time-consuming and technically beyond your reach. Nothing could be further from the truth. In some cases it's almost ridiculously easy, and the results will beat commercial sodas hands-down, every time.

Homemade soda always starts with a flavor base. Some flavor bases are quick and simple. Others require more preparation and ingredients. Once prepared, the base can be used right away or refrigerated for spur-of-the-moment refreshment any time. In this book, I size the recipes for simple flavor bases for a single glass to give you flexibility. For flavor bases that are more complex, or those that can be used to make a variety of sodas, I give recipes for making them in bulk.

Once you have your base, it is time to add bubbles and turn your syrup into soda. I use three different methods of carbonation in this book:

 SELTZER

 SIPHON

 FERMENTATION

For easy homemade soda that does not require any special equipment, you can simply mix your flavor base with bottled seltzer and drink up. Carbonating soda with a siphon is also very easy, but you do need that specialized gear (see page 22). Or you can brew your soda in bottles with yeast: the least expensive but most time-consuming method.

I have included with each recipe instructions for each carbonation method that is appropriate for it. Not all sodas can be carbonated by all methods. A carbonated fruit juice, for example, would be weakened by a dilution of water or seltzer, so its recipe may specify only the siphon method of carbonation. Similarly, the recipe for a flavor base that needs to be fermented for flavor as well as carbonation, such as a honey soda, will specify only the fermentation method.

Ingredients

In undertaking to supply you with a wide variety of soda recipes, I have at times employed ingredients that might be new to you. Use this partial list as a guide to help you understand, procure, and use your ingredients to their best advantage.

Sweeteners

Sweetness is one of the defining characteristics of soda. Although it is easy to make soft drinks with less sugar than is found in commercial products, all sodas need some sweetness.

Granulated Sugars

Granulated sugars must be dissolved in liquid before they can be added to beverages. The easiest way to do this is to make simple syrup (see below), a solution of equal parts sugar and water. Any granulated sugar can be cooked into simple syrup.

Granulated white sugar is the most common sugar, extracted from the sap of sugarcane and sugar beets (pure cane sugar uses only sugarcane sap). During refinement, the syrupy juice (molasses) is separated from the sugar crystals, leaving behind white table sugar.

Brown sugar is granulated sugar that retains some of its molasses or has had molasses added back to it. It has a slight savory character that is well suited for root beers and colas.

Raw sugar is cane sugar that has been partially refined but has not been washed of all of its molasses. Raw sugar is sold in various forms, including turbinado sugar, Demerara sugar, and muscovado sugar. It can be used in any soda in the same manner as granulated white sugar and brown sugar.

Evaporated coconut palm sugar is a pale brown sugar made from the sap of the coconut palm, with a mild honeylike flavor. Its glycemic index is just about one-third that of cane sugar. It can be used in any soda in the same manner as granulated white sugar and brown sugar.

White   Brown

Palm   Raw

Making Simple Syrup

COMBINE EQUAL PARTS WATER AND SUGAR in a saucepan over medium heat. Stir just until the sugar dissolves; when the sugar granules are no longer visible, stop stirring. The syrup will continue to clear as it approaches a boil. As soon as it comes to a boil, remove the pan from the heat and let cool to room temperature. Store the syrup in the refrigerator, where it will keep for up to two months.

Liquid Sweeteners

Liquid sweeteners have an advantage over granulated sweeteners in that they do not have to be dissolved in order to be used in making beverages. This allows you to make a flavor base without cooking.

Agave syrup, also known as agave nectar, is made from the boiled juice of the agave cactus. Pale gold with a thin honeylike consistency, it is a less-refined alternative to simple syrup, and can be substituted for it in recipes.

Honey is a purely natural sweetener. With its bold floral fragrance, honey can be assertive in a soda and should be used only when its flavor is expressly desired. Unless you know you want a strong honey flavor, stick to pale mild honeys, like those of clover and orange blossom. Honey is sweeter than sugar syrup and should be used in a 3:4 ratio to simple syrup (three parts honey for every four parts simple syrup called for in a recipe).

Molasses is the main by-product of sugar refinement, containing all of the vitamins, minerals, and flavorful miconutrients that are filtered from sugarcane during manufacturing. It is not nearly as sweet as sugar but can be used to add color and richness to dark-colored sodas. The different grades of molasses, from palest (mildest) to darkest (strongest), are light, dark, and blackstrap.

Artificial Sweeteners

A full discussion of the artificial sweeteners commonly found in soft drinks is on page 17. I can't recommend using any of them when making soda at home, because they all produce off flavors. Also, because they do not have calories, they cannot be used for making fermented sodas; yeasts will not feed from them. (Although our taste buds can be fooled into thinking there's energy where there is none, yeasts are not as gullible.)

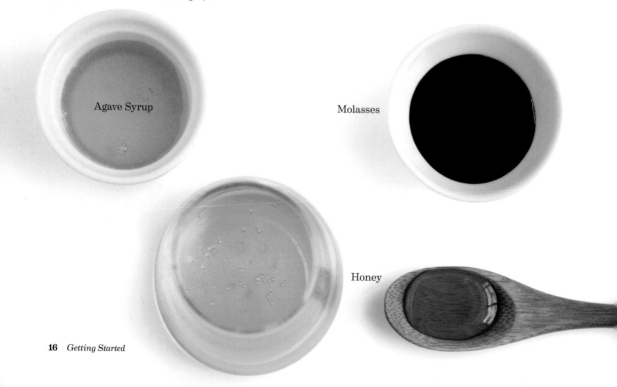

Agave Syrup

Molasses

Honey

//

Sugar by Any Other Name
Doesn't Taste as Sweet

SWEETENERS ARE SUBSTANCES, some naturally derived from plants (natural sweeteners) and some manufactured in laboratories (artificial sweeteners), that attempt to deliver the desirable qualities of sugar, like a sensation of sweetness, without the undesirable ones, like calories (a boon for people who have trouble metabolizing sugar, like those with diabetes). The only problem is that nothing else tastes quite like sugar, and all nonsugar sweeteners miss the flavor boat. Many have strong aftertastes, or they have a sweetness taste pattern that peaks early or finishes abruptly. In order to mitigate the deficiencies of nonsugar sweeteners, commercial soft drink manufacturers often use several in tandem. The most common sweeteners used in soda production, other than sugar and high-fructose corn syrup, are the following:

ASPARTAME, marketed under the trade names Equal, NutraSweet, and Canderel, is currently included in the formula of more than 6,000 commercial foods and beverages. Aspartame is 200 times sweeter than sugar and has minimal aftertaste. Its calorie content is similar to that of sugar by weight, but because it can be used in much smaller amounts, the number of calories it contributes to foods is negligible. Aspartame is synthesized from amino acids, and when it is heated it breaks down into those component parts and loses its sweetness.

CYCLAMATES, the first artificial sweeteners, were discovered in 1937 and approved for use as artificial sweeteners in 1958. They are 50 times sweeter than sugar and were originally used in conjunction with saccharin to boost sweetness in diet sodas, such as Tab. But a 1969 study linked cyclamates to cancerous tumors in rats and mice, and in October of that year they were banned in the United States. Follow-up studies have failed to duplicate the results of the 1969 research, but cyclamates are still outlawed in the United States, although they are used in place of saccharin in Canada (where saccharin is banned) and are common in European sodas.

SACCHARIN, another early artificial sweetener (it was first synthesized in 1878), is about 30 times sweeter than sugar but has a strong metallic aftertaste, which can be effectively subdued by teaming it with cyclamates. In 1977 the FDA petitioned Congress for a ban on saccharin, which was never enacted, but the publicity caused almost all soda manufacturers to switch to aspartame. In countries where cyclamates and saccharin are both legal, they are commonly used together in the manufacturing of sugar-free soft drinks.

SUCRALOSE, sold under the trade name Splenda, has very little aftertaste, which has made it very popular. Since its initial launch in 1991 in Canada, and 1998 in the States, sucralose has captured a large part of the sugar-free beverage market, and it is now used in more than 4,500 food and beverage products. It is twice as sweet as saccharin, four times as sweet as aspartame, and 600 times sweeter than sugar. Sucralose has 83 percent of the calories of sugar, but because it is used in such small quantities, most products sweetened with sucralose are permitted to say they have 0 calories.

ACESULFAME POTASSIUM, marketed as Sunett, is about 200 times sweeter than sugar and about 25 percent as sweet as sucralose. It is usually blended with aspartame or sucralose.

Flavorings

Soft drink flavors come from the fruits, roots, barks, leaves, and other parts of aromatic plants. In some cases recipes call for the plant parts themselves: burdock root, for example, or mint leaf. In other cases recipes may call for an extract, in which the aromatic components of a plant are extracted, concentrated, and suspended in alcohol. Still other recipes may call for essential oils, the volatile oils that give plants their characteristic scents and are potent flavoring agents.

Hundreds of plants fall into the flavoring category. Here's some information on the most common ones:

Birch bark lends a mild wintergreen flavor to brewed sodas. Birch beer, flavored with sassafras and birch, is a classic American brew. Birch bark is usually sold in homebrew stores.

Bitter Orange (Bergamot) is highly aromatic, and its dried peel is an essential part of cola flavor. The dried peel and its extract are usually available in spice shops, or any store with a good spice selection. They can be pricey.

Burdock root is a traditional ingredient in American root beers. It has a mild sweet flavor similar to that of artichoke. Dried burdock root is available in most Asian groceries and homebrew stores.

Cinnamon has several species, but they all fall into two types. Ceylon cinnamon is thin and mild, with a faint fragrance of allspice. Southeast Asian cinnamon, also called cassia, is both stronger and more common. The best grade comes from Vietnam and is sold as Saigon cinnamon. Use it in sticks, rather than ground. The sticks can be found in most grocery stores.

Ginger, a common soda ingredient, is very aromatic, at once spicy and cooling. It is widely available fresh in the produce section of grocery stores, and it can be found whole and dried in most spice shops.

Birch bark

Burdock root

Cinnamon

Bitter Orange

Star anise

Lemongrass, a perennial herb from central Asia, contains high levels of citral, the pungent aromatic component of lemon oil. It yields a rich lemon flavor without the acid of lemon juice, which can disrupt the fermentation of yeasted sodas. Lemon zest is similar in flavor and can be substituted. Lemongrass is available in most Asian markets and in the produce section of well-stocked grocery stores.

Licorice root provides the well-known strong and sweet flavor of black licorice candy. Dried licorice root is sold in natural food stores and homebrew stores. Anise seed and dried star anise are suitable substitutes.

Sarsaparilla is similar in flavor to sassafras, but a little milder. Many plants go by the name sarsaparilla. Southern-clime sarsaparilla (*Smilax* spp.) is the traditional root-beer flavoring. Most of the supply we get in North America comes from Mexico; it's commonly sold in homebrew stores. Wild sarsaparilla (*Aralia* spp.) is more common in North America and is sometimes used as a substitute for true sarsaparilla. Small young sarsaparilla roots, known as "root bark" are less pungent and are usually preferred for soda making, although fully mature roots give fine results.

Sassafras is the most common flavoring for root beers of all types. Its root bark is very strong and should be used with caution, especially if combined with other flavors. It is easily overpowering. Dried sassafras is available in homebrew stores.

Star anise, the dried fruit of an Asian evergreen, tastes like licorice, with hints of clove and cinnamon. The flavor is strong, so use star anise with caution. It is available dried in the spice section of most grocery stores but can be found much more cheaply at Asian markets.

Sarsaparilla

Lemongrass

Sassafras

Ginger

Licorice

Fermentation and Mouthfeel

The sensual charm of many sodas can be augmented by fermenting them with yeast and/or thickening the flavor base with a complex sugar (polysaccharide). Yeasts produce carbonation as they improve the flavor of a soda base in myriad ways, metabolizing some of the sugar in the base into acidic and savory flavors. Not all sodas benefit from fermentation. The subtle but complex aromas in a cola, for instance, are flattened by exposure to yeast, whereas the more overt pungent flavor of root beer is tamed and mellowed through fermentation. On the other hand, both root beer and cola benefit from the small amount of viscosity they get from the addition of a polysaccharide, like maltodextrin or gum arabic.

Yeasts

There are hundreds of species of wild yeasts and several dozen cultivated strains. Each one will give you slightly different results in the time required to ferment sodas, in the degree of carbonation, and in the flavor of the finished sodas.

Bread yeast (*Saccharomyces cerevisiae*) is the most commonly available, and though you can use it for brewing soda, the finished flavors of the soft drinks can be coarse and perceptibly yeasty. Bread yeast works rapidly, so the fermentation may take only half as long as when you're using other yeasts, and the soda will not store as long without becoming overly carbonated.

Beer yeast is better. You can get both granulated ale and lager yeasts through homebrewing supply houses. Ale yeasts (*Saccharomyces cerevisiae*) are more readily available and are bit more aggressive than lager yeasts, so you will need less of them. Lager yeasts (*Saccharomyces uvarum*) work more slowly and produce cleaner-tasting sodas.

Champagne or wine yeast (*Saccharomyces bayanus*) is the one I most prefer. This strain of yeast is very delicate. It works slowly, so the carbonation builds gradually and your sodas are less likely to overcarbonate during storage. Most importantly, the residual flavors of this yeast are imperceptible, allowing you to make the most subtle sodas without worrying about the development of a yeasty aftertaste.

Polysaccharides

Polysaccharides are complex sugars that provide the soft creamy mouthfeel that is an essential part of the flavor profile of some sodas, particularly root beers and colas. Two polysaccharides — maltodextrin and gum arabic — are of particular value. Both are available wherever nutritional supplements are sold and in many brewing supply houses.

Maltodextrin is made by breaking large starch molecules into smaller sugar chains. Because it is chemically between starch and sugar, maltodextrin thickens liquids subtly, and it helps give sodas a creamy consistency. In addition, by causing soda to linger on the tongue, a little maltodextrin gives our taste buds more time to perceive all of the soda's flavors, enhancing our experience.

Gum arabic (also known as gum acacia) is extracted from the sap of various sub-Saharan acacia trees. Like other gums, gum arabic has the ability to absorb liquid in an amount that is many times its volume, so a little bit thickens the consistency of a soda, giving it a velvety mouthfeel and causing the liquid to pass over the tongue more slowly so that our perception of the soda's flavor increases.

Soda siphon

Equipment

It's not the intention of this book to give you directions for setting up a soda-production facility. I know it is possible to equip your soda setup with far more than what I list here, but for making soda for yourself, your family, and your close circle of friends, this collection should suffice.

Pots: Use stainless-steel or enamel-clad cookware for brewing flavor bases and mixing sodas. For small batches to consume at home, all you should need is a 2- to 3-quart saucepan and a 2- to 3-gallon stockpot.

Plastic pail: A 5-gallon food-grade plastic pail is helpful for sanitizing bottles and mixing up large batches of soda.

Funnels: A funnel made of stainless steel or food-grade plastic is needed to fill soda bottles.

Strainer: A fine-mesh stainless-steel strainer is helpful for straining out solid ingredients from the flavor base.

Soda siphon: A quart-size soda siphon allows you to carbonate juices and flavor bases mechanically, without diluting them with seltzer. A sealed siphon will keep soda fresh for about five days. (See page 22 for more about siphons.)

Bottles: If you plan to brew sodas, you will want to store your sodas in bottles to capture the gas of the fermentation process. (See page 24 for more about bottling.)

Thermometer: An instant-read thermometer is helpful for determining the temperature of liquids for fermentation.

Scale: You will need a digital scale that measures in 0.1-gram increments if you want to make flavor bases using concentrated flavor extracts, such as the essential oils used for making cola syrup (page 100).

Juicer: A juice extractor is helpful for juicing vegetables and pulpy fruits, like pineapples and pears.

....

The Allure of Siphons

I have always been a sucker for carbonated comedy. Whether it's Margaret Dumont taking a shot of seltzer in the kisser from the bottle hiding in Harpo's pants or a full-out clown fizz bomb blitzkrieg in the center ring, the appearance of a soda siphon always comes with a titillation of expectation. Soda siphons are sophisticated (imagine Fred Astaire dressing his single malt with a quick spritz from a chrome-and-crystal siphon) and nostalgic, harking back to a time of garter-armed bartenders who knew how to concoct a perfect gin fizz, even though they wouldn't know the first thing about handling a mechanical soda gun.

The first patented siphon, the *siphon champenois*, built in 1829 by two French jewelers, was little more than a hollow corkscrew that was inserted through the cork of a sparkling beverage, allowing the user to dispense the carbonated liquid without dissipating its fizz. It was followed by many dozens of designs patented between 1830 and 1939, mostly in France and the United States, for pressurized valves that improved the capabilities of sealed bottles to hold and dispense a gaseous liquid. Modern soda siphons are still built the same way. The only difference is that early siphons needed to be filled by a soda manufacturer, and now siphons can be used to both carbonate and dispense soda at home.

Antique soda siphons used to be readily available and relatively cheap at yard sales and flea markets, but now they have become fairly pricey. The most coveted types are made from Bohemian glass, touted in the nineteenth century to be strong enough to withstand the intense pressure inside a siphon bottle. Early siphon bottles were sometimes encased in wire mesh to contain flying glass if an overpressurized bottle burst. One of the most collectible designs was the gasogene or seltzogene, built from two interconnecting wire-encased globes, in which a reactive mixture of acid and base was combined in the top section and water was siphoned into it from the bottom.

Today there are several manufacturers of soda siphons for the home. They come with their own carbonation methods, usually disposable pressurized CO_2 cartridges that are screwed into the siphon to release the gas. Modern siphon "bottles" are all made from metal and no longer pose an explosion problem. Popular brands include iSi, Liss, and SodaStream.

How to Work a Soda Siphon

1. Clean all parts of the siphon with warm, soapy water and rinse well. Let the base container of the siphon cool before using.

2. Assemble the siphon according to the manufacturer's directions to prepare it for filling.

3. Fill the base container with cold liquid (a mixture of flavor base and water if making a flavored soda or filtered water if making seltzer water).

4. Insert the siphon tube and screw on the top securely.

5. Remove the protective cap and insert a fresh CO_2 charger, with the nipple facing the open end of the cover.

6. Screw the loaded charger cover back onto the base container, tightening it slowly but completely, until you hear the gas discharge into the container.

7. Shake the entire container vigorously for at least 15 seconds to distribute the carbon dioxide into the liquid.

8. Unscrew the charger cover and discard the dispensed CO_2 charger. Replace the protective cap onto the threading.

9. Dispense the carbonated liquid by gently squeezing the trigger.

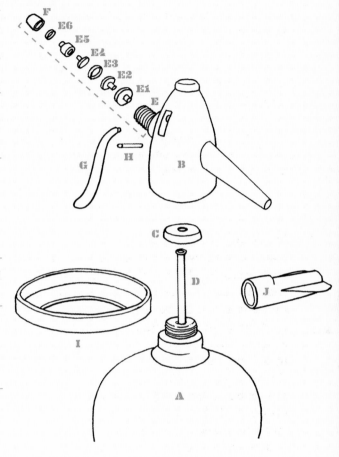

A Base container
B Head
C Neck insertion gasket
D Siphon tube
E Admission valve threaded casing
E1 Admission valve rubber seat gasket
E2 Admission valve
E3 Screw nut for admission valve
E4 Needle or pin
E5 Rubber packing
E6 Thread ring or threaded collar
F Protective cap
G Lever
H Peg for lever
I Rubber stiffener for bottom of bottle
J Charger cover

Refreshment in a Bottle

Carbonation is fleeting. Because carbon dioxide is gaseous, it wants to escape the confines of the liquid it was forced into. Sealed in a bottle, the gas is dispersed and relatively stable, but as soon as the bottle is opened the carbon dioxide takes any path it can find to get out. That's where bubbles come from.

Have you ever noticed that a sealed bottle of soda isn't bubbly? That's because the gas in a bottle of soda takes the form of bubbles only when it is on the move. As soon as you open a bottle of carbonated beverage, air from the outside enters the bottle along with a gazillion tiny particles of dust and such. The suspended carbon dioxide latches on to these particles and separates from the water, each molecule forming a little bubble as it hitches a ride up and out. That's why when you open a bottle of soda, the bubbling is most active first on the surface and moves toward the bottom of the bottle only after it has been open for a few seconds.

The sole purpose of bottling is the preservation of carbonation. When you're carbonating through yeast fermentation, sealing soda in a bottle is the only way to capture the gas. But if you are creating homemade sodas in a siphon, or simply by adding commercially carbonated seltzer, bottling soda is not necessary.

Heavy glass bottles, particularly the clunky, old-timey bail-top bottles with porcelain stoppers that you can still pick up at yard sales and second-hand stores, are nostalgic embellishments to the art of bottling your own soda, but I prefer plastic. The carbonation trapped in a bottle of homebrewed soda is far greater than the pressure in a bottle of homebrewed beer, and for that reason the standard-weight

Number of Bottles Needed per Gallon

The number of bottles you will need for bottling your soda depends on the size of your bottles and the size of your batch of soda.

Bottle Size
12 fluid ounces (1½ cups)

11
Bottles per Gallon

Bottle Size
16 fluid ounces (2 cups)

8
Bottles per Gallon

bottles used for bottling home brewski are not strong enough for homebrewed soda — they are likely to explode.

Screw-top plastic soda bottles are readily available and far safer. Because they expand as the carbonation in the bottle grows, they provide a built-in gauge for judging the degree of carbonation in the bottle. When they feel rock hard, the soda is ready to be refrigerated. Screw tops can be reused, but they should not be used more than three times. After that, their rate of failure rises exponentially.

Sanitizing Bottles

Bottles can be reused any number of times, but they must be cleaned and sanitized with each use. Glass bottles can be run through a dishwasher to sanitize them, but most plastic bottles will melt at a dishwasher's sanitizing drying temperature. To sanitize plastic soda bottles, wash them well with hot, soapy water using a soft bottle brush, rinse them completely, and let them sit in a sanitizing solution made from 1 teaspoon household bleach mixed with $\frac{1}{2}$ gallon water (137 ppm bleach to water) for 10 minutes. Rinse and then let them air-dry.

Soda Storage

Because carbon dioxide is more soluble at refrigerated temperatures, all sealed bottles of soda, regardless of their means of carbonation, will stay effervescent longer when stored chilled. A charged soda siphon will keep its carbonation for at least five days in the refrigerator, but a resealed opened bottle of seltzer or soda will lose its bubbles in about 24 hours, even when stored chilled.

If you've carbonated your sodas by fermenting them with yeast, you'll need to

Bottle Size
20 fluid ounces (2½ cups)

7
Bottles per Gallon

4
Bottles per Gallon

Bottle Size
1 liter

be cautious of overcarbonation. Though fermentation requires a certain length of time to develop the flavor of a soda, the buildup of carbon dioxide doesn't stop once the optimal effervescence has been reached. Sodas that bubble over upon being opened have overcarbonated, either because they were brewed with too much yeast or because they were left fermenting for too long.

It is good practice to refrigerate sodas as soon as you think they are nearing full carbonation. Getting a soda cold makes the yeast go dormant, which slows down carbonation, and makes the soda less likely to gush out the top upon opening. To avoid gushers it is best to consume refrigerated sodas within a few weeks of producing them. Sodas containing live yeast that are left in the refrigerator for more than a month will most assuredly gush upon opening. If you find that you're not consuming all of the soda from a batch in a few weeks, make smaller batches.

Problem Solving

Following are some common soda-making problems you might experience.

Too much carbonation: In a yeasted soda, you either added too much yeast to the batch or allowed the soda to ferment too long. The fix is to use less yeast or ferment for less time with the next batch. For the current overcarbonated batch, you can diminish the amount of soda you lose when opening a bottle by setting the bottle in a sink and slowly unscrewing the cap just a bit, allowing carbon dioxide to leak out without opening the cap enough to release any liquid.

In a siphon-carbonated soda, overcarbonation could mean that the siphon was overfilled with liquid, creating excessive pressure inside the siphon and forcing too much gas into the liquid. Just dispense some of the soda, and the problem should fix itself.

Too little carbonation: In a yeasted soda, you may not have let the bottles sit long enough before refrigerating them, you may have used too little yeast in the batch, or perhaps the soda was acidic and therefore weakened the yeast. In all cases the bottles just needed to sit longer before being cooled. If just a single bottle is undercarbonated, rather than a whole batch, probably the cap was faulty. The only solution is to drink it.

No carbonation: In a yeasted soda, lack of carbonation indicates that either you forgot to add the yeast, or the yeast died. Sometimes you get a bad batch of yeast. Other times there's not enough sugar in the soda to support the yeast, or the liquid is too hot when you add the yeast and the high temperatures kill them. Unfortunately there's no fix.

Off taste: Usually this means a sanitation problem. Throw out the batch and clean up (for information about sanitizing bottles, see page 25).

2

Recipes for Soda Drinks

Honeydew Mint Seltzer, page 46

CHAPTER ONE

Sparkling Waters

*B*ottled sparkling water has been commercially marketed in the United States since 1807, when advances in the production of glass bottles allowed the first natural spring waters to be sealed and sold, but back then mineral waters were consumed as medicine, not as refreshment. The notion of drinking sparkling water for pleasure is a fairly recent phenomenon.

Perrier, the sparkling water from Languedoc in the south of France, is largely given credit for starting the current bottled water craze in the United States. The Perrier company, named for Dr. Louis Perrier, who owned the spring for a brief period from 1898 to 1903, began selling bottled water in Europe at the beginning of the twentieth century, and in 1976 Perrier water began selling in the States. By 1988, Perrier held 80 percent of the imported water market in the United States, and in that same year it introduced flavored sparkling waters.

Although all soft drinks are predominantly water, sparkling waters are in a class by themselves. They retain the beneficial aura of mineral water from natural springs, even when made from municipal water supplies. Most consumers view sparkling water as more healthful than sweet soda pops, and bottled-water manufacturers have followed suit by fortifying their products with vitamins, minerals, antioxidants, and natural extracts that claim to boost energy, fight disease, and reverse the signs of aging.

Though the old claim that natural spring waters have health-giving properties is a bit exaggerated, at the very least, water is our best source of hydration. If our essential animal requirement for water can be enhanced with the sensual allure of a little flavor or some carbonation and be amended by a few vitamins, our bodies are all the better for it.

A Seltzer Time Line

1741
The word *seltzer* as the name for carbonated water appears in print for the first time, referring to the mineral water *Selterser Wasser* (water of Selters), from the Prussian town of Niederselters.

1772
Joseph Priestley publishes a method for artificially carbonating water.

1807
Man-made soda waters are sold in New York City.

1832
John Matthews, a British immigrant living in New York, builds a small carbonating machine for pharmacies, called a soda fountain. (The early connection between carbonated water and pharmacies sprang from the belief that carbonation in and of itself had medicinal value.)

1840s
Flavored seltzers become a standard item in drugstore soda fountains.

1880s–1920
Seltzer is increasingly favored as an alternative to alcoholic carbonated beverages.

1920
Prohibition is declared, boosting the sale of all nonalcoholic soft drinks, including seltzer.

1930s
The association of seltzer with the Jewish community in New York springs from its popularity as a beverage that can be served with any kosher meal. Bottled seltzers were some of the first products to receive kosher certification.

1933
Prohibition is repealed. In an attempt to distance their product from its temperance connections and medicinal roots, seltzer manufacturers begin to rename it "club soda" to appeal to patrons of chic supper clubs. Today, club soda is distinguished from seltzer by the addition of a small amount of salt.

1955
SodaStream (founded in 1903 by Gilbey Gin in London) introduces a bottled water carbonation system for the home. It makes seltzer or flavored sodas in 8-ounce bottles.

1986
Bottled flavored seltzers, which appeared in the United States market only a few years before, hit annual sales of $250 million.

1987
FDA cracks down on two seltzer companies for adding high-fructose corn syrup to flavored seltzer, saying that sweetened seltzer had to be marketed as "soda," not "seltzer."

2002
SodaStream introduces a home carbonation system with recyclable gas cartridges in the United States.

2010
Bariloche, seltzer packaged in a recyclable plastic siphon, from Argentina, begins test marketing in the United States.

mineral water

The health benefits of natural sparkling mineral waters have been valued for nearly two thousand years. Typically, natural mineral water contains sulfur, calcium, magnesium, and potassium. By combining liquid supplements with natural flavors and carbonated water, you can create your own fortified water that delivers a full dose of all the minerals needed to maintain your bones, your cardiovascular health, and a strong immune system.

MULTIMINERAL SYRUP

1 tablespoon liquid multi-mineral supplement

1 teaspoon agave syrup or simple syrup (page 15)

⅛ teaspoon finely grated lemon zest

ENOUGH FOR 1 SERVING

Mix the liquid minerals, agave syrup, and lemon zest, stirring until blended.

 TO MIX WITH SELTZER

1 batch multimineral syrup

1½ cups seltzer

1 SERVING

Pour the multimineral syrup into a tall glass. Add the seltzer and stir briefly to combine. Add ice and serve.

vitamin water

The health benefits of vitamins were recognized long before we had names for them. Ancient Egyptians knew that eating liver cures night blindness (a symptom of vitamin A deficiency), and as early as 1614 physicians knew that the acid in certain fruits eliminates symptoms of scurvy, but it was not until the twentieth century that vitamins themselves were recognized and isolated. Although it's possible to get all the vitamins you need by eating a balanced diet plentiful in fruits and vegetables, most of us can use a little help. Here's a tasty beverage that will boost your vitamin intake with every glass.

MULTIVITAMIN SYRUP

¼ cup orange juice

1 tablespoon liquid multi-vitamin supplement

1 teaspoon honey

¼ teaspoon finely grated orange zest

ENOUGH FOR 1 SERVING

Mix the orange juice, liquid vitamins, honey, and orange zest, stirring until blended.

 TO MIX WITH SELTZER

1 batch multivitamin syrup

1¼ cups seltzer

1 SERVING

Pour the syrup into a tall glass. Add the seltzer and stir briefly to combine. Add ice and serve.

energy water

Commercial energy drinks are loaded with sugar and stimulants, like caffeine and guarana. Although you can purchase stimulating chemicals and use them to make energy sodas at home, having a canister of pure caffeine in your house, especially if you have young children, is not a great idea: chemical stimulants are lethally toxic if consumed indiscriminately. With that in mind I offer you this formula for a homemade energy drink that contains the caffeine of a single cup of espresso (about 75 mg), the calories of an average soft drink (106 kcal), and a trace amount of protein.

COFFEE SYRUP

3 tablespoons strong brewed coffee, preferably espresso

1½ tablespoons honey

1½ teaspoons heavy cream

ENOUGH FOR 1 SERVING

Mix the coffee, honey, and heavy cream, stirring until blended.

 TO MIX WITH SELTZER

1 batch coffee syrup

1¼ cups seltzer

1 SERVING

Pour the syrup into a tall glass. Slowly add the seltzer. When the mixture foams up, stir briefly to reduce the foam, and then add the remaining seltzer. Add ice and serve.

lime sparkling water

The flavor and health benefits of citrus come in two layers. The juice is bright and sweet, loaded with vitamin C (ascorbic acid) and natural sugar, and the peel has rich citrus oils containing limonene, which has been shown to help ward off cancer. This quickly prepared sparkling water gives you the flavor and health benefits of both.

LIME SYRUP

Finely grated zest and juice of ½ lime

1 tablespoon agave syrup or simple syrup (page 15)

ENOUGH FOR 1 SERVING

Mix the lime zest, lime juice, and syrup, stirring until blended.

 TO MIX WITH SELTZER

1 batch lime syrup
1⅓ cups seltzer

1 SERVING

Pour the lime syrup into a tall glass. Add the seltzer and stir just to combine. Add ice and serve.

sweet soy soda

All legumes are good sources of protein, but the soybean is unusually well endowed. It has double the amount of protein as other beans, with a near perfect composition of amino acids for human consumption. And when the beans are soaked and ground, the resulting mash can be pressed to deliver soy milk: a translucent liquid dispersed with droplets of protein and fat similar to the structure of animal milk, but with fewer calories, less saturated fat, no cholesterol, and more protein. All of that is captured in this sweet soda.

SOY MILK SYRUP

¼ cup vanilla soy milk

1 tablespoon agave syrup or simple syrup (page 15)

ENOUGH FOR 1 SERVING

Mix the soy milk and syrup, stirring until blended.

 TO MIX WITH SELTZER

1 batch soy milk syrup
1¼ cups seltzer

1 SERVING

Pour the soy milk syrup into a tall glass. Add the seltzer and stir just to combine. Add ice and serve.

slightly salty caramel seltzer

Fleur de sel, *the delicate bloom that forms on the surface of seawater under the perfect alignment of sun and wind, finds its soulmate in buttery caramel candies. This ultimately decadent soda water is the quaffable incarnation of that pairing. The syrup requires a little work, so it's most efficient to produce enough to make several glasses at once.*

SALTED CARAMEL SYRUP

½ cup sugar

½ cup whole milk

1 teaspoon fleur de sel

ENOUGH FOR 3 SERVINGS

Melt the sugar in a medium skillet over medium heat until pale golden, stirring constantly, about 5 minutes.

Remove from the heat and carefully stir in the milk; the liquid will foam and bubble vigorously. Keep stirring until the caramelized sugar and milk are completely combined. If necessary, return the pan to medium heat to fully dissolve the sugar in the milk. Then let cool to room temperature and stir in the fleur de sel.

The syrup can be stored in the refrigerator for up to 2 weeks. Warm to room temperature in a microwave or in a saucepan over low heat before mixing with seltzer.

 TO MIX WITH SELTZER

3 tablespoons salted caramel syrup

1⅓ cups seltzer

1 SERVING

Pour the syrup into a tall glass. Add the seltzer and stir just until blended. Add ice and serve.

blazing inferno chile water

Hot peppers (Capsicum spp.) comprise a huge family of at least fifty thousand varieties, ranging from sweet pimientos to incendiary habañeros. Though hot pepper sauces are not quite as varied, there is still a huge range. Spice this soda to your preference, balancing the fire with some sweetness to bring out the fruity sweet and sour flavors of the hot sauce.

HOT PEPPER SYRUP

- 1 tablespoon medium-hot pepper sauce (such as Frank's RedHot) or hot pepper sauce (such as Huy Fong Sriracha)
- 3 tablespoons agave syrup or simple syrup (page 15)

ENOUGH FOR 3 SERVINGS

Combine the hot pepper sauce and agave syrup and whisk together until smooth.

The syrup can be stored in the refrigerator for up to 1 month.

 TO MIX WITH SELTZER

- 1 tablespoon hot pepper syrup
- 1⅓ cups seltzer

1 SERVING

Pour the syrup into a tall glass. Add the seltzer and stir just until blended. Add ice and serve.

 TO CARBONATE WITH A SIPHON

- 4 cups water
- 1 batch hot pepper syrup

3 SERVINGS

Combine the water and syrup in a 1-quart soda siphon. Charge with CO_2 according to the manufacturer's directions. Siphon-charged sodas can be stored in the siphon in a refrigerator for up to 5 days. Disperse as desired into tall glasses filled with ice, and serve.

M I X O L O G Y

//

sparkling spicy bloody mary

Prepare the hot pepper syrup as described at left, then carbonate as desired.

Pour 1½ ounces (3 tablespoons) vodka over ice cubes in a tall glass. Add 3 ounces (6 tablespoons) Blazing Inferno Chile Water and 3 ounces (6 tablespoons) tomato juice. Stir just until blended.

//

sparkling spicy vodka spritzer

Prepare the hot pepper syrup as described at left, then carbonate as desired.

Pour 1½ ounces (3 tablespoons) vodka over ice cubes in a wine glass. Add 4 ounces (½ cup) Blazing Inferno Chile Water. Stir just to combine. Garnish with lime.

//

sparkling screwdriver

Prepare the citrus syrup as described on page 40, then carbonate as desired.

Pour 1½ ounces (3 tablespoons) vodka over ice cubes in a tall glass. Add 3 ounces (6 tablespoons) Zesty Sparkling Water (page 40) and 3 ounces (6 tablespoons) orange juice. Stir just until blended.

//

bubbling bloody mary

Prepare the celery seed syrup as described on page 41, then carbonate as desired.

Pour 1½ ounces (3 tablespoons) vodka over ice cubes in a tall glass. Add 3 ounces (6 tablespoons) Celrtzer (page 41) and 3 ounces (6 tablespoons) tomato juice. Stir just until blended. Garnish with a celery stick.

zesty sparkling water

Citrus zest oozes oils that yield all the citrus flavor and fragrance of the fruit without the acid. For this soda, citrus zest is steeped into a concentrated syrup. The recipe is written for three servings so that it fits easily into a 1-quart soda siphon, but if you want to make larger batches it can be multiplied. When you grate the zest from the citrus fruit, avoid the white pith under the skin, which can be bitter.

CITRUS SYRUP

½ cup water

¼ cup sugar

Finely grated zest of
1 orange, 1 lemon, or
2 limes

ENOUGH FOR 3 SERVINGS

Combine the water, sugar, and citrus zest in a small saucepan. Bring to a simmer over medium heat, and let simmer, uncovered, for 7 to 8 minutes, until the liquid reduces to one-third of its original volume (about ¼ cup). Remove from the heat and let cool to room temperature. Strain out the solids, reserving the liquid.

The syrup can be stored in the refrigerator for up to 2 weeks.

TO MIX WITH SELTZER

1 tablespoon citrus syrup
1⅓ cups seltzer

1 SERVING

Pour the syrup into a tall glass. Add the seltzer and stir just until blended. Add ice and serve.

TO CARBONATE WITH A SIPHON

4 cups water
1 batch citrus syrup

3 SERVINGS

Combine the water and syrup in a 1-quart soda siphon. Charge with CO_2 according to the manufacturer's directions. Siphon-charged sodas can be stored in the siphon in a refrigerator for up to 5 days. Disperse as desired into tall glasses filled with ice, and serve.

Also see Mixology recipe on page 39.

celrtzer

Dr. Brown's Cel-Ray was first manufactured in 1869 in Brooklyn, New York. It was originally dubbed a "tonic," though it is unlikely that the soda was ever therapeutic or that there ever was a Dr. Brown. Celery sodas are flavored with celery seed, sugar, and salt, and they are identified most closely with Jewish deli food, stemming from the days when the Dr. Brown products were the only kosher sodas. This sparkling celery soda is ever so slightly bitter and not too sweet. It is one of the most refreshing of soft drinks.

CELERY SEED SYRUP

¾ cup water

2 tablespoons celery seed

2 tablespoons sugar

¼ teaspoon fine sea salt

ENOUGH FOR 3 SERVINGS

Combine the water, celery seed, sugar, and salt in a small saucepan. Bring to a simmer over medium heat, and let simmer, uncovered, for 7 to 8 minutes, until reduced to about ¼ cup. Strain out the solids, and set the syrup aside to cool.

The syrup can be stored in the refrigerator for up to 1 month.

TO MIX WITH SELTZER

1 tablespoon celery seed syrup

1⅓ cups seltzer

1 SERVING

Pour the syrup into a tall glass. Add the seltzer and stir just until blended. Add ice and serve.

TO CARBONATE WITH A SIPHON

4 cups water

1 batch celery seed syrup

3 SERVINGS

Combine the water and syrup in a 1-quart soda siphon. Charge with CO_2 according to the manufacturer's directions. Siphon-charged sodas can be stored in the siphon in a refrigerator for up to 5 days. Disperse as desired into tall glasses filled with ice, and serve.

Also see Mixology recipe on page 39.

goji water

The goji berry has been a sought-after medicinal fruit in Chinese medicine for six thousand years. It has reputed benefit for the eyes, muscles, liver, and immune system. Though its efficacy is still debated, lab tests have shown goji to have high levels of the antioxidants beta-carotene, zeaxanthin, lutein, lycopene, and xanthophylls. Goji has a pronounced sweet-tart flavor, a little like that of sweetened cranberries.

GOJI SYRUP

2 tablespoons unsweetened goji juice (see note)

1 tablespoon agave syrup or simple syrup (page 15)

¼ teaspoon balsamic vinegar

ENOUGH FOR 3 SERVINGS

Combine the goji juice, agave syrup, and vinegar, and whisk together until smooth.

The syrup can be stored in the refrigerator for up to 1 month.

Note: Goji juice can be fairly pricey. If you want to save some money, you can make a facsimile of goji juice by pouring 1 cup boiling water over ½ cup coarsely chopped dried goji berries and letting the berries steep until the infusion cools to room temperature. Then strain out the solids, reserving the liquid.

 ## TO MIX WITH SELTZER

1 tablespoon goji syrup

1⅓ cups seltzer

1 SERVING

Pour the syrup into a tall glass. Add the seltzer and stir just until blended. Add ice and serve.

 ## TO CARBONATE WITH A SIPHON

4 cups water

1 batch goji syrup

3 SERVINGS

Combine the water and syrup in a 1-quart soda siphon. Charge with CO_2 according to the manufacturer's directions. Siphon-charged sodas can be stored in the siphon in a refrigerator for up to 5 days. Disperse as desired into tall glasses filled with ice, and serve.

honey cardamom fizzy water

Dark brown, oily, and pungent, cardamom seeds emit an intoxicating aroma of camphor, eucalyptus, and lemon when bruised with a mallet. In this recipe, that palate-expanding experience is captured in honey syrup.

HONEY SYRUP

- 16 green cardamom pods
- ⅓ cup honey
- ¼ cup water
- 2 teaspoons lemon juice

ENOUGH FOR 3 SERVINGS

Spread the cardamom pods in a single layer on a solid work surface. Pound the pods with a hammer, meat pounder, or small heavy skillet until the pods are crushed and the cardamom seeds inside are bruised.

Combine the crushed cardamom pods, honey, water, and lemon juice in a small saucepan. Bring to a simmer over medium heat, and let simmer, uncovered, for 4 to 5 minutes, until the liquid reduces to one-third of its original volume (about ¼ cup). Remove from the heat and set aside to cool for 15 minutes. Strain out the solids, reserving the liquid.

The syrup can be stored in the refrigerator for up to 1 month.

TO MIX WITH SELTZER

- 1 tablespoon honey syrup
- 1⅓ cups seltzer

1 SERVING

Pour the syrup into a tall glass. Add the seltzer and stir just until blended. Add ice and serve.

TO CARBONATE WITH A SIPHON

- 4 cups water
- 1 batch honey syrup

3 SERVINGS

Combine the water and syrup in a 1-quart soda siphon. Charge with CO_2 according to the manufacturer's directions. Siphon-charged sodas can be stored in the siphon in a refrigerator for up to 5 days. Disperse as desired in tall glasses filled with ice, and serve.

fragrant vanilla water

Heady vanilla notes blend with the caramel flavor of tropical coconut palm sugar in this inspired combination. The palm sugar and vanilla reinforce each other's perfumes, resulting in a subtle flavor and intoxicating aroma.

VANILLA SYRUP

¾ cup water

½ vanilla bean, split lengthwise

¼ cup evaporated coconut palm sugar

ENOUGH FOR 3 SERVINGS

Combine the water, vanilla bean, and palm sugar in a small saucepan, and stir well. Bring to a simmer over medium heat, stirring occasionally until the sugar dissolves; let simmer, uncovered, about 5 minutes, until the syrup is reduced to ⅓ cup.

Remove from the heat and let cool to room temperature. Remove the vanilla bean, and scrape the seeds from the pod into the syrup.

The syrup can be stored in the refrigerator for up to 1 month.

TO MIX WITH SELTZER

1¾ tablespoons vanilla syrup

1⅓ cups seltzer

1 SERVING

Pour the syrup into a tall glass. Add the seltzer and stir just until blended. Add ice and serve.

TO CARBONATE WITH A SIPHON

4 cups water

1 batch vanilla syrup

3 SERVINGS

Combine the water and syrup in a 1-quart soda siphon. Charge with CO_2 according to the manufacturer's directions. Siphon-charged sodas can be stored in the siphon in a refrigerator for up to 5 days. Disperse as desired into tall glasses filled with ice, and serve.

lychee water

The season for fresh lychees is short, about a month in the middle of the summer, but canned lychees work perfectly well in this beverage, which is honey-sweet (from the natural sugars in the lychee) and ever so slightly tangy (from slices of pickled ginger). Lychees are rich in vitamin C.

LYCHEE GINGER MUDDLE

2 lychees, peeled and pitted if fresh, or drained if canned

1 slice pickled ginger (sushi ginger)

ENOUGH FOR 1 SERVING

Muddle the lychees and ginger in the bottom of a tall glass.

 ## TO MIX WITH SELTZER

1½ cups seltzer

1 batch lychee ginger muddle

1 SERVING

Add the seltzer to the muddled fruit and stir briefly to combine. Add ice and serve.

POP CULTURE

Got Moxie?

MOXIE SODA ORIGINATED AS MOXIE NERVE FOOD in 1876, created by Dr. Augustin Thompson from an unnamed tropical plant (turns out it was gentian root) he claimed had been discovered by his (fictitious) friend Lieutenant Moxie. This herbal panacea was advertised as a medication to guard against "paralysis, softening of the brain, nervousness, and insomnia." The original version was not carbonated, but in 1884 sparkling water was added to the formula, and Moxie was soon distributed in bottles and through soda fountains. Calvin Coolidge drank Moxie, as did Boston Red Sox star Ted Williams. The Catawissa Bottling Company of Pennsylvania is the current producer of Moxie.

honeydew mint seltzer

A ripe honeydew melon is hard to find. That's because these melons do not ripen further after being harvested and do not travel well after ripening. Look for melons that have a creamy yellow (rather than pale green) cast to the skin and a pronounced honeydew aroma. If you can't find a ripe specimen, you can substitute watermelon. Either way, this naturally sweet sparkling water is one of the most refreshing summer beverages imaginable.

HONEYDEW JUICE

½ ripe honeydew, rind and seeds discarded, flesh coarsely chopped

2 dozen fresh mint leaves, finely chopped

Big pinch of sea salt

ENOUGH FOR 4 SERVINGS

Mash the honeydew and mint leaves with a vegetable masher into a loose, wet purée. Set a strainer over a small bowl and scrape the purée into the strainer, so that it drains into the bowl below. Stir the purée gently as it strains to get as much liquid through as possible without forcing any solids into the strained liquid. Discard the solids, and stir the salt into the liquid.

The purée can be stored in the refrigerator for up to 2 days, but it is best to use it immediately.

 TO MIX WITH SELTZER

½ cup honeydew juice
1 cup seltzer

1 SERVING

Pour the juice into a tall glass. Add the seltzer and stir just until blended. Add ice and serve.

 Mixology

Prepare the honeydew juice as described above, then carbonate with seltzer.

honeydew mint julep

Add 1 ounce (2 tablespoons) vodka and 1 teaspoon honey to a glass of Honeydew Mint Seltzer.

sparkling rose water

Rose water, a steam-distilled elixir of rose petals, is to Middle Eastern cooking what vanilla is to Western cooking. A frequent ingredient in baking and sweet beverages, it has an ethereal fragrance that is at once innocent and intoxicating, and highly exotic to the uninitiated American palate. The floral aroma is quite subtle and blends beautifully with the slightly musky notes of honey. Think of this recipe as the foreign-born cousin of vanilla-scented cream soda.

ROSE WATER SYRUP

2 teaspoons rose water

½ teaspoon honey, preferably orange blossom

ENOUGH FOR 1 SERVING

Mix the rose water and honey, stirring until blended.

 ## TO MIX WITH SELTZER

1 batch rose water syrup

1½ cups seltzer

1 SERVING

Pour the syrup into a tall glass. Add the seltzer and stir just until blended. Add ice and serve.

barely sweet white grape water

More noble potables owe their pedigree to grapes than to any other fruit, yet all but a few are decidedly alcoholic, since the sugar in grapes is highly susceptible to fermentation. In this grape-infused soft drink, the natural sugars of grapes are amended with a few raisins (drying the grapes concentrates the sugars) and then tamed with a hint of white wine vinegar (the acidic fermentation of grape juice). The combined effect is barely sweet and tongue-tinglingly grapey.

GRAPE SYRUP

- 2¾ cups unsweetened white grape juice
- ⅓ cup golden raisins, coarsely chopped
- 1½ teaspoons white wine vinegar

ENOUGH FOR 4 SERVINGS

Combine ½ cup grape juice and the raisins in a small saucepan. Bring to a simmer over medium heat, then remove from the heat and let cool, about 30 minutes. Strain out the raisins and combine the raisin-flavored grape juice with the remaining 2¼ cups grape juice and the vinegar.

The syrup can be stored in the refrigerator for up to 2 weeks.

 TO MIX WITH SELTZER

- ⅔ cup grape syrup
- ⅔ cup seltzer

1 SERVING

Pour the syrup into a tall glass. Add the seltzer and stir just until blended. Add ice and serve.

 Mixology

Prepare the grape syrup as described above, then carbonate with seltzer.

deconstructed bubbly

Add 1 ounce (2 tablespoons) vodka to a glass of Barely Sweet White Grape Water.

a hint of chocolate mint water

Chocolate soda water may be an acquired taste, but the mutual attraction of chocolate and mint registers so naturally on the palate, and the mentholated refreshment of mint beverages is so universal, that concocting a sparkling water of chocolate and mint seemed worth a try. It proved to be far more seductive than I ever anticipated. The chocolate is embracing and warm, the mint aerating and cool, and the carbonation tickles and nudges everyone to play together nicely.

MINT CHOCOLATE SYRUP

- ¼ cup unsweetened cocoa powder
- ¼ cup finely chopped fresh mint leaves
- 3 tablespoons sugar
- ⅓ cup cold water

ENOUGH FOR 3 SERVINGS

Combine the cocoa, mint, and sugar in a small saucepan. Add the water and whisk until smooth. Bring to a simmer over medium heat, stirring constantly. Let simmer for 1 minute, then remove from the heat, let cool, and strain out the solids.

This syrup can be stored in the refrigerator for up to 1 week.

TO MIX WITH SELTZER

- 2 tablespoons mint chocolate syrup
- 1⅓ cups seltzer

1 SERVING

Pour the syrup into a tall glass. Add the seltzer and stir just until blended. Add ice and serve.

TO CARBONATE WITH A SIPHON

- 4 cups water
- 1 batch mint chocolate syrup

3 SERVINGS

Combine the water and syrup in a 1-quart soda siphon. Charge with CO_2 according to the manufacturer's directions. Siphon-charged sodas can be stored in the siphon in a refrigerator for up to 5 days. Disperse as desired into tall glasses filled with ice, and serve.

Raspberry Lime Rickey, page 59

CHAPTER TWO

Fruit Sodas

*B*ecause ripe fruit is high in sugar, fruit juices are easily carbonated by wild yeast and were among the first carbonated beverages drunk for refreshment. It is therefore not surprising that while medicinal sodas made from herb teas were commonplace at early pharmacy soda fountains, the first flavored soda fountain beverages sold purely for refreshment were combinations of fruit juice and carbonated water.

To this day, all fruit sodas are made by one of these two methods: either fruit juice is fermented with yeast until it is naturally carbonated (such as sparkling cider), or a base of fruit juice or fruit and sweetener is artificially carbonated with sparkling water (such as orange soda). Yeast fermentation produces full-flavored drinks with a creamy mouthfeel. Fruit sodas made from artificial carbonation tend to be sweeter and thinner, characteristics that increase their refreshment quotient.

When fruit sodas are made via the artificial carbonation method, in which a fruity base is diluted with sparkling water, the sodas retain some of the nutrition of the fruit but can have far fewer calories than straight fruit juice, a quality that endears them to dieters. With that said, remember that commercially produced fruit sodas are mainly fruit-flavored sugar water, not a carbonated juice base. They can have just as many calories as standard sweet sodas, and can be just as void of nutrition, which for many people is the main impetus behind making their own fruit sodas.

The recipes that follow start with either bottled fruit juice or a fresh fruit purée. When using a purée you will have to strain the fruit to rid it of excess pulp, which could otherwise cause the soda to separate as it sits. You can instead use a juice extractor to make the fruit bases for recipes calling for a purée, thereby eliminating the need to strain. However, if you do so you will have to increase the amount of fruit in the recipes, anywhere from 50 to 100 percent, depending on the fruit's pulpiness, in order to produce enough fruit base to make the ratios in the recipes come out correctly.

sparkling watermelon

Watermelon is so sweet and juicy that it is practically a beverage right off the vine. A bit of added water makes it truly quaffable. Watermelon is lower in sugar than other melons (6.2 percent, as opposed to the 7.8 percent of cantaloupe and 8.6 percent of honeydew), but it is also very low in sodium (1 percent, as opposed to the 16 percent of cantaloupe and 18 percent of honeydew), which means it can be bland when juiced. A little bit of sea salt takes care of that. A glass of watermelon juice tastes sweet but has only 60 calories.

WATERMELON JUICE

¼–⅓ seedless watermelon (about 4½ pounds)

½ cup water

½ teaspoon coarse sea salt

ENOUGH FOR 4 SERVINGS

Cut the rind from the watermelon and chop the flesh into small pieces, trapping any juices that flow out. Combine the chopped watermelon flesh, collected juices, and water in a blender or food processor. Process until puréed.

Set a strainer over a large bowl and pass the puréed melon through the strainer, stirring the loose purée gently as it strains to get as much liquid through as possible without forcing any solids into the strained liquid. Discard the solids, and stir the salt into the watermelon liquid.

Note: Because watermelon juice is so naturally watery, it cannot be diluted with seltzer into a sparkling beverage. It must be carbonated in a soda siphon.

TO CARBONATE WITH A SIPHON

1 batch watermelon juice

4 SERVINGS

Pour the juice into a 1-quart soda siphon. Charge with CO_2 according to the manufacturer's directions. Siphon-charged sodas can be stored in the siphon in a refrigerator for up to 5 days. Disperse as desired into tall glasses filled with ice, and serve. Garnish with more sea salt, if desired.

orange honey ginger ale

Before refrigeration, ginger was commonly added to beer to counteract off flavors that could develop when the fermentation process went awry. The practice has waned, but the appreciation for ginger-flavored beverages has not. Ginger is a unique aromatic ingredient, one of the few that burns and cools simultaneously. With its pronounced floral character, it has an affinity for both honey and orange. Select a mild honey, such as orange blossom, for this soda. If the honey is too bold it will fight with the ginger and overpower the orange flavor. This soda may take slightly longer that usual to ferment due to the acidity of the orange juice.

ORANGE HONEY GINGER SYRUP

- 1 quart water
- 2¼ cups sugar
- ¾ cup mild honey, such as orange blossom
- 3 ounces fresh gingerroot, peeled and grated (about ½ cup)

Juice of 1 orange

ENOUGH FOR 1 GALLON BREWED GINGER ALE

Combine the water, sugar, honey, ginger, and orange juice in a large saucepan, and stir to combine. Bring to a simmer over medium heat, stirring occasionally until the sugar dissolves, then let simmer, uncovered, for 30 minutes. Remove from the heat, let cool for 30 minutes, and strain out the solids.

This syrup can be stored in the refrigerator for up to 2 months.

 ## TO MIX WITH SELTZER

- ⅓ cup orange honey ginger syrup
- 2 tablespoons orange juice
- 1½ cups seltzer

1 SERVING

Pour the syrup and juice into a tall glass. Add the seltzer and stir just until blended. Add ice and serve.

TO CARBONATE WITH A SIPHON

3 cups water
⅔ cup orange honey ginger syrup
⅓ cup orange juice

3 SERVINGS

Combine the water, syrup, and juice in a 1-quart soda siphon. Charge with CO_2 according to the manufacturer's directions. Siphon-charged sodas can be stored in the siphon in a refrigerator for up to 5 days. Disperse as desired into tall glasses filled with ice, and serve.

 ## TO BREW

2 quarts lukewarm (80 to 90°F) water
1 batch orange honey ginger syrup
¼ teaspoon champagne yeast (*Saccharomyces bayanus*)
1 quart orange juice

1 GALLON

Combine the water and syrup in a large container. Test the temperature; the mixture should be at a warm room temperature, from 75 to 80°F. (If it is too hot, let it sit until it cools a bit. If it is too cold, warm it over low heat.) Add the yeast and stir until it is completely dissolved. Stir in the orange juice.

Pour the mixture into sanitized plastic bottles (see page 25) using a sanitized kitchen funnel, leaving 1¼ inches of air space at the top of each bottle. Seal the bottles. Store for 4 to 6 days at room temperature. When the bottles feel rock hard, the soda is fully carbonated. Refrigerate for at least 1 week before serving; drink within 3 weeks to avoid overcarbonation.

 ### *Mixology*

Prepare the orange honey ginger syrup as described at left, then carbonate as desired.

ginger honey rummy

Pour 2 ounces (¼ cup) golden rum over ice in a tall glass. Add 6 ounces (¾ cup) Orange Honey Ginger Ale and stir briefly. Garnish with an orange slice.

black lemonade

This serious soda is like biting into a fresh lemon peppered with a hint of chile and a glaze of caramel richness. The sensation is hard to define, but there is something about the midnight hue, the sultry mouthfeel of citrus oil, and the intriguing combination of clove, sage, and sweetness that sets the taste receptors on boggle. Crazy rarely tastes this delicious.

SPICED LEMONADE SYRUP

- ⅔ cup water
- Finely grated zest and juice of 2 lemons
- ¼ teaspoon finely grated nutmeg
- 2 cloves
- 3 fresh sage leaves, or ¼ teaspoon rubbed sage
- Pinch of crushed chile flakes
- 1 cup sugar
- 1 tablespoon browning sauce, such as Kitchen Bouquet

ENOUGH FOR 3 SERVINGS

Combine the water, lemon zest, nutmeg, cloves, sage, and chile flakes in a large saucepan. Stir in the sugar. Bring to a boil, stirring until the sugar dissolves, and let boil for 1 minute. Remove from the heat and stir in the lemon juice and browning sauce. Let cool, then strain.

This syrup can be stored in the refrigerator for up to 2 weeks.

TO MIX WITH SELTZER

- ⅓ cup spiced lemonade syrup
- 1 cup seltzer

1 SERVING

Pour the syrup into a tall glass. Add the seltzer and stir just until blended. Add ice and serve.

TO CARBONATE WITH A SIPHON

3 cups water
1 batch spiced lemonade
   syrup

3 SERVINGS

Combine the water and syrup in a 1-quart soda siphon. Charge with CO_2 according to the manufacturer's directions. Siphon-charged sodas can be stored in the siphon in a refrigerator for up to 5 days. Disperse as desired into tall glasses filled with ice, and serve.

Soda and Health Risks

IN 2005 THE CENTER FOR SCIENCE IN THE PUBLIC INTEREST published a report, "Liquid Candy: How Soft Drinks are Harming Americans' Health," examining the increased consumption of soft drinks, especially by children and teenagers, and the increased incidence of obesity, diabetes, tooth decay, osteoporosis, and kidney stones in the population at large. The report recommended stopping the sale and advertising of soft drinks in schools, requiring medical professionals to ask patients about their soft drink consumption, and the levying of taxes on soft drink sales to pay for a mass-media campaign to improve diet and promote exercise.

sparkling honey lemonade

The combination of honey and lemon is embraced as a soothing cure for coughs, sore throats, and colds, as a digestive aid, and as a weight-loss method. I would like to make the case for its power to produce pure delectable pleasure. The two ingredients complement one another as they spar on the palate — the honey syrupy and floral, the lemon bright, fruity, and acidic — delivering a rambunctious, full-flavored mouthful in every swallow. Few foods fulfill that kind of promise with such simplicity.

LEMON HONEY SYRUP

6 tablespoons honey

6 tablespoons lemon juice

ENOUGH FOR 3 SERVINGS

Mix the honey and lemon juice, stirring until blended.

The syrup can be stored in the refrigerator for up to 1 week.

 ## TO MIX WITH SELTZER

¼ cup lemon honey syrup
1 cup seltzer

1 SERVING

Pour the syrup into a tall glass. Add the seltzer and stir just until blended. Add ice and serve.

 ## TO CARBONATE WITH A SIPHON

3 cups water
1 batch lemon honey syrup

3 SERVINGS

Combine the water and syrup in a 1-quart soda siphon. Charge with CO_2 according to the manufacturer's directions. Siphon-charged sodas can be stored in the siphon in a refrigerator for up to 5 days. Disperse as desired into tall glasses filled with ice, and serve.

raspberry lime rickey

Rickeys can be alcoholic or not, and made with any fruit and practically any liquor. The common ingredients they all share are lime juice, sugar, and soda water. The drink is said to have been named for English colonel Joseph Rickey, who was stationed in Washington DC in the late 1800s and reputedly concocted the libation at Shoomaker's, a local bar. The Cuban mojito is a modern-day rendition of the rickey.

RASPBERRY LIME SYRUP

1 cup raspberries

¼ cup freshly squeezed lime juice

1 cup sugar

ENOUGH FOR 3 SERVINGS

Mash the raspberries in a small saucepan with a vegetable masher. Stir in the lime juice and sugar until combined. Warm over low heat, stirring often, until the sugar dissolves and the raspberries have released all of their liquid. Bring to a boil, and then remove from the heat. Let cool to room temperature and then strain.

This syrup can be stored in the refrigerator for up to 2 days, but is best used immediately.

 TO MIX WITH SELTZER

⅔ cup raspberry lime syrup

1 cup seltzer

Lime wedge

1 SERVING

Pour the syrup into a tall glass. Add the seltzer and stir just until blended. Add ice and serve. Garnish with a wedge of lime.

Mixology

rosy rickey

Add 1 ounce (2 tablespoons) gin to a glass of carbonated Raspberry Lime Rickey.

rickey julep

Replace the raspberries in the raspberry lime syrup with mint leaves, then carbonate with seltzer. Add 1 ounce (2 tablespoons) bourbon to each glass of soda.

strawberry pomegranate soda

Pomegranate juice is loaded with antioxidants that help the body fight diseases of all sorts. Its intense flavor is matched by its overt tartness. In this soda, the pomegranate's pucker is tempered by the floral sweetness of strawberries.

STRAWBERRY POMEGRANATE SYRUP

- 1 pint strawberries, hulled and coarsely chopped
- 1 cup sugar
- 1 cup unsweetened pomegranate juice, fresh (page 61) or bottled

ENOUGH FOR 3 SERVINGS

Combine the strawberries and sugar in a small bowl and let sit for 10 minutes. Combine the mixture with the pomegranate juice in a blender or food processor and purée. Set a strainer over a small bowl and scrape the purée into the strainer, so that the liquid drains into the bowl below.

Stir the purée gently as it strains to get as much liquid through as possible without forcing any solids into the strained liquid. Discard the solids, reserving the liquid. You should have about 2 cups.

The syrup can be stored in the refrigerator for up to 2 days, but is best used immediately.

TO MIX WITH SELTZER

⅔ cup strawberry
pomegranate syrup
⅔ cup seltzer

1 SERVING

Pour the syrup into a tall glass. Add the seltzer and stir just until blended. Add ice and serve.

 TO CARBONATE WITH A SIPHON

2 cups water
1 batch strawberry pomegranate syrup

3 SERVINGS

Combine the water and syrup in a 1-quart soda siphon. Charge with CO_2 according to the manufacturer's directions. Siphon-charged sodas can be stored in the siphon in a refrigerator for up to 5 days. Disperse as desired into tall glasses filled with ice, and serve.

Fresh Pomegranate Juice

THERE ARE TWO METHODS for making fresh pomegranate juice. Either one will make about 1 cup of juice from a medium-size pomegranate.

METHOD 1: Cut the pomegranate in half along its equator. Working with one half at a time, place the fruit, cut side down, on a square of double-thick cheesecloth that has been dampened with water. Wrap the corners of the cheesecloth up around the pomegranate and squeeze the juice into a container.

METHOD 2: Cut a pomegranate in quarters. Scoop the seeds and flesh into a food processor equipped with a knife blade. Process until the juice separates from the seeds and pulp. Strain out the solids, reserving the juice.

grapagne

Naturally carbonated grape soda lives on the road between grape juice and wine. The main difference is that in grape soda, the carbon dioxide produced by the yeasts consuming the juice's sugar is trapped in the bottle, and the fermentation is stopped as soon as the desired level of carbonation is achieved. This also limits the amount of fruit sugar that converts into alcohol, producing a soda that is ever so slightly alcoholic, vigorously fizzy, and subtly sugared — a sweet teetotaling version of champagne.

This recipe does not begin with a flavor base. Follow the complete brewing instructions to make two quarts of Grapagne.

 TO BREW

2 quarts unsweetened white or purple grape juice, at room temperature (75 to 80°F)

⅛ teaspoon champagne yeast (*Saccharomyces bayanus*)

2 QUARTS

Combine the grape juice and yeast, and stir until the yeast is dissolved.

Pour the mixture into sanitized plastic bottles (see page 25) using a sanitized kitchen funnel, leaving 1¼ inches of air space at the top of each bottle. Seal the bottles. Store for 2 to 4 days at room temperature. When the bottles feel hard, the soda is fully carbonated. Refrigerate for at least 1 week before serving; drink within 3 weeks to avoid overcarbonation.

kiwi lime soda

Pair the tutti-frutti grapey sweetness of ripe kiwi with the fragrant acidity of freshly squeezed lime juice and you have a natural soda that is perfectly balanced. The only challenge is leaching the juice from the pulpy fruit. That's easily accomplished by heating the mashed kiwi with sugar. Because sugar is hydroscopic (water-attracting), it leaches the juice from the kiwi without any squeezing or puréeing.

KIWI LIME SYRUP

- 4 ripe kiwis, peeled and coarsely chopped
- 1 cup sugar
- ¼ cup freshly squeezed lime juice

ENOUGH FOR 3 SERVINGS

Mash the kiwis and sugar in a small saucepan with a vegetable masher. Warm over low heat, stirring often, until the sugar dissolves and the kiwis have released their liquid. Bring to a boil, and then remove from the heat and let cool to room temperature. Stir in the lime juice; strain. You should have about 1½ cups syrup.

The syrup can be stored in the refrigerator for up to 5 days.

 ## TO MIX WITH SELTZER

- ½ cup kiwi lime syrup
- 1 cup seltzer

1 SERVING

Pour the syrup into a tall glass. Add the seltzer and stir just until blended. Add ice and serve.

 ## TO CARBONATE WITH A SIPHON

- 2½ cups water
- 1 batch kiwi lime syrup

3 SERVINGS

Combine the water and syrup in a 1-quart soda siphon. Charge with CO_2 according to the manufacturer's directions. Siphon-charged sodas can be stored in the siphon in a refrigerator for up to 5 days. Disperse as desired into tall glasses filled with ice, and serve.

blueberry cinnamon soda

The fragrance of blueberries is subtle and fleeting — spectacular when the berries are freshly picked, but lacking when they are cooked and puréed. Blueberries need a boost of sweetness, acid, or, best of all, cinnamon: the spicy bark's woody bite is just what a blueberry needs to bloom and become its best self.

BLUEBERRY SYRUP

1 pint blueberries

¼ cup red wine or unsweetened purple grape juice

1 cup sugar

1 cinnamon stick, broken into small pieces

ENOUGH FOR 3 SERVINGS

Mash berries, wine, and sugar in a small saucepan with a vegetable masher; stir in the cinnamon. Warm over low heat, stirring often, until the sugar dissolves and the blueberries have released their liquid. Bring to a boil, and then remove from the heat, let cool to room temperature, and strain. You should have about 2 cups syrup.

The syrup can be stored in the refrigerator for up to 5 days.

 TO MIX WITH SELTZER

⅔ cup blueberry syrup

⅔ cup seltzer

1 SERVING

Pour the syrup into a tall glass. Add the seltzer and stir just until blended. Add ice and serve.

 TO CARBONATE WITH A SIPHON

2 cups water

1 batch blueberry syrup

3 SERVINGS

Combine the water and syrup in a 1-quart soda siphon. Charge with CO_2 according to the manufacturer's directions. Siphon-charged sodas can be stored in the siphon in a refrigerator for up to 5 days. Disperse as desired into tall glasses filled with ice, and serve.

"sloe" fizz

Sloe, the berry of the blackthorn bush, looks like a swollen blueberry and tastes somewhere between a blueberry and a plum. It is the flavoring of sloe gin, a rendition of English gin infused with sloe in place of juniper berries. Sloe gin is red from the berry's juice, which is extracted by macerating the fruit in sugar. It is combined with seltzer to create a sloe gin fizz, a classic nineteenth-century cocktail. This nonalcoholic version uses a combination of blueberry and prune juices to approximate the flavor and color of sloe.

BLUEBERRY PRUNE JUICE

½ cup unsweetened blueberry juice

½ cup unsweetened prune juice

¼ teaspoon almond extract

ENOUGH FOR 3 SERVINGS

Combine the blueberry juice, prune juice, and almond extract, stirring to combine.

The syrup can be stored in the refrigerator for up to 5 days.

 TO MIX WITH SELTZER

⅓ cup blueberry prune juice

1 cup seltzer

1 SERVING

Pour the juice into a tall glass. Add the seltzer and stir just until blended. Add ice and serve.

TO CARBONATE WITH A SIPHON

3 cups water

1 batch blueberry prune juice

3 SERVINGS

Combine the water and juice in a 1-quart soda siphon. Charge with CO_2 according to the manufacturer's directions. Siphon-charged sodas can be stored in the siphon in a refrigerator for up to 5 days. Disperse as desired into tall glasses filled with ice, and serve.

original orange crush

SECRET FORMULA

Orange Crush was created in 1915 by Neil Callen Ward, a chemist in Los Angeles who solved the perishability problems of orange juice by creating an orange beverage solely from the oils in the peel. Orange juice was added briefly to the formula in 1921, but today's beverage contains no juice.

ORANGE ZEST SYRUP

1½ cups sugar

¼ cup finely grated orange zest

1 cup water

½ teaspoon citric acid

½ teaspoon gum arabic

2 drops yellow food coloring

1 drop red food coloring

ENOUGH FOR 3 SERVINGS

Combine the orange zest and sugar in small saucepan. Add the water, stir, and bring to a simmer over medium heat, stirring just until the sugar dissolves. Stir in the citric acid and gum arabic, then remove from the heat, let cool to room temperature, and strain. Stir in the food coloring.

This syrup can be stored in the refrigerator for up to 1 month.

 TO MIX WITH SELTZER

½ cup orange zest syrup
1 cup seltzer

1 SERVING

Pour the syrup into a tall glass. Add the seltzer and stir just until blended. Add ice and serve.

 TO CARBONATE WITH A SIPHON

2½ cups water
1 batch orange zest syrup

3 SERVINGS

Combine the water and syrup in a 1-quart soda siphon. Charge with CO_2 according to the manufacturer's directions. Siphon-charged sodas can be stored in the siphon in a refrigerator for up to 5 days. Disperse as desired into tall glasses filled with ice, and serve.

Soda vs. Pop

WHAT'S IN A NAME? Would that which we call "soda" by any other name taste as sweet? No, it seems. The United States is divided between soda drinkers, pop drinkers, and, in the South, a good many coke (with a small *c*) drinkers, where a soft drink by any manufacturer is still called *coke*.

The name *soda* apparently derives from its connection to sodium, a mineral commonly found in natural spring water. Its use in association to carbonation was first recorded in 1802. The name *pop,* on the other hand, was first used in 1812 to describe the sound a cork made when pulled from a bottle of carbonated beverage.

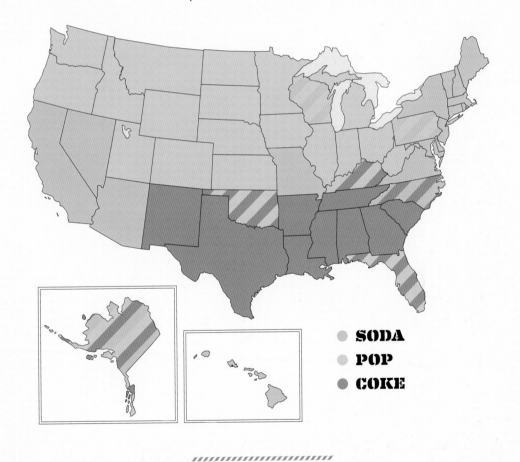

- SODA
- POP
- COKE

Introductory Dates of Beverage Terms

1798	1809	1812	1863	1880	1909	1920
soda water	ginger pop	pop	soda pop	soft drink	coke	cola

fruit cola

The hard-to-pin-down yet familiar flavor of cola is at heart little more than citrus flavored with coriander (see Natural Cola, page 104). Once we know the basic formula, it becomes fun to fiddle with, which is exactly what we're doing here. The citrus base is a natural for mixing with other fruit flavors, and to my palate, the one that fits seamlessly is plum or prune. Prune juice is one of the great culinary secrets, an all-purpose fruit flavor that adds richness, natural sweetness, and a generic fruitiness that few people can pinpoint. Prune and cola — quite a mysterious couple.

PRUNE COLA SYRUP

1⅛ cups prune juice

6 tablespoons Natural Cola syrup (page 104)

ENOUGH FOR 3 SERVINGS

Combine the prune juice and cola syrup, stirring until blended.

The syrup can be stored in the refrigerator for up to 5 days.

TO MIX WITH SELTZER

½ cup prune cola syrup
1 cup seltzer

1 SERVING

Pour the syrup into a tall glass. Add the seltzer and stir just until blended. Add ice and serve.

TO CARBONATE WITH A SIPHON

2½ cups water
1 batch prune cola syrup

3 SERVINGS

Combine the water and syrup in a 1-quart soda siphon. Charge with CO_2 according to the manufacturer's directions. Siphon-charged sodas can be stored in the siphon in a refrigerator for up to 5 days. Disperse as desired into tall glasses filled with ice, and serve.

maraschino ginger ale

Maraschino is a cherry-infused alcohol that derives much of its flavor from benzaldehyde, the potent aromatic in cherry pits. Benzaldehyde's flavor is easily replicated with a few drops of pure almond extract. When added to a glass of ginger ale it generates instant time travel, transporting our palates back to childhood days of sipping maraschino-tinted Shirley Temples at the bar, just like the sophisticates we emulated.

This recipe does not begin with a flavor base. Follow the complete mixing instructions to make one serving of Maraschino Ginger Ale.

 ## TO MIX WITH GINGER ALE

1½ cups Ginger Ginger Ale (page 108) or purchased ginger ale
¼ teaspoon almond extract

1 SERVING

Combine the ginger ale and almond extract in a tall glass, stirring just until blended. Fill with ice and serve.

 ### *Mixology*

Prepare the Maraschino Ginger Ale as described above.

drunken shirley temple

Pour 1 ounce (2 tablespoons) whiskey over a few ice cubes in a sour glass. Top with 3 to 4 ounces (6 to 8 tablespoons) Maraschino Ginger Ale. Garnish with a cherry.

fruity root beer

The tang of root beer is so pronounced that it easily trumps almost any other flavor it is paired with. The trick is not to try to compete, but to complement. Unobtrusive fruit juices like apple and pear are frequently paired with more assertive juices in the manufacturing of commercial fruit beverages. This easy mixed drink takes advantage of the same phenomenon. Apple juice blends effortlessly with root beer flavoring, making it mellower and smoother.

APPLE ROOT BEER SYRUP

1⅛ cups apple juice

6 tablespoons Rooty Toot Root Beer syrup (page 88) or purchased root beer syrup (see Resources)

ENOUGH FOR 3 SERVINGS

Combine the apple juice and root beer syrup, stirring until blended.

The syrup can be stored in the refrigerator for up to 5 days.

TO MIX WITH SELTZER

½ cup apple root beer syrup
1 cup seltzer

1 SERVING

Pour the syrup into a tall glass. Add the seltzer and stir just until blended. Add ice and serve.

TO CARBONATE WITH A SIPHON

2½ cups water
1 batch apple root beer syrup

3 SERVINGS

Combine the water and syrup in a 1-quart soda siphon. Charge with CO_2 according to the manufacturer's directions. Siphon-charged sodas can be stored in the siphon in a refrigerator for up to 5 days. Disperse as desired into tall glasses filled with ice, and serve.

Original Formula for Dr Pepper Discovered?

IN THE SUMMER OF 2008, Bill Waters of Tulsa, Oklahoma, was antiquing in the Texas Panhandle. He happened upon an old apothecary ledger filled with formulas and bought it for $200, thinking that something that old might be worth more. It turns out that the ledger was from Morrison's Old Corner Drug Store in Waco, Texas, the same store that first served Dr Pepper soda. On the book's cover was a faded title, *Castles Formulas* (John Castle was a partner of W. B. Morrison and its druggist as early as 1880). One of the formulas, titled "D Peppers Pepsin Bitters," was of particular interest, because early soda bases were very similar to bitters and were sold as digestive aids. Dr Pepper was first served at the Old Corner Drug Store in 1885. Could this be the original Dr Pepper formula? Representatives from Snapple, which now owns Dr Pepper, say that the formula is nothing like the formula they use, but that is not to say that the discovered formula is not an early version.

very cherry cola

Think about it! Cherry flavor is no more like a fresh cherry than carob is like chocolate. Although we may associate cherry flavor with cherries, it is mostly because the foods it flavors are commonly dyed red. It looks like a cherry, but it tastes like . . . almond extract. That's right. The flavor of all cherry-flavored concoctions is almond. The aromatic in almond extract is benzaldehyde, a toxic substance derived from bitter almonds and detoxified of cyanide for consumption. Benzaldehyde is also found in the pits of most drupe fruits, like apricots, prunes, and, most notably, cherries.

ALMOND COLA SYRUP

9 tablespoons Natural Cola syrup (page 104)

¾ teaspoon almond extract

ENOUGH FOR 3 SERVINGS

Combine the cola syrup and almond extract, stirring until blended.

The syrup can be stored in the refrigerator for up to 2 weeks.

TO MIX WITH SELTZER

3 tablespoons almond cola syrup

1 cup seltzer

1 SERVING

Pour the syrup into a tall glass. Add the seltzer and stir just until blended. Add ice and serve.

TO CARBONATE WITH A SIPHON

3 cups water

1 batch almond cola syrup

3 SERVINGS

Combine the water and syrup in a 1-quart soda siphon. Charge with CO_2 according to the manufacturer's directions. Siphon-charged sodas can be stored in the siphon in a refrigerator for up to 5 days. Disperse as desired into tall glasses filled with ice, and serve.

Fruity Coca-Cola

AMENDING COCA-COLA WITH FRUIT FLAVORS was a popular trick of drugstore soda jerks in the 1950s. Cherry and lemon were the most popular additions. The Coca-Cola Company did not produce a bottled cherry-flavored Coke until 1985; lemon came along in 2001.

pomegranate elixir

Merriman-Webster's definition of elixir *includes this hyperbole: "a substance held capable of prolonging life indefinitely." I'm not sure whether this concoction qualifies, but it certainly packs enough antioxidants to come close. Antioxidants help your body neutralize free radicals, which have been implicated in the growth of cancerous cells and in cell aging.*

BLUEBERRY POMEGRANATE JUICE

1 cup unsweetened blueberry juice, fresh or bottled

1 cup unsweetened pomegranate juice, fresh (page 61) or bottled

1 tablespoon agave syrup or simple syrup (page 15)

ENOUGH FOR 3 SERVINGS

Combine the blueberry juice, pomegranate juice, and agave syrup, stirring until blended.

The syrup can be stored in the refrigerator for up to 2 days.

 ## TO MIX WITH SELTZER

⅔ cup blueberry pomegranate juice
⅔ cup seltzer

1 SERVING

Pour the juice into a tall glass. Add the seltzer and stir just until blended. Add ice and serve.

TO CARBONATE WITH A SIPHON

2 cups water
1 batch blueberry pomegranate juice

3 SERVINGS

Combine the water and juice in a 1-quart soda siphon. Charge with CO_2 according to the manufacturer's directions. Siphon-charged sodas can be stored in the siphon in a refrigerator for up to 5 days. Disperse as desired into tall glasses filled with ice, and serve.

tropical passion

Passion fruit, native to tropical and subtropical parts of South America, has a hard husk and hard seeds embedded in its pulp. The fruits are a pain to deal with, so I usually use passion fruit juice for making soda. The juice is often sold blended with a nondescript fruit juice, like apple or white grape, to stretch it. This is actually beneficial, as straight passion fruit can be overpowering. The fruit has a strong, penetrating aroma that is tutti-frutti, floral, and musky. In this soda, the intensity is tamed with sweet-tart pineapple juice and a touch of vanilla.

PASSION FRUIT– PINEAPPLE JUICE

1½ cups unsweetened passion fruit juice

½ cup unsweetened pineapple juice

¼ teaspoon vanilla extract

ENOUGH FOR 3 SERVINGS

Combine the passion fruit juice, pineapple juice, and vanilla extract, stirring until blended. The syrup can be stored in the refrigerator for up to 5 days.

 ## TO MIX WITH SELTZER

⅔ cup passion fruit– pineapple juice

⅔ cup seltzer

1 SERVING

Pour the juice into a tall glass. Add the seltzer and stir just until blended. Add ice and serve.

 ## TO CARBONATE WITH A SIPHON

2 cups water

1 batch passion fruit– pineapple juice

3 SERVINGS

Combine the water and juice in a 1-quart soda siphon. Charge with CO_2 according to the manufacturer's directions. Siphon-charged sodas can be stored in the siphon in a refrigerator for up to 5 days. Disperse as desired into tall glasses filled with ice, and serve.

strawberry pineapple soda

Because ripe pineapples bruise easily and don't travel well, and because the fruit doesn't ripen after being picked, processed pineapple products like juice and canned fruit that are made from fully ripened fruit frequently taste better than the fresh pineapples available to most consumers. That's why I don't waste my time juicing my own pineapples for beverages. Strawberries are another matter. Strawberry juice, because of its low acidity, is highly perishable. In this light sparkling soda, the strawberry juice is fresh and the pineapple juice is processed — the best of both worlds.

STRAWBERRY PINEAPPLE PURÉE

- 1 pint fresh strawberries, hulled and coarsely chopped
- 1½ tablespoons sugar, preferably raw cane
- 1 cup unsweetened pineapple juice

ENOUGH FOR 3 SERVINGS

Combine the strawberries and sugar in a small bowl and let sit for about 20 minutes, until the mixture is very wet. Combine the mixture with the pineapple juice in a blender or food processor and purée.

Set a strainer over a small bowl and scrape the purée into the strainer, so that the liquid drains into the bowl below. Stir the purée gently as it strains to get as much liquid as possible without forcing any solids into the strained liquid. Discard the solids, reserving the liquid. You should have about 2 cups.

The purée can be stored in the refrigerator for up to 1 day, but is best if used immediately.

 TO MIX WITH SELTZER

- ⅔ cup strawberry pineapple purée
- ⅔ cup seltzer

1 SERVING

Spoon the purée into a tall glass. Add the seltzer and stir just until blended. Add ice and serve.

 ## TO CARBONATE WITH A SIPHON

2 cups water
1 batch strawberry
pineapple purée

3 SERVINGS

Combine the water and purée in a 1-quart soda siphon. Charge with CO_2 according to the manufacturer's directions. Siphon-charged sodas can be stored in the siphon in a refrigerator for up to 5 days. Disperse as desired into tall glasses filled with ice, and serve.

cardamom apricot soda

Cardamom is one of the few spices that is equally at home in savory and sweet preparations. Quite pungent, with hints of lemon and ginger, it is completely delicious when teamed with drupe fruits like plums, peaches, and my favorite, apricots. Like other pulpy fruits, apricots are difficult to juice, so bottled nectar is the best source.

CARDAMOM APRICOT SYRUP

⅔ cup water

2 tablespoons sugar, preferably raw cane

2 tablespoons crushed cardamom seeds

1⅓ cups apricot nectar

ENOUGH FOR 3 SERVINGS

Combine the water, sugar, and cardamom in a small saucepan. Bring to a boil over medium heat, stirring until the sugar dissolves. Remove from the heat and let cool to room temperature. Strain out the cardamom seeds, then stir in the apricot nectar.

The syrup can be stored in the refrigerator for up to 2 days.

TO MIX WITH SELTZER

⅔ cup cardamom apricot syrup

⅔ cup seltzer

1 SERVING

Pour the syrup into a tall glass. Add the seltzer and stir just until blended. Add ice and serve.

TO CARBONATE WITH A SIPHON

2 cups water

1 batch cardamom apricot syrup

3 SERVINGS

Combine the water and syrup in a 1-quart soda siphon. Charge with CO_2 according to the manufacturer's directions. Siphon-charged sodas can be stored in the siphon in a refrigerator for up to 5 days. Disperse as desired into tall glasses filled with ice, and serve.

cucumber celery tonic

I know what you're thinking — this is the chapter on fruit sodas, and there's no way that cucumber is a fruit. Hold on. It's not sweet, like an apple or a grape, but a fruit it is. What cucumbers are missing in sugar, they make up for in refreshment. Cucumbers are cool, clean, and so full of water that all you need to do is grind them up to turn them into the most thirst-quenching of soft drinks. This one is sweetened with syrup flavored with celery seed.

CUCUMBER PURÉE

- 1 cup water
- ½ cup sugar
- 3 tablespoons celery seed
- ¼ teaspoon fine sea salt
- 1 large cucumber, trimmed, peeled, and cut into chunks

ENOUGH FOR 3 SERVINGS

Combine the water, sugar, celery seed, and salt in a small saucepan over medium heat. Bring to a simmer, and stir just until the sugar dissolves. Remove from the heat, let cool to room temperature, and strain.

Combine the syrup and cucumber in a blender or food processor and purée until smooth. Pass through a strainer to make sure that the mixture is completely smooth.

The purée can be stored in the refrigerator for up to 2 weeks.

 ## TO MIX WITH SELTZER

- ⅔ cup cucumber purée
- ⅔ cup seltzer

1 SERVING

Spoon the purée into a tall glass. Add the seltzer and stir just until blended. Add ice and serve.

 ## TO CARBONATE WITH A SIPHON

- 2 cups water
- 1 batch cucumber purée

3 SERVINGS

Combine the water and purée in a 1-quart soda siphon. Charge with CO_2 according to the manufacturer's directions. Siphon-charged sodas can be stored in the siphon in a refrigerator for up to 5 days. Disperse as desired into tall glasses filled with ice, and serve.

 Also see Mixology recipe on page 81.

balsamic date soda

Dates are the sweetest of dried fruits, saturated with so much sugar that their skin practically crystallizes from the concentration. Aged balsamic vinegar has a similar character, containing so much natural sugar that it is really more dessert sauce than acidifier. Combine the two and any additional sweetener becomes superfluous. The flavor of this soda is both familiar and exotic, combining the musky caramelized qualities of dates with the oaky, plummy aromas of balsamic.

DATE PURÉE

12 large dates, preferably Medjool, pitted and coarsely chopped

1 cup boiling water

1½ teaspoons balsamic vinegar

ENOUGH FOR 3 SERVINGS

Combine the dates and boiling water in a small bowl. Mash the dates with the back of a fork, working the mixture into a coarse paste. Pass through a sieve to remove bits of skin and undissolved pieces of date. Stir in the balsamic vinegar.

The purée can be stored in the refrigerator for up to 2 days.

TO MIX WITH SELTZER

¼ cup date purée

1 cup seltzer

1 SERVING

Spoon the purée into a tall glass. Add the seltzer and stir just until blended. Add ice and serve.

TO CARBONATE WITH A SIPHON

3 cups water

1 batch date purée

3 SERVINGS

Combine the water and purée in a 1-quart soda siphon. Charge with CO_2 according to the manufacturer's directions. Siphon-charged sodas can be stored in the siphon in a refrigerator for up to 5 days. Disperse as desired into tall glasses filled with ice, and serve.

Fruit Soda

M I X O L O G Y

///

mediterranean port of call

Prepare the date purée as described at left, then carbonate as desired.

Pour 2 ounces (¼ cup) port wine into a wine glass and stir in 4 ounces (½ cup) Balsamic Date Soda.

///

jean lafitte on the rocks

Prepare the date purée as described at left, then carbonate as desired.

Pour 1 ounce (2 tablespoons) golden rum over a few ice cubes in a rocks glass. Fill glass with Balsamic Date Soda and add a dash of bitters.

///

spiked gazpacho

Prepare the cucumber purée as described on page 79, then carbonate as desired.

Pour 1 ounce (2 tablespoons) vodka over ice in a tall glass. Add 3 ounces (6 tablespoons) vegetable cocktail juice and 3 ounces (6 tablespoons) Cucumber Celery Tonic (page 79). Stir just to blend, and garnish with a wedge of lime.

bittersweet grapefruit soda

The oil-rich zest of lemons, limes, and oranges is sweet, but grapefruit zest still contains some of the alkaloids from the pith and has a bitter aftertaste that I have emphasized in this soda by cooking it in bitter quinine water. The bitterness is offset by sugar syrup for a sophisticated bittersweet soda.

GRAPEFRUIT TONIC SYRUP

- 1 cup sugar
- 1 cup uncarbonated Home-made Tonic (page 166) or flat purchased tonic water
- Finely grated zest and juice of 2 large grapefruit
- ½ teaspoon fine sea salt

ENOUGH FOR 3 SERVINGS

Combine the sugar, tonic, and grapefruit zest in a small saucepan. Bring to a boil over medium heat, stirring just until the sugar dissolves. Remove from the heat, let cool to room temperature, and strain out the zest. Add the sea salt and grapefruit juice, stirring until the salt dissolves.

The syrup can be stored in the refrigerator for up to 2 days.

TO MIX WITH SELTZER

- ⅔ cup grapefruit tonic syrup
- ⅔ cup seltzer

1 SERVING

Pour the syrup into a tall glass. Add the seltzer and stir just until blended. Add ice and serve.

TO CARBONATE WITH A SIPHON

- 2 cups water
- 1 batch grapefruit tonic syrup

3 SERVINGS

Combine the water and syrup in a 1-quart soda siphon. Charge with CO_2 according to the manufacturer's directions. Siphon-charged sodas can be stored in the siphon in a refrigerator for up to 5 days. Disperse as desired into tall glasses filled with ice, and serve.

Mixology

Prepare the grapefruit tonic syrup as described at left, then carbonate as desired.

bitter relief

Mix 1½ ounces (3 tablespoons) vodka and 4 ounces (½ cup) Bittersweet Grapefruit Soda in an old-fashioned glass. Add several ice cubes and drizzle in ½ ounce (1 tablespoon) Campari.

sparkling grapefruit cosmo

Put a martini glass in the freezer for at least 5 minutes. Rim the glass with sugar. Fill a cocktail shaker with ice. Add 1½ ounces (3 table-spoons) vodka and 4 ounces (½ cup) Bittersweet Grapefruit Soda. Stir to chill (do not shake), and strain into the prepared glass. Garnish with a grapefruit section, if desired. Serve chilled.

POP CULTURE

Fresca, the Sophisticate's Soda

WHEN THE COCA-COLA COMPANY INTRODUCED the calorie-free grapefruit-flavored soft drink Fresca in 1963, the American public met its first adult-rated soda. Decidedly tangy, with a sharp citric acid edge, Fresca delivered a lingering bittersweet aftertaste, which was partly due to its artificial sweetener, but more importantly paid homage to the bitter alkaloids that give grapefruit its discriminating not-for-kids edge. The adult image stuck, for better or worse, and although Fresca was President Lyndon Johnson's beverage of choice (he kept a refrigerator stocked with it in the Oval Office) and the NHL's favored refresher in 1967 (a presage to Gatorade), its adult appeal kept it from full-blown mainstream acceptance.

For almost three decades Fresca maintained a die-hard cult following. In the years since 2000, its popularity has begun to grow — enough so that in 2005 Coca-Cola reintroduced the soft drink with an updated sleek logo and a campaign with the an emphasis on discriminating sophistication.

Grapefruit continues to be a fringe soft drink flavor. Pepsi never came out with a Fresca clone, but there are several grapefruit sodas sold internationally: Kiss Grapefruit (a boutique bottled retro soda from Orca Beverage in Mukilteo, Washington) is made with sugar and grapefruit juice; Izze Sparkling Grapefruit soda boasts a full serving of juice in a 12-ounce bottle; and Jarritos Toronja is a natural grapefruit soda produced and bottled in Mexico. Coca-Cola also markets Fresca in Mexico, but there it is made with sugar rather than aspartame, the calorie-free sweetener in the current U.S. product.

CHAPTER THREE

Root

Cola

*I*n the early days of American beverage making, brewers did not make a distinction between nonalcoholic and alcoholic potables. Anything was adequate to wash down dinner, and a batch of sassafras tea or sweet apple cider left out where wild yeasts were apt to get into them might be fresh one night, mildly bubbly the next, and alcoholic by the end of the week. When it came to homemade beverages, alcohol content was a matter of degree, and only teetotalers made much of a distinction between soft and hard drinks. Well into the late nineteenth century, the most common beverages in the American colonies were whiskey and beer, and the fermentation techniques used to make these alcoholic beverages became the basis for making soft drinks as well.

Fermentation begins with heating water with some sort of flavorful vegetation, like roots, herbs, flowers, barks, seeds, or fruits, to create a flavor base. Fruits and their seeds (particularly starchy grains) are naturally sweet enough to support fermentation without additional sugar. Fermentation of other types of vegetation requires sugar to be added. Before the availability of cheap refined cane sugar in the mid-1700s, that sugar came from fruit, honey, and sometimes molasses.

After about an hour of simmering, the vegetation releases its flavors and sugars into the liquid, which is then cooled to a little warmer than room temperature and mixed with yeast. Yeasts are tiny organisms that feed off sugar, just like the rest of us, and given the right conditions they will grow and multiply. In the course of their life they respire (mostly carbon dioxide) and excrete (mostly alcohol).

Making beverages, both carbonated and alcoholic, involves playing with the conditions under which yeasts thrive and using the by-products of their life cycle, carbon dioxide and alcohol, to produce different styles of beverage. If our goal is an alcoholic beer, the yeast is encouraged to consume as much sugar as it can in pursuit of a certain concentration of alcohol. Because we don't care as much about carbonation, the container in which the beer ferments is burped occasionally to keep the pressure from building up.

Yeasts cannot live in liquid with an alcohol content of more than 20 percent. For alcoholic beers the fermentation is usually stopped below 12 percent, which leaves some sugar in the brew. This residual sugar is enough to allow the yeast to continue to produce CO_2 after bottling, creating a slightly effervescent beverage.

Nonalcoholic beer is made in basically the same way, except the beer is bottled as soon as the yeast is added. Fermentation takes place right in the bottle, so all of the carbon dioxide produced by the yeast gets trapped in the beer. Because there is a limited amount of pressure that can build up in the bottle before it is in danger of

bursting, fermentation has to be stopped after a day or two (by chilling the bottles), resulting in a beer that is barely alcoholic and still quite sweet. Early American root cellars were filled with bottles of alcoholic and nonalcoholic beers, along with the roots and orchard fruits from which they were brewed.

Roots are the place where plants store starch (for long-term energy), sugars (for immediate energy), and large aggregate molecules (mostly pigments and aromatic phenols) that protect the plant and fight disease. These components tend to make roots flavorful, colorful, and sweet, all qualities that make delicious and beautiful beverages. The most common roots for making root beers are the most pungent ones: burdock, ginger, licorice, sarsaparilla, and sassafras.

Fruits, which are more delicate than roots, are also full of sugar, but because they do not store as well as roots, they have in the past been less available for making beverages on a regular basis. Common fruits for fermentation include berries, apples, pears, and citrus.

Leaves and flowers (including herbs) and seeds and bark (including spices) have neither enough substance nor enough sugar to be the main ingredients in a fermented beverage, but they can be added for flavor. Cola is the most popular fermented soda that is principally flavored with herbs and spices.

rooty toot root beer

Root beer is a complex brew, radiating the wintergreen aroma of birch, the tang of sassafras, the woodsiness of sarsaparilla, and the palate-pumping pungency of licorice root. Modify those root flavors with floral vanilla beans and the fruity esters plentiful in raisins and you have one of the most sophisticated flavor combinations ever devised. In this chapter you'll find more than half a dozen recipes for root beers; this one is beautifully balanced and rich-tasting. It gets its creamy mouthfeel from the addition of maltodextrin (available from most brewing supply houses and natural food stores).

ROOT BEER SYRUP

- 4½ cups water
- ¼ cup raisins, coarsely chopped
- 2 ounces dried sassafras root
- ¼ ounce dried wintergreen leaves
- 4 star anise
- ½ vanilla bean, cut into three pieces
- 2 cups light brown sugar
- 2 tablespoon maltodextrin (optional)

ENOUGH FOR 1 GALLON BREWED ROOT BEER

Combine the water, raisins, sassafras, wintergreen, star anise, and vanilla in a large saucepan. Bring to a simmer over medium heat, stirring occasionally; let simmer, uncovered, for 15 minutes.

Blend the brown sugar and maltodextrin (if using), and gradually add the mixture to the simmering root infusion, stirring until the sugar dissolves. Then remove from the heat, let cool for 30 minutes, and strain.

This syrup will keep in the refrigerator for up to 2 months.

 ## TO MIX WITH SELTZER

- ½ cup root beer syrup
- 1½ cups seltzer

1 SERVING

Pour the syrup into a tall glass. Add the seltzer and stir just until blended. Add ice and serve.

TO CARBONATE WITH A SIPHON

3 cups water
1 cup root beer syrup

3 SERVINGS

Combine the water and syrup in a 1-quart soda siphon. Charge with CO_2 according to the manufacturer's directions. Siphon-charged sodas can be stored in the siphon in a refrigerator for up to 5 days. Disperse as desired into tall glasses filled with ice, and serve.

TO BREW

3 quarts lukewarm (80–90°F) water
1 batch root beer syrup
⅛ teaspoon champagne yeast (*Saccharomyces bayanus*)

1 GALLON

Combine the water and syrup in a large container. Test the temperature; the mixture should be at a warm room temperature, from 75 to 80°F. (If it is too hot, let it sit until it cools a bit. If it is too cold, warm it over low heat.) Add the yeast and stir until it is completely dissolved.

Pour the mixture into sanitized plastic bottles (see page 25) using a sanitized kitchen funnel, leaving 1¼ inches of air space at the top of each bottle. Seal the bottles. Store for 2 to 4 days at room temperature. When the bottles feel rock hard, the soda is fully carbonated.

Refrigerate for at least 1 week before serving; drink within 3 weeks to avoid overcarbonation.

Mixology

These cocktails can be made with any kind of root beer.

root beer beer

Combine equal parts chilled root beer and dark beer.

blackbeard

Add 1 ounce (2 tablespoons) Captain Morgan's Spiced Rum to 12 ounces (1½ cups) root beer. Serve over ice.

r&r beer

Add 2 ounces (¼ cup) dark rum to 12 ounces (1½ cups) root beer and serve over ice in a highball glass.

malibeer

Add 2 ounces (¼ cup) coconut rum to 10 ounces (1¼ cups) root beer and serve over ice in a highball glass, topped with a squeeze of lime juice.

Charles Hires and the Root Beer Business

CHARLES HIRES, A PHILADELPHIA PHARMACIST, is known as the inventor of root beer, even though root beer is one of those foods whose exact origin is impossible to pinpoint. By the time Hires was born in 1851, many dozens of well-known recipes for teas and fermented soft drinks made from various barks, roots, leaves, and seeds were known as "root teas" or "root beers." Every colonial housewife had at least one. Hires's claim to fame is that he took a traditional root tea formula and manufactured it as a powdered concentrate that could be sold to pharmacies to be batched into a beverage by adding water and sugar and fermenting it with yeast, thereby streamlining and standardizing the process of brewing medicinal root elixirs. To his credit Hires also suggested serving root beer chilled, changing what was commonly thought of as a medicine into a refreshment.

Hires sold his root beer locally and then introduced it internationally at the Centennial Exposition held in Philadelphia in 1876, the first official World's Fair in the United States, which attracted about 10 million visitors, more than 20 percent of the population of the United States. In 1890 he established the Charles E. Hires Company, which sold root beer powder along with a formula for mixing and fermenting it; the company started selling a premixed bottled version in 1893.

Hires had his beverage analyzed to prove that it "contained less alcohol than a loaf of bread" and promoted it as a temperance drink to "purify the blood and make rosy cheeks." Hires's Root Beer kits were sold until 1980 for the homebrewing of root beer, although from the time that bottled root beer was introduced it far outsold the homemade product.

not-too-sweet sarsaparilla

When brewed and sweetened, the roots of sarsaparilla (Smilax spp.), a native American plant, have a flavor not unlike that of sassafras, the dominant flavor in traditional root beers. Because sarsaparilla is similar to but more subtle than sassafras, the two are often brewed together, but I find that sarsaparilla is easily overshadowed by sassafras, so I use very little of the latter. The flavor of this root beer is amended with wintergreen, which gives it a birch-beer quality.

SARSAPARILLA SYRUP

4½ cups water

5 ounces dried sarsaparilla root, chopped

1 ounce dried sassafras root, chopped

¼ ounce dried wintergreen leaves

4 cups dark brown sugar

2 tablespoon maltodextrin (optional)

ENOUGH FOR 1 GALLON BREWED SARSAPARILLA

Combine the water, sarsaparilla, sassafras, and wintergreen in a large saucepan. Bring to a simmer over medium heat, stirring occasionally; let simmer, uncovered, for 15 minutes.

Blend the brown sugar and maltodextrin (if using), and gradually add the mixture to the simmering root infusion, stirring until the sugar dissolves. Then remove from the heat, let cool to room temperature, and strain.

This syrup will keep in the refrigerator for up to 2 months.

 ## TO MIX WITH SELTZER

½ cup sarsaparilla syrup

1½ cups seltzer

1 SERVING

Pour the syrup into a tall glass. Add the seltzer and stir just until blended. Add ice and serve.

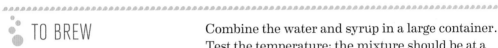

TO CARBONATE WITH A SIPHON

3 cups water
1 cup sarsaparilla syrup

3 SERVINGS

Combine the water and syrup in a 1-quart soda siphon. Charge with CO_2 according to the manufacturer's directions. Siphon-charged sodas can be stored in the siphon in a refrigerator for up to 5 days. Disperse as desired into tall glasses filled with ice, and serve.

TO BREW

3 quarts lukewarm (80–90°F) water
1 batch sarsaparilla syrup
⅛ teaspoon champagne yeast (*Saccharomyces bayanus*)

1 GALLON

Combine the water and syrup in a large container. Test the temperature; the mixture should be at a warm room temperature, from 75 to 80°F. (If it is too hot, let it sit until it cools a bit. If it is too cold, warm it over low heat.) Add the yeast and stir until it is completely dissolved.

Pour the mixture into sanitized plastic bottles (see page 25) using a sanitized kitchen funnel, leaving 1¼ inches of air space at the top of each bottle. Seal the bottles. Store for 2 to 4 days at room temperature. When the bottles feel rock hard, the soda is fully carbonated.

Refrigerate for at least 1 week before serving; drink within 3 weeks to avoid overcarbonation.

7-root beer

Seven is a powerful number, and in this sweet and savory root beer, seven is the factor that pushes the flavor ante beyond the ordinary. Some of these roots (sarsaparilla, sassafras, burdock, and licorice) have to be purchased dried, while others, such as ginger, carrot, and parsnip, are readily available fresh.

7-ROOT SYRUP

4½ cups water

1 ounce fresh gingerroot, thinly sliced

½ ounce dried sarsaparilla root, chopped

½ ounce dried sassafras root, chopped

¼ ounce dried burdock root, chopped

¼ ounce dried licorice root, chopped

1 large carrot, coarsely shredded

1 large parsnip, coarsely shredded

4 cups dark brown sugar

1 teaspoon gum arabic

ENOUGH FOR 1 GALLON BREWED ROOT BEER

Combine the water, ginger, sarsaparilla, sassafras, burdock, licorice, carrot, and parsnip in a large saucepan. Bring to a simmer over medium heat, stirring occasionally; let simmer, uncovered, for 15 minutes.

Blend the brown sugar and gum arabic. Gradually add the sugar mixture to the simmered root infusion, stirring until the sugar dissolves. Then remove from the heat, let cool to room temperature, and strain.

This syrup will keep in the refrigerator for up to 2 months.

TO MIX WITH SELTZER

½ cup 7-root syrup
1½ cups seltzer

1 SERVING

Pour the syrup into a tall glass. Add the seltzer and stir just until blended. Add ice and serve.

TO CARBONATE WITH A SIPHON

3 cups water
1 cup 7-root syrup

3 SERVINGS

Combine the water and syrup in a 1-quart soda siphon. Charge with CO_2 according to the manufacturer's directions. Siphon-charged sodas can be stored in the siphon in a refrigerator for up to 5 days. Disperse as desired into tall glasses filled with ice, and serve.

TO BREW

3 quarts lukewarm (80–90°F) water
1 batch 7-root syrup
⅛ teaspoon champagne yeast (*Saccharomyces bayanus*)

1 GALLON

Combine the water and syrup in a large container. Test the temperature; the mixture should be at a warm room temperature, from 75 to 80°F. (If it is too hot, let it sit until it cools a bit. If it is too cold, warm it over low heat.) Add the yeast and stir until it is completely dissolved.

Pour the mixture into sanitized plastic bottles (see page 25) using a sanitized kitchen funnel, leaving 1¼ inches of air space at the top of each bottle. Seal the bottles. Store for 2 to 4 days at room temperature. When the bottles feel rock hard, the soda is fully carbonated.

Refrigerate for at least 1 week before serving; drink within 3 weeks to avoid overcarbonation.

Mixology

Prepare the root beer syrup as described at left, then carbonate as desired.

root and rye

Add 2 ounces (¼ cup) rye or Canadian whiskey to 10 ounces (1¼ cups) root beer, and serve over ice in a tall glass.

birch beer

Birch beer is a classic European herbal beer from the seventeenth century. Birch bark adds to the fermentation a tangy mentholated aeration that is pronounced but ethereal. The brew requires other more substantial flavors to give it body, which is why birch beers are still based on sassafras for their flavor. Because sassafras root is relatively potent and birch flavor is fleeting, I always hold back on the sassafras.

BIRCH SYRUP

4½ cups water

6 ounces dried birch bark, chopped

1 ounce sassafras root

Finely grated zest and juice of 1 lemon

3 cloves

½ vanilla bean, cut into three pieces

4 cups dark brown sugar

2 tablespoons maltodextrin (optional)

ENOUGH FOR 1 GALLON BREWED BIRCH BEER

Combine water, birch bark, sassafras root, lemon zest and juice, cloves, and vanilla in a large saucepan. Bring to a simmer over medium heat, stirring occasionally; let simmer, uncovered, for 15 minutes.

Blend the brown sugar and maltodextrin (if using), and gradually add the mixture to the simmering root infusion, stirring until the sugar dissolves. Then remove from the heat, let cool to room temperature, and strain.

This syrup will keep in the refrigerator for up to 2 months.

 ## TO MIX WITH SELTZER

½ cup birch syrup

1½ cups seltzer

1 SERVING

Pour the syrup into a tall glass. Add the seltzer and stir just until blended. Add ice and serve.

TO CARBONATE WITH A SIPHON

3 cups water
1 cup birch syrup

3 SERVINGS

Combine the water and syrup in a 1-quart soda siphon. Charge with CO_2 according to the manufacturer's directions. Siphon-charged sodas can be stored in the siphon in a refrigerator for up to 5 days. Disperse as desired into tall glasses filled with ice, and serve.

TO BREW

3 quarts lukewarm (80–90°F) water
1 batch birch syrup
⅛ teaspoon champagne yeast (*Saccharomyces bayanus*)

1 GALLON

Combine the water and syrup in a large container. Test the temperature; the mixture should be at a warm room temperature, from 75 to 80°F. (If it is too hot, let it sit until it cools a bit. If it is too cold, warm it over low heat.) Add the yeast and stir until it is completely dissolved.

Pour the mixture into sanitized plastic bottles (see page 25) using a sanitized kitchen funnel, leaving 1¼ inches of air space at the top of each bottle. Seal the bottles. Store for 2 to 4 days at room temperature. When the bottles feel rock hard, the soda is fully carbonated.

Refrigerate for at least 1 week before serving; drink within 3 weeks to avoid overcarbonation.

Mixology

Prepare the birch syrup as described at left, then carbonate as desired.

beermeister

Add 2 ounces (¼ cup) Jägermeister herbal liqueur to 12 ounces (1½ cups) Birch Beer, and serve over ice in a tall glass.

spruce beer

Spruce's piney terpene flavor is an acquired taste. Drinking a soda made exclusively from spruce twigs would be not unlike imbibing the essence of forest, but when blended with more traditional root beer flavors (such as sassafras and sarsaparilla) and especially a good hit of ginger, spruce's pine essence is refreshing and cooling. Spruce beer was an American colonial favorite, since spruce had preserving qualities similar to those of hops.

SPRUCE SYRUP

4½ cups water

1½ cups molasses

2 ounces sassafras root, chopped

3 tablespoons chopped fresh gingerroot

¾ teaspoon oil of spruce

3 cups dark brown sugar

2 tablespoons maltodextrin (optional)

ENOUGH FOR 1 GALLON BREWED SPRUCE BEER

Combine the water, molasses, sassafras, ginger, and spruce oil in a large saucepan. Bring to a simmer over medium heat, stirring occasionally; let simmer, uncovered, for 5 minutes.

Blend the brown sugar and maltodextrin (if using), and gradually add the mixture to the simmering root infusion, stirring until the sugar dissolves. Then remove from the heat, let cool to room temperature, and strain.

This syrup will keep in the refrigerator for up to 2 months.

Wintergreen Root Beer: Substitute ½ teaspoon wintergreen essential oil for spruce oil.

 TO MIX WITH SELTZER

½ cup spruce syrup

1½ cups seltzer

1 SERVING

Pour the syrup into a tall glass. Add the seltzer and stir just until blended. Add ice and serve.

TO CARBONATE WITH A SIPHON

3 cups water

1 cup spruce syrup

3 SERVINGS

Combine the water and syrup in a 1-quart soda siphon. Charge with CO_2 according to the manufacturer's directions. Siphon-charged sodas can be stored in the siphon in a refrigerator for up to 5 days. Disperse as desired into tall glasses filled with ice, and serve.

TO BREW

3 quarts lukewarm (80–90°F) water

1 batch spruce syrup

⅛ teaspoon champagne yeast (*Saccharomyces bayanus*)

1 GALLON

Combine the water and syrup in a large container. Test the temperature; the mixture should be at a warm room temperature, from 75 to 80°F. (If it is too hot, let it sit until it cools a bit. If it is too cold, warm it over low heat.) Add the yeast and stir until it is completely dissolved.

Pour the mixture into sanitized plastic bottles (see page 25) using a sanitized kitchen funnel, leaving 1¼ inches of air space at the top of each bottle. Seal the bottles. Store for 2 to 4 days at room temperature. When the bottles feel rock hard, the soda is fully carbonated.

Refrigerate for at least 1 week before serving; drink within 3 weeks to avoid overcarbonation.

POP CULTURE

Root Beer Restaurants

EARLY SODA MAKERS frequently sold their wares at stands, but Roy Allen and Frank Wright, the owners of A&W Root Beer, were the first to build a full-service restaurant chain based on a soft drink. In the early 1920s they opened the first A&W drive-in restaurant, featuring "tray-boys" offering curbside service. By 1933 there were more than 170 franchised A&W outlets, and in 1960 there were 2,000 nationwide.

SECRET FORMULA

curiosity cola

Why anyone other than a rival soda manufacturer would want the secret formula for a product as readily available and affordable as Coca-Cola is beyond me, but if trying to duplicate Coke sounds like a fun challenge, try this recipe. It is my rendition of a formula that has been floating around on the Internet for years. Reputedly it is the secret formula for Coke, but I don't think so (it sure doesn't taste like Coke). My efforts have yielded something that most of my friends find delicious. Some find it a bit fruity, others a little too bitter, but most appreciate the balance.

COLA SYRUP

- 10 grams citric acid
- 1 gram lemon edible essential oil
- 1 gram orange edible essential oil
- 0.5 gram bergamot edible essential oil or neroli edible essential oil
- 0.5 gram cinnamon edible essential oil
- 0.5 gram lime edible essential oil
- 0.2 gram coriander edible essential oil
- 0.1 gram nutmeg edible essential oil
- 0.5 gram gum arabic
- 1 quart boiling water
- 2 pounds sugar
- ¼ cup (72 g) browning sauce, such as Kitchen Bouquet
- ½ teaspoon vanilla extract

ENOUGH FOR 5 QUARTS BREWED COLA

Combine the citric acid, lemon oil, orange oil, bergamot oil, cinnamon oil, lime oil, coriander oil, nutmeg oil, and gum arabic in a large heat-proof bowl, and stir to blend. Add the boiling water and mix well with a small whisk. Add the sugar, whisking until it dissolves. Stir in the browning sauce and vanilla and let cool.

This syrup will keep in the refrigerator for up to 2 months.

Notes and Warnings: You will need a gram scale to measure out the ingredients. One gram of essential oil is equal to about 50 drops.

Not all essential oils are safe for human consumption. Look for essential oils labeled "food-grade" or "edible." See Resources for two Internet sources.

TO MIX WITH SELTZER

½ cup cola syrup
1½ cups seltzer

1 SERVING

Pour the syrup into a tall glass. Add the seltzer and stir just until blended. Add ice and serve.

 ## TO CARBONATE WITH A SIPHON

3¼ cups water
¾ cup cola syrup

3 SERVINGS

Combine the water and syrup in a 1-quart soda siphon. Charge with CO_2 according to the manufacturer's directions. Siphon-charged sodas can be stored in the siphon in a refrigerator for up to 5 days. Disperse as desired into tall glasses filled with ice, and serve.

 ## TO BREW

4 quarts lukewarm (80 to 90°F) water
1 batch cola syrup
⅛ teaspoon champagne yeast (*Saccharomyces bayanus*)

5 QUARTS

Combine the water and syrup in a large container. Test the temperature; the mixture should be at a warm room temperature, from 75 to 80°F. (If it is too hot, let it sit until it cools a bit. If it is too cold, warm it over low heat.) Add the yeast and stir until it is completely dissolved.

Pour the mixture into sanitized plastic bottles (see page 25) using a sanitized kitchen funnel, leaving 1¼ inches of air space at the top of each bottle. Seal the bottles. Store for 2 to 4 days at room temperature. When the bottles feel rock hard, the soda is fully carbonated.

Refrigerate for at least 1 week before serving; drink within 3 weeks to avoid overcarbonation.

Selling Refreshment

ALMOST FROM THE START, THE POPULARITY OF BOTTLED SOFT DRINKS has had more to do with image than with what's in the bottle. Let's face it, Coke and Pepsi are not all that different. Our allegiance to one brand or another has more to do with conception than perception. This fact has not been lost on soft drink manufacturers. The battle for world dominance between Coke and Pepsi has been going on for more than 70 years.

COKE SLOGANS VS. PEPSI SLOGANS

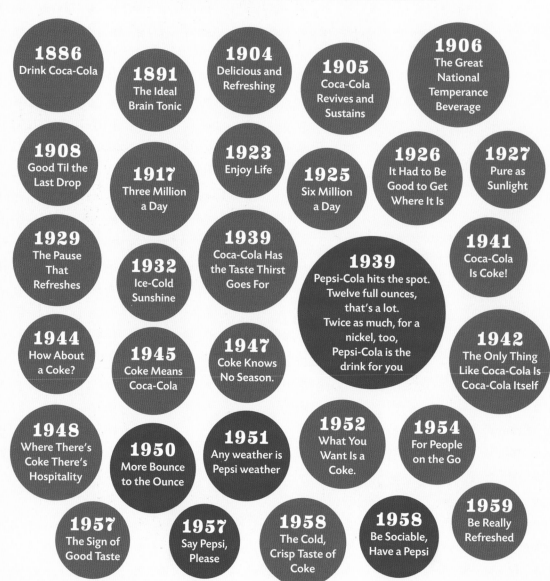

1886 Drink Coca-Cola

1891 The Ideal Brain Tonic

1904 Delicious and Refreshing

1905 Coca-Cola Revives and Sustains

1906 The Great National Temperance Beverage

1908 Good Til the Last Drop

1917 Three Million a Day

1923 Enjoy Life

1925 Six Million a Day

1926 It Had to Be Good to Get Where It Is

1927 Pure as Sunlight

1929 The Pause That Refreshes

1932 Ice-Cold Sunshine

1939 Coca-Cola Has the Taste Thirst Goes For

1939 Pepsi-Cola hits the spot. Twelve full ounces, that's a lot. Twice as much, for a nickel, too, Pepsi-Cola is the drink for you

1941 Coca-Cola Is Coke!

1944 How About a Coke?

1945 Coke Means Coca-Cola

1947 Coke Knows No Season.

1942 The Only Thing Like Coca-Cola Is Coca-Cola Itself

1948 Where There's Coke There's Hospitality

1950 More Bounce to the Ounce

1951 Any weather is Pepsi weather

1952 What You Want Is a Coke.

1954 For People on the Go

1957 The Sign of Good Taste

1957 Say Pepsi, Please

1958 The Cold, Crisp Taste of Coke

1958 Be Sociable, Have a Pepsi

1959 Be Really Refreshed

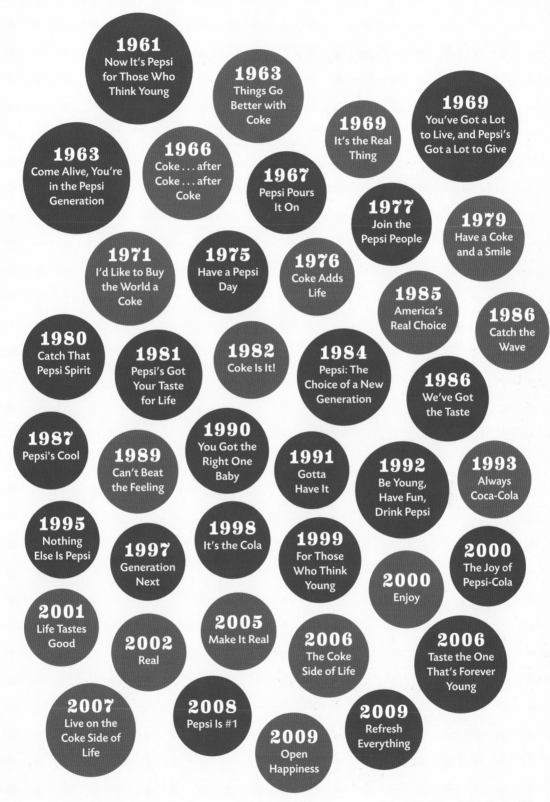

1961 Now It's Pepsi for Those Who Think Young

1963 Things Go Better with Coke

1969 It's the Real Thing

1969 You've Got a Lot to Live, and Pepsi's Got a Lot to Give

1963 Come Alive, You're in the Pepsi Generation

1966 Coke...after Coke...after Coke

1967 Pepsi Pours It On

1977 Join the Pepsi People

1979 Have a Coke and a Smile

1971 I'd Like to Buy the World a Coke

1975 Have a Pepsi Day

1976 Coke Adds Life

1985 America's Real Choice

1986 Catch the Wave

1980 Catch That Pepsi Spirit

1981 Pepsi's Got Your Taste for Life

1982 Coke Is It!

1984 Pepsi: The Choice of a New Generation

1986 We've Got the Taste

1987 Pepsi's Cool

1989 Can't Beat the Feeling

1990 You Got the Right One Baby

1991 Gotta Have It

1992 Be Young, Have Fun, Drink Pepsi

1993 Always Coca-Cola

1995 Nothing Else Is Pepsi

1997 Generation Next

1998 It's the Cola

1999 For Those Who Think Young

2000 Enjoy

2000 The Joy of Pepsi-Cola

2001 Life Tastes Good

2002 Real

2005 Make It Real

2006 The Coke Side of Life

2006 Taste the One That's Forever Young

2007 Live on the Coke Side of Life

2008 Pepsi Is #1

2009 Open Happiness

2009 Refresh Everything

natural cola

Extracts aren't necessary for cola flavor. After all, those extracts originally started as real ingredients, so why not go right to the source? This formula yields a beautiful cola concoction using all fresh and dried ingredients, readily available in most home refrigerators and spice cupboards. The one ingredient you might have to search for is gum arabic. It's there for mouthfeel rather than flavor, so if you don't have it, your cola will still be delicious; it will just seem a little thin.

COLA SYRUP

1 quart water

Finely grated zest and juice of 1 lemon

Finely grated zest and juice of 1 lime

Finely grated zest and juice of 2 oranges

3 large (5-inch) cinnamon sticks, broken into small pieces

2 tablespoons dried bitter orange peel

2 teaspoons coriander seed

¼ teaspoon finely grated nutmeg

1 teaspoon gum arabic (optional)

2 pounds sugar

¼ cup browning sauce, such as Kitchen Bouquet

½ teaspoon vanilla extract

ENOUGH FOR 5 QUARTS BREWED COLA

Combine the water, lemon zest, lime zest, orange zest, cinnamon, bitter orange peel, coriander seed, nutmeg, and gum arabic (if using) in a large saucepan. Whisk together until the gum arabic dissolves. Stir in the sugar and bring to a boil, stirring until the sugar dissolves. Boil for 1 minute.

Remove from the heat and stir in the lemon, lime, and orange juices, along with the browning sauce and vanilla. Let cool, then strain.

This syrup will keep in the refrigerator for up to 2 weeks.

TO MIX WITH SELTZER

½ cup cola syrup
1½ cups seltzer

1 SERVING

Pour the syrup into a tall glass. Add the seltzer and stir just until blended. Add ice and serve.

TO CARBONATE WITH A SIPHON

3¼ cups water
¾ cup cola syrup

3 SERVINGS

Combine the water and syrup in a 1-quart soda siphon. Charge with CO_2 according to the manufacturer's directions. Siphon-charged sodas can be stored in the siphon in a refrigerator for up to 5 days. Disperse as desired into tall glasses filled with ice, and serve.

TO BREW

4 quarts lukewarm (80–90°F) water
1 batch cola syrup
⅛ teaspoon champagne yeast (*Saccharomyces bayanus*)

5 QUARTS

Combine the water and syrup in a large container. Test the temperature; the mixture should be at a warm room temperature, from 75 to 80°F. (If it is too hot, let it sit until it cools a bit. If it is too cold, warm it over low heat.) Add the yeast and stir until it is completely dissolved.

Pour the mixture into sanitized plastic bottles (see page 25) using a sanitized kitchen funnel, leaving 1¼ inches of air space at the top of each bottle. Seal the bottles. Store for 2 to 4 days at room temperature. When the bottles feel rock hard, the soda is fully carbonated.

Refrigerate for at least 1 week before serving; drink within 3 weeks to avoid overcarbonation.

Mixology

Prepare the cola syrup as described at left, then carbonate as desired.

kentucky cola

Pour 1 ounce (2 tablespoons) Jack Daniels over ice cubes in a tall glass, and fill with cola.

mind bender

Pour 1 ounce (2 tablespoons) dark rum and 1 ounce (2 tablespoons) golden tequila over ice cubes in a tall glass, and fill with cola.

cherry cola

Pour 1 ounce (2 tablespoons) cherry liqueur and 1 ounce (2 tablespoons) light rum over ice in a rocks glass, and fill with cola. Garnish with a cherry.

sour cherry cola

Rather than flavoring plain cola with cherry syrup, I brewed this cherry cola using dried sour cherries in place of some of the citrus that is the usual cola flavoring. The cherry flavor is both more subtle and more pervasive. Instead of being cola with a cherry afterglow, it is a cherry-spiced soda.

CHERRY COLA SYRUP

1 quart water

1 cup dried sour red cherries, finely chopped

Finely grated zest and juice of 2 oranges

3 large (5-inch) cinnamon sticks, broken into small pieces

2 tablespoons dried bitter orange peel

2 teaspoons coriander seed

¼ teaspoon finely grated nutmeg

1 teaspoon gum arabic (optional)

2 pounds sugar

¼ cup browning sauce, such as Kitchen Bouquet

½ teaspoon vanilla extract

¼ teaspoon almond extract

ENOUGH FOR 5 QUARTS BREWED COLA

Combine the water, cherries, orange zest, cinnamon, bitter orange peel, coriander seed, nutmeg, and gum arabic (if using) in a large saucepan. Whisk together until the gum arabic dissolves. Stir in the sugar and bring to a boil, stirring until the sugar dissolves. Boil for 1 minute.

Remove from the heat and stir in the orange juice, browning sauce, vanilla, and almond extract. Let cool, then strain.

This syrup can be stored in the refrigerator for up to 2 weeks.

Medjool Cola: Follow the recipe for Sour Cherry Cola, substituting eight dried Medjool dates, pitted and finely chopped, for the dried sour cherries and the zest and juice of one large lemon for one of the oranges.

 TO MIX WITH SELTZER

½ cup cherry cola syrup

1½ cups seltzer

1 SERVING

Pour the syrup into a tall glass. Add the seltzer and stir just until blended. Add ice and serve.

TO CARBONATE WITH A SIPHON

3¼ cups water
¾ cup cherry cola syrup

3 SERVINGS

Combine the water and syrup in a 1-quart soda siphon. Charge with CO_2 according to the manufacturer's directions. Siphon-charged sodas can be stored in the siphon in a refrigerator for up to 5 days. Disperse as desired into tall glasses filled with ice, and serve.

TO BREW

4 quarts lukewarm (80 to 90°F) water
1 batch cherry cola syrup
⅛ teaspoon champagne yeast (*Saccharomyces bayanus*)

5 QUARTS

Combine the water and syrup in a large container. Test the temperature; the mixture should be at a warm room temperature, from 75 to 80°F. (If it is too hot, let it sit until it cools a bit. If it is too cold, warm it over low heat.) Add the yeast and stir until it is completely dissolved.

Pour the mixture into sanitized plastic bottles (see page 25) using a sanitized kitchen funnel, leaving 1¼ inches of air space at the top of each bottle. Seal the bottles. Store for 2 to 4 days at room temperature. When the bottles feel rock hard, the soda is fully carbonated.

Refrigerate for at least 1 week before serving; drink within 3 weeks to avoid overcarbonation.

POP CULTURE

The Origins of Coca-Cola

IN 1863, FRENCH CHEMIST ANGELO MARIANI created a popular elixir by infusing coca leaves in Bordeaux wine. The resulting tonic, Vin Mariani, contained about 6 mg of cocaine per fluid ounce and was popular with many contemporary celebs, including Queen Victoria and Pope Pius X. John Pemberton, an Atlanta pharmacist, though neither queen nor pope, was also enamored, and he decided he could do better. He developed Pemberton's French Wine Coca, brewed from coca leaf, kola nut, and damiana. He was sent scrambling in 1885 when Atlanta enacted temperance laws that made the alcohol in his tonic (but not the coca) illegal. He reformulated, taking out the alcohol, resulting in an early version of Coca-Cola, which was originally sold as a soda fountain medicinal elixir, mixed with carbonated water.

ginger ginger ale

The combination of fresh and dried ginger gives this ginger ale an extra layer of flavor, a potent floral aroma, and minimal heat. Because the flavor develops during fermentation, this soda must be made with yeast.

This recipe does not begin with a flavor base. Follow the complete brewing instructions to make one gallon of Ginger Ginger Ale.

TO BREW

3½ quarts water

3 ounces fresh ginger-root, coarsely grated

1 (1-inch) length dried ginger

1 pound sugar

1 tablespoon apple cider vinegar

⅛ teaspoon champagne yeast (*Saccharomyces bayanus*)

1 GALLON

Combine the water, fresh ginger, and dried ginger in a large saucepan. Bring to a simmer over medium heat, stirring occasionally. Let simmer, uncovered, for 15 minutes. Then add the sugar and vinegar, stirring until the sugar dissolves.

Remove from the heat and let cool until the mixture reaches warm room temperature, from 75 to 80°F. Strain out the ginger. Add the yeast, stirring until it is completely dissolved.

Pour the mixture into sanitized plastic bottles (see page 25) using a sanitized kitchen funnel, leaving 1¼ inches of air space at the top of each bottle. Seal the bottles. Store for 3 to 5 days at room temperature. When the bottles feel rock hard, the soda is fully carbonated.

Refrigerate for at least 1 week before serving; drink within 3 weeks to avoid overcarbonation.

Mixology

Prepare the Ginger Ginger Ale as described above.

ginger screwdriver

Pour 1 ounce (2 tablespoons) vodka and 4 ounces (½ cup) orange juice over ice in a tall glass, and top up with Ginger Ginger Ale.

szechuan ginger beer

The schizoid effect of ginger on the palate — at once hot and cooling — is reinforced in this recipe with an added kick of aromatic Szechuan pepper-corns. This pepper, named after its native Szechuan province of China, is the dried berry of prickly ash (Zanthoxylum spp.) and is not related to the vine peppercorn (Piper nigrum) commonly served at tables. It has a fruity, floral fragrance that is a wonderful complement to the pungency of ginger.

This recipe does not begin with a flavor base. Follow the complete brewing instructions to make one gallon of Szechuan Ginger Beer.

 TO BREW

3½ quarts water
4 ounces fresh ginger-
root, coarsely grated
1 tablespoon Szechuan
peppercorns
1 pound sugar
2 tablespoons unflavored
rice vinegar
⅛ teaspoon champagne
yeast (*Saccharomyces
bayanus*)

1 GALLON

Combine the water, ginger, and peppercorns in a large pot. Bring to a simmer over medium heat. Let simmer for 5 minutes, then add the sugar and vinegar, stirring until the sugar dissolves. Remove from the heat and let cool until the mixture reaches warm room temperature, from 75 to 80°F. Strain out the ginger and peppercorns. Add the yeast, stirring until it is completely dissolved.

Pour the mixture into sanitized plastic bottles (see page 25) using a sanitized kitchen funnel, leaving 1¼ inches of air space at the top of each bottle. Seal the bottles. Store for 3 to 5 days at room temperature. When the bottles feel rock hard, the soda is fully carbonated.

Refrigerate for at least 1 week before serving; drink within 3 weeks to avoid overcarbonation.

molasses beer

Molasses, a by-product of sugar refinement, contains all of the minerals, vitamins, and simple and complex carbohydrates filtered from raw cane sugar when it is purified, making it much less sweet and far more savory than sugar. These savory elements lend this rich mahogany-hued soda the meatiness of a dark beer, like stout or porter.

This recipe does not begin with a flavor base. Follow the complete brewing instructions to make one gallon of Molasses Beer.

TO BREW

- 3½ quarts water
- 2 cups light or dark molasses
- 3 cinnamon sticks
- 1½ cups sugar
- 1 tablespoon maltodextrin (optional)
- 2 teaspoons vanilla extract
- ⅛ teaspoon champagne yeast (*Saccharomyces bayanus*)

ABOUT 1 GALLON

Combine the water, molasses, and cinnamon in a large saucepan over high heat. Bring to a boil, then reduce the heat and let simmer, uncovered, for 15 minutes. Blend the sugar and maltodextrin (if using), and add the mixture to the simmering molasses mixture, stirring until the sugar dissolves.

Remove from the heat and let cool to warm room temperature, from 75 to 80°F. Strain out the solids, and add the vanilla and yeast, stirring until the yeast is dissolved.

Pour the mixture into sanitized plastic bottles (see page 25) using a sanitized kitchen funnel, leaving 1¼ inches of air space at the top of each bottle. Seal the bottles. Store for 2 to 4 days at room temperature. When the bottles feel rock hard, the soda is fully carbonated.

Refrigerate for at least 1 week before serving; drink within 3 weeks to avoid overcarbonation.

Mixology

Prepare the Molasses Beer as described above.

black rum

Combine 4 ounces (½ cup) Molasses Beer and 2 ounces (¼ cup) dark rum. Pour over ice and serve.

fermented honey soda

Like nonalcoholic mead, this soda has a pronounced honey flavor with barely a hint of the cloying sweetness of fresh honey. It has a beautiful golden hue, but because the yeast remains in the bottle, it is not crystal clear. You can alter the flavor and color of the soda by varying the honey you use. I usually use a neutral-tasting honey, like orange blossom or clover.

This recipe does not begin with a flavor base. Follow the complete brewing instructions to make one gallon of Fermented Honey Soda.

TO BREW

3¼ quarts lukewarm
(80 to 90°F) water

3 cups honey

⅛ teaspoon champagne
yeast (*Saccharomyces bayanus*)

1 GALLON

Combine the water and honey in a large container. Test the temperature; the mixture should be at a warm room temperature, from 75 to 80°F. (If it is too hot, let it sit until it cools a bit. If it is too cold, warm it over low heat.) Add the yeast and stir until it is completely dissolved.

Pour the mixture into sanitized plastic bottles (see page 25) using a sanitized kitchen funnel, leaving 1¼ inches of air space at the top of each bottle. Seal the bottles. Store for 2 to 4 days at room temperature. When the bottles feel rock hard, the soda is fully carbonated.

Refrigerate for at least 1 week before serving; drink within 3 weeks to avoid overcarbonation.

Mixology

Prepare the Fermented Honey Soda as described above.

sparkling mead

Add 1 ounce (2 tablespoons) brandy to 8 ounces (1 cup) Fermented Honey Soda. Serve over ice.

honey bee

Add 2 ounces (¼ cup) gin to 8 ounces (1 cup) Fermented Honey Soda. Serve over crushed ice, garnished with a lemon wedge.

coffee chocolate stout

Similar in character to Molasses Beer (page 110), this recipe takes on a more roasted caramelized character with the addition of cocoa (dark roasted cocoa beans), dark roasted coffee, and unsulfured (dark) molasses. It's comparable to a porter beer.

COFFEE SYRUP

- 3 cups water
- ½ cup unsweetened cocoa powder
- ½ cup finely ground dark roasted coffee
- ½ cup unsulfured dark molasses
- 1 tablespoon caraway seed
- 2 cinnamon sticks
- 1 vanilla bean, cut into three pieces
- 3 cups dark brown sugar
- 2 tablespoon maltodextrin (optional)

ENOUGH FOR 1 GALLON BREWED SODA

Combine the water, cocoa, coffee, molasses, caraway seed, cinnamon, and vanilla in a large saucepan, and stir to blend. Bring to a simmer over medium heat, stirring occasionally; let simmer, uncovered, for 3 minutes. Blend the sugar and maltodextrin (if using), and gradually add the mixture to the simmering syrup, stirring until the sugar dissolves. Remove from the heat, let cool, and strain through a damp coffee filter or very fine mesh strainer.

This syrup will keep in the refrigerator for up to 2 months.

 TO MIX WITH SELTZER

- ½ cup coffee syrup
- 1½ cups seltzer

1 SERVING

Pour the syrup into a tall glass. Add the seltzer and stir just until blended. Add ice and serve.

TO CARBONATE WITH A SIPHON

3 cups water
1 cup coffee syrup

3 SERVINGS

Combine the water and syrup in a 1-quart soda siphon. Charge with CO_2 according to the manufacturer's directions. Siphon-charged sodas can be stored in the siphon in a refrigerator for up to 5 days. Disperse as desired into tall glasses filled with ice, and serve.

TO BREW

3 quarts lukewarm (80–90°F) water
1 batch coffee syrup
⅛ teaspoon champagne yeast (*Saccharomyces bayanus*)

1 GALLON

Combine the water and syrup in a large container. Test the temperature; the mixture should be at a warm room temperature, from 75 to 80°F. (If it is too hot, let it sit until it cools a bit. If it is too cold, warm it over low heat.) Add the yeast and stir until it is completely dissolved.

Pour the mixture into sanitized plastic bottles (see page 25) using a sanitized kitchen funnel, leaving 1¼ inches of air space at the top of each bottle. Seal the bottles. Store for 2 to 4 days at room temperature. When the bottles feel rock hard, the soda is fully carbonated.

Refrigerate for at least 1 week before serving; drink within 3 weeks to avoid overcarbonation.

Mixology

Prepare the coffee syrup as described at left, then carbonate as desired.

sparkling black velvet
Combine equal parts chilled Coffee Chocolate Stout and champagne in a chilled pilsner glass.

lime ginseng ginger root beer

Ginseng root contains ginsenosides, a class of steroids that includes several substances, like digitalis, used in the treatment of heart disease. Although traditional applications for ginseng root include treatments for stress, male impotence, and type II diabetes, clinical studies on humans have not supported any therapeutic effects (although animal studies have shown ginseng to promote increased libido and sexual activity). I make no libido promises in regard to this root beer. I can say that it is highly refreshing, clean tasting, cooling, and fragrant. Does that turn you on?

GINSENG GINGER SYRUP

4½ cups water

⅓ cup ground dried ginseng root, or contents of 6 ginseng-root tea bags

1 (5-inch) length of fresh gingerroot, coarsely chopped

Finely grated zest and juice of 3 limes

1 vanilla bean, cut into three pieces

4 cups evaporated coconut palm sugar

2 tablespoons maltodextrin (optional)

ENOUGH FOR 1 GALLON BREWED ROOT BEER

Combine the water, ginseng, ginger, lime zest and juice, and vanilla bean in a large saucepan, and stir to blend. Bring to a simmer over medium heat, stirring occasionally; let simmer, uncovered, for 10 minutes. Blend the sugar and maltodextrin (if using), and gradually add the mixture to the simmering syrup, stirring until the sugar dissolves. Let simmer for 2 minutes, stirring occasionally. Then remove from the heat, let cool, and strain.

This syrup will keep in the refrigerator for up to 2 months.

TO MIX WITH SELTZER

½ cup ginseng ginger
 syrup
1½ cups seltzer

1 SERVING

Pour the syrup into a tall glass. Add the seltzer and stir just until blended. Add ice and serve.

TO CARBONATE WITH A SIPHON

3 cups water
1 cup ginseng ginger
 syrup

3 SERVINGS

Combine the water and syrup in a 1-quart soda siphon. Charge with CO_2 according to the manufacturer's directions. Siphon-charged sodas can be stored in the siphon in a refrigerator for up to 5 days. Disperse as desired into tall glasses filled with ice, and serve.

TO BREW

3 quarts lukewarm
 (80–90°F) water
1 batch ginseng ginger
 syrup
⅛ teaspoon champagne
 yeast (*Saccharomyces
 bayanus*)

1 GALLON

Combine the water and syrup in a large container. Test the temperature; the mixture should be at a warm room temperature, from 75 to 80°F. (If it is too hot, let it sit until it cools a bit. If it is too cold, warm it over low heat.) Add the yeast and stir until it is completely dissolved.

Pour the mixture into sanitized plastic bottles (see page 25) using a sanitized kitchen funnel, leaving 1¼ inches of air space at the top of each bottle. Seal the bottles. Store for 2 to 4 days at room temperature. When the bottles feel rock hard, the soda is fully carbonated.

Refrigerate for at least 1 week before serving; drink within 3 weeks to avoid overcarbonation.

anise licorice root beer

Star anise, the dried star-shaped fruit of an Asian evergreen, is pungent with the aroma of licorice and hints of clove and cinnamon. Together, star anise and licorice root create a flavor so full-bodied and powerful that just a few ounces will flavor a whole barrel of root beer. In this aromatic soda I have amended the licorice-anise partnership with vanilla bean for its floral top notes, clove for depth, and brown sugar for mellowness.

ANISE LICORICE SYRUP

- 4½ cups water
- 4 ounces dried licorice root, chopped
- 4 star anise
- 3 cloves
- 1 vanilla bean, cut into three pieces
- 4 cups dark brown sugar
- 2 tablespoon maltodextrin (optional)

ENOUGH FOR 1 GALLON BREWED ROOT BEER

Combine the water, licorice, star anise, cloves, and vanilla bean in a large saucepan. Bring to a simmer over medium heat, stirring occasionally; let simmer, uncovered, for 15 minutes. Blend the brown sugar and maltodextrin (if using), and gradually add the mixture to the simmering syrup, stirring until the sugar dissolves. Let simmer for 2 minutes, stirring occasionally. Then remove from the heat, let cool, and strain.

This syrup will keep in the refrigerator for up to 2 months.

 TO MIX WITH SELTZER

- ½ cup anise licorice syrup
- 1½ cups seltzer

1 SERVING

Pour the syrup into a tall glass. Add the seltzer and stir just until blended. Add ice and serve.

TO CARBONATE WITH A SIPHON

3 cups water
1 cup anise licorice syrup

3 SERVINGS

Combine the water and syrup in a 1-quart soda siphon. Charge with CO_2 according to the manufacturer's directions. Siphon-charged sodas can be stored in the siphon in a refrigerator for up to 5 days. Disperse as desired into tall glasses filled with ice, and serve.

TO BREW

3 quarts lukewarm (80–90°F) water
1 batch anise licorice syrup
⅛ teaspoon champagne yeast (*Saccharomyces bayanus*)

1 GALLON

Combine the water and syrup in a large container. Test the temperature; the mixture should be at a warm room temperature, from 75 to 80°F. (If it is too hot, let it sit until it cools a bit. If it is too cold, warm it over low heat.) Add the yeast and stir until it is completely dissolved.

Pour the mixture into sanitized plastic bottles (see page 25) using a sanitized kitchen funnel, leaving 1¼ inches of air space at the top of each bottle. Seal the bottles. Store for 2 to 4 days at room temperature. When the bottles feel rock hard, the soda is fully carbonated.

Refrigerate for at least 1 week before serving; drink within 3 weeks to avoid overcarbonation.

Mixology

Prepare the anise licorice syrup as described at left, then carbonate as desired.

black licorice

Add 1 ounce (2 tablespoons) Pernod, Sambuca, or other anise-flavored liqueur to 8 ounces (1 cup) Anise Licorice Root Beer and serve over ice.

hardly hard cider

At one time almost all apple cider was alcoholic, but since the days of Prohibition, apple cider has been pasteurized to keep it from fermenting, making it pungently sweet. In this mildly fermented cider the yeast is allowed to feed off the sugars for 3 to 4 days, yielding a just slightly sweet cider in which the tartness and fragrance of the apple shine through. It is highly refreshing, and surprisingly thirst-quenching for a fruit drink.

This recipe does not begin with a flavor base. Follow the complete brewing instructions to make one gallon of Hardly Hard Cider.

 TO BREW

> 1 gallon apple cider
> 1¾ cups light brown sugar
> 2 cinnamon sticks, broken into small pieces
> ⅛ teaspoon champagne yeast (*Saccharomyces bayanus*)
>
> 1 GALLON

Combine the cider, sugar, and cinnamon in a large pot over medium heat. Bring to a simmer, stirring occasionally to dissolve the sugar. Then remove from the heat and let cool to warm room temperature, from 75 to 80°F. Remove the cinnamon and add the yeast, stirring until it is completely dissolved.

Pour the mixture into sanitized plastic bottles (see page 25) using a sanitized kitchen funnel, leaving 1¼ inches of air space at the top of each bottle. Seal the bottles. Store for 3 to 5 days at room temperature. When the bottles feel rock hard, the soda is fully carbonated.

Refrigerate for at least 1 week before serving; drink within 3 weeks to avoid overcarbonation.

 Mixology

Prepare the Hardly Hard Cider as described above.

mulling mulled cider

Add 1 ounce (2 tablespoons) brandy to 8 ounces (1 cup) Hardly Hard Cider.

Kombucha Tips

KOMBUCHA IS A FERMENTED TEA. It has a tart, refreshing flavor and a naturally light carbonation. The carbonation can vary from batch to batch, but generally the longer you let the beverage ferment, the fizzier it becomes. Before you start brewing the kombucha recipes on pages 120, 122, and 150, you'll need to know some background information.

KOMBUCHA STARTER CULTURE (MOTHER)
Kombucha starter culture, also known as kombucha "mother," contains a combination of acetic acid bacteria (mother of vinegar) and one or more yeasts. The culture, which looks and feels like a leftover congealed pancake, goes by various names, including "mushroom" and "SCOBY" (an acronym for "symbiotic colony of bacteria and yeast").

You can purchase a kombucha starter culture from suppliers on the Internet or get one from a kombucha-making acquaintance. Every time you brew a batch of kombucha, the mother culture gives birth to a "baby." You can reuse the mother, or if the baby is big enough it can become a mother culture itself. Baby cultures can vary in size. If they are thicker than ¼ inch they can be used on their own, but if they are thin they should be paired with a thicker mother. Once a baby is used to make a new batch of kombucha, it graduates to mother status.

KOMBUCHA STARTER TEA
In addition to a starter culture, you will need a starter tea to brew kombucha. For your first batch, this can be store-bought kombucha tea, or starter tea obtained from a kombucha-brewing friend. In a pinch, you can substitute vinegar. Then, every time you make kombucha, reserve a small amount (about ½ cup) of finished fermented tea mixed with an equal part of distilled white vinegar. This liquid is called "starter tea." Pour it over the kombucha starter culture (mother) and store in the refrigerator.

KOMBUCHA EQUIPMENT DETAILS AND CARE
It is best to wash any piece of equipment that the fermenting tea will contact with vinegar rather than tap water. The starter culture for kombucha thrives in an acidic environment and alkaline substances in hard tap water can dilute the acidity.

Metals are highly interactive with acids so it is best to use glass storage containers for kombucha. If you use a glass jar with a metal lid, cover the mouth of jar with a layer of plastic wrap before putting on the lid, to keep the contents from coming into contact with metal.

You can use stainless steel pans to heat the tea before fermentation, since stainless steel is a fairly inert metal that will not react with the kombucha.

orange kombucha

There seems to be an unending supply of anecdotal evidence about the health benefits of kombucha and nothing scientific to support them. Kombucha fans claim that it boosts energy, sharpens mental capabilities, and strengthens the immune system. In the name of transparency I admit that I am one of those fans. Please do try a batch and see how you like it.

This recipe does not begin with a flavor base. Follow the complete brewing instructions to make three servings of Orange Kombucha.

Note: Before you make you first batch of kombucha, see Kombucha Tips (page 119) to familiarize yourself with some important background concepts.

 TO BREW

Distilled white vinegar
for rinsing equipment
1 quart spring water or
filtered water
¼ cup sugar
5 black tea bags
½ cup kombucha starter
tea (see Kombucha
Tips, page 119)
1 kombucha starter
culture (called
"mother"; see Kom-
bucha Tips, page 119)
½ cup distilled white
vinegar
½ cup orange juice

3 SERVINGS

1. Rinse out a medium stainless-steel saucepan with distilled vinegar. Add the water to the pan and bring to a boil over medium-high heat. As soon as the water boils, add the sugar and stir to dissolve. Remove from the heat, add the tea bags, cover, and let sit for 20 minutes. Rinse a slotted spoon with vinegar and use it to remove the tea bags from the pot.

Rinse a large (at least 1½-quart) glass jar with distilled vinegar. Pour the sweet tea into the glass jar and let cool to room temperature, about 2 hours.

2. Stir the starter tea into the sweet tea and add the starter culture ("mother"). Cover the jar with a coffee filter, cheesecloth, or other material that will keep out debris but allow air to circulate. Secure with a rubber band. Set in a warm, dark place to ferment for 8 to 12 days (a spot in the basement near a water heater works well).

3 As the kombucha ferments a new starter culture (called a "baby") will form on the surface, while the mother will either float beneath it or sink to the bottom of the jar. Strings may extend between the two cultures. When the new baby culture is almost as big as its mother, it's time to taste-test the kombucha. Stick a straw partway into the liquid, cover the end still in the air with a finger, and withdraw the straw from the liquid, thereby removing a dropperful. Taste the kombucha you've captured in the straw. If it is refreshingly tart, it's ready. If not, let the kombucha ferment longer.

4 When the kombucha is fully fermented, preserve the starter culture and starter tea for your next batch of kombucha. Rinse your hands with distilled vinegar, and then lift the mother and baby to a clean glass bowl or glass jar that has been rinsed with vinegar. Pour about ½ cup of the unfiltered kombucha over the culture, and add the ½ cup distilled white vinegar. This liquid is starter tea. Cover tightly and store in the refrigerator for up to 1 to 2 months. (If you're using a jar for storage instead and it has a metal lid, cover the jar with a layer of plastic wrap first, before putting on the lid, to keep the contents from coming into contact with metal.)

5 Filter the remaining kombucha through a damp coffee filter or several layers of damp cheesecloth into a clean glass jar. Stir in the orange juice and seal the jar with a plastic or plastic-wrap-lined lid. Let sit at room temperature for 2 to 4 days, until the kombucha is bubbly, and then chill for 24 hours. Serve over ice.

green tea kombucha

Green tea kombucha is lighter in color and flavor than its black tea brethren, which is why I spike it with a little honey and mint. As a general rule, if you want to add any flavoring other than tea to kombucha, you should do so only after the fermentation is complete. Kombucha culture is notoriously fickle and can refuse to grow when its environment isn't acidic enough, or when it is infused with competing botanicals. I tend to shy away from adding anything other than tea and sugar until after I have removed the culture.

This recipe does not begin with a flavor base. Follow the complete brewing instructions to make three servings of Green Tea Kombucha.

Note: Before you make you first batch of kombucha, see Kombucha Tips (page 119) to familiarize yourself with some important background concepts.

 TO BREW

Distilled white vinegar
   for rinsing equipment
5 cups spring water or
   filtered water
¼ cup sugar
5 green tea bags
½ cup kombucha starter
   green tea (see Kom-
   bucha Tips, page 119)
1 kombucha starter
   culture (called
   "mother"; see Kom-
   bucha Tips, page 119)
1 mint tea bag
½ cup distilled white
   vinegar
1 tablespoon honey

3 SERVINGS

1 Rinse out a medium stainless-steel saucepan with distilled vinegar. Add 4 cups of the water to the pan and bring to a boil over medium-high heat. As soon as the water boils, add the sugar and stir to dissolve. Remove from the heat, add the tea bags, cover, and let sit for 20 minutes. Rinse a slotted spoon with vinegar and use it to remove the tea bags from the pot.

Rinse a large (at least 1½-quart) glass jar with distilled vinegar. Pour the sweet tea into the glass jar and let cool to room temperature, about 2 hours.

2 Stir the starter tea into the sweet tea and add the starter culture ("mother"). Cover the jar with a coffee filter, cheesecloth, or other material that will keep out debris but allow air to circulate. Secure with a rubber band. Set in a warm, dark place to ferment for 8 to 12 days (a spot in the basement near a water heater works well).

3 As the kombucha ferments a new starter culture (called a "baby") will form on the surface, while the mother will either float beneath it or sink to the bottom of the jar. Strings may extend between the two cultures. When the new baby culture is almost as big as its mother, it's time to taste-test the kombucha. Stick a straw partway into the liquid, cover the end still in the air with a finger, and withdraw the straw from the liquid, thereby removing a dropperful. Taste the kombucha you've captured in the straw. If it is refreshingly tart, it's ready. If not, let the kombucha ferment longer.

4 When the kombucha is fully fermented, preserve the starter culture and starter tea for your next batch of kombucha. Rinse your hands with distilled vinegar, and then lift the mother and baby to a clean glass bowl or glass jar that has been rinsed with vinegar. Pour about ½ cup of the unfiltered kombucha over the culture, and add the ½ cup distilled white vinegar. This liquid is starter tea. Cover tightly and store in the refrigerator for up to 1 to 2 months. (If you're using a jar for storage instead and it has a metal lid, cover the jar with a layer of plastic wrap first, before putting on the lid, to keep the contents from coming into contact with metal.)

5 Bring the remaining 1 cup water to a boil. Stir in the honey, and let the mixture boil until it is reduced to about ½ cup. Remove from the heat, add the mint tea bag, and let sit for 5 minutes. Remove the tea bag.

6 Filter the remaining kombucha through a damp coffee filter or several layers of damp cheesecloth into a clean glass jar. Stir in the mint tea and seal the jar with a plastic or plastic-wrap-lined lid. Let sit at room temperature for 2 to 4 days, until the kombucha is bubbly, and then chill for 24 hours. Serve over ice.

CHAPTER FOUR

Herbal & Healing

Sodas

Waters

*𝒥*n the beginning, sodas were brewed from pungent plant parts, not to extract their flavor, but to reap their medicinal chemicals. Plants excel at biochemistry. Animals run from danger, but plants cannot. To defend themselves plants have developed chemicals that discourage potential predators. A biochemical that may kill an insect might just be enough to dilate the blood vessels of a larger animal, like a human, improving circulation. A small amount of caffeine destroys the nervous system of most insects. It affects our nerves too, but in the right amount it is just enough to stimulate and quicken our nerve responses, not enough to undermine them.

Root beers started out as herbal teas, cola was originally a painkiller, and ginger ale is a time-honored digestive aid. In other words, the contemporary addiction to functional beverages — drinks constructed around a specific nutrient content or to treat a particular ailment — is nothing new. Functional beverages fall into two categories:

LIFESTYLE DRINKS, DESIGNED TO ENHANCE BEHAVIOR

These include energy and alertness drinks, sedating drinks, and sports beverages.

HEALTH DRINKS, DESIGNED TO COMBAT PARTICULAR AILMENTS

There are drinks that either fight ailments (arthritis, headache) or strengthen bodily systems (immune boosters, digestive aids).

Vitamin A Tonic, page 134

For the recipes in this chapter, I have relied as much as possible on whole ingredients that are naturally rich in the chemicals that are typically included in commercial functional beverages. My recipes for energy drinks rely on stimulating ingredients like coffee, tea, and chocolate, rather than extracts of caffeine. To aid digestion I might include ginger, mint, or chile peppers, but not isolated gingerole, menthol, or capsaicin. Above all, these recipes have been formulated to taste good. Of course a soda can be healthful, but it must still excite our taste and thirst.

ginseng soda

Ginseng has been used in Chinese medicine for millennia, mostly in the treatment of sexual dysfunction, particularly male impotence. I don't want to get your hopes up, but a study done by the Southern Illinois University School of Medicine found that ginseng enhanced sexual performance in laboratory animals. Drink up!

GINSENG SYRUP

1 cup water

¼ cup sugar

4 ginseng-root tea bags

1 tablespoon honey

1 teaspoon unflavored rice vinegar

ENOUGH FOR 3 SERVINGS

Bring the water to a boil. As soon as the water boils, add the sugar, stirring until it dissolves. Remove from the heat, add the tea bags, cover, and let sit for 20 minutes. Then remove the tea bags, stir in the honey and vinegar, and let cool to room temperature.

This syrup will keep in the refrigerator for up to 2 weeks.

 ## TO MIX WITH SELTZER

⅓ cup ginseng syrup
1¼ cups seltzer

1 SERVING

Pour the syrup into a tall glass. Add the seltzer and stir just until blended. Add ice and serve.

 ### *Mixology*

Prepare the ginseng syrup as described above, then carbonate with seltzer.

ginseng spritzer

Mix equal parts chilled Ginseng Soda and chilled white wine in a wine glass.

ginseng gin

Pour 1 to 2 ounces (2 to 4 tablespoons) Dutch-style gin, such as Hendrick's, over ice in a tall glass, add a splash of bitters, and top up the glass with Ginseng Soda. Garnish with lime wedge.

Energy Drinks

IN 1982, DIETRICH MATESCHITZ, an Austrian entrepreneur, was sitting at a bar in the Mandarin Hotel in Hong Kong experiencing the Asian phenomenon of "tonic drinks," the early name for functional beverages. He liked what he tasted, and by 1987 he had developed the formula, packaging, and marketing strategy for Red Bull and had begun selling it in Austria. Red Bull soon became (and remains) the top-selling energy beverage in the world. With its selection of ingredients and overtly mineral flavor profile, Red Bull has become the gold standard that almost all energy beverages emulate.

Energy drinks are designed to deliver a compact gulp of energy and nutrition. Let's take these aspects one at a time.

COMPACT GULP: Energy drinks come in small packages. Originally launched in 8-ounce cans (diminutive in the world of 2-liter soft drink bottles), now the powerhouse of energy drinks has been shrunk to shots, packing the same energy and nutrition boost as the larger package in a 1- to 2-ounce shooter.

ENERGY: The energy comes from sugar and trimethylxanthine ($C_8H_{10}N_4O_2$), the chemical term for caffeine. The substance can go by several different names: caffeine, when coming from coffee, chocolate, or kola nuts; guaranine, when coming from guarana seeds; and mateine, when coming from yerba maté. Any of these names could appear on a label of an energy drink. They all refer to the same chemical stimulant, most commonly known as caffeine.

NUTRITION: As you might expect, nutrition in energy drinks usually centers around performance, with various nutrients touted as enhancing physical or mental capabilities. Taurine, for example, is an amino acid that is thought to have antioxidant properties and that in some studies has been linked to an increase in athletic performance. Glucuronolactone is a complex carbohydrate that reputedly detoxifies the body. Most energy drinks feature a number of B vitamins, including inositol (involved in the breakdown of fats and cholesterol and in moderating the activity of the neurotransmitter serotonin), niacin (affects brain activity and metabolic levels), pantothenol (a.k.a. pantothenic acid, critical to metabolism and the synthesis of macronutrients), pyridoxine (moderates the cardiovascular system), and vitamin B_{12} (essential for brain and nerve functions and the formation of blood plasma).

brain juice

Extracts from the leaf of the ginkgo tree (Ginkgo biloba) *reputedly improve blood flow, particularly in the small capillaries of the brain, thereby enhancing concentration and decreasing the symptoms of vertigo. Ginkgo extract is available wherever nutritional supplements are sold. Store it in the refrigerator and mix up a glass of this juice whenever you need a brain boost. Note that ginkgo leaves contain allergens similar to those in poison ivy and should be avoided by those who have strong reactions to poison ivy. Also, some people report headaches as a side effect of consuming ginkgo.*

GINKGO ORANGE JUICE

1 tablespoon liquid ginkgo biloba extract

1 teaspoon honey

¼ cup orange juice

ENOUGH FOR 1 SERVING

Combine the gingko biloba, honey, and orange juice, stirring to blend.

 ## TO MIX WITH SELTZER

1 batch ginkgo orange juice

1¼ cups seltzer

1 SERVING

Pour the juice into a tall glass. Add the seltzer and stir just until blended. Add ice and serve.

 Mixology

Prepare the ginkgo orange juice as described above, then carbonate with seltzer.

 the addled brain

Pour 1 to 2 ounces (2 to 4 tablespoons) vodka over ice in a tall glass and top up the glass with Brain Juice. Garnish with an orange slice.

açai super soda

The açai palm tree (Euterpe oleracea) *produces both the hearts of palm used in salads and the açai berry, ranked among the world's most nutritious foods. Because the fresh fruit spoils quickly after being picked, it is not found fresh outside its growing region, which is mostly in Brazil. But its juice and the dried fruit are widely available. Açai berry is rich in antioxidants (mainly cyanidins) and anthocyanins, which have been shown to boost the body's immune system. The grapefruit juice cuts the sweetness of the açai.*

AÇAI GRAPEFRUIT JUICE

1½ cups açai juice

½ cup grapefruit juice, preferably fresh

ENOUGH FOR 3 SERVINGS

Combine the açai and grapefruit juices, stirring to blend.

This juice will keep in the refrigerator for up to 2 weeks.

 ## TO MIX WITH SELTZER

⅔ cup açai grapefruit juice
⅔ cup seltzer

1 SERVING

Pour the juice into a tall glass. Add the seltzer and stir just until blended. Add ice and serve.

 ## TO CARBONATE WITH A SIPHON

2 cups water
1 batch açai grapefruit juice

3 SERVINGS

Combine the water and juice in a 1-quart soda siphon. Charge with CO_2 according to the manufacturer's directions. Siphon-charged sodas can be stored in the siphon in a refrigerator for up to 5 days. Disperse as desired into tall glasses filled with ice, and serve.

 ### Mixology

Prepare the açai grapefruit juice as described above, then carbonate as desired.

açai punch

Pour 1 ounce (2 tablespoons) vodka and 1 ounce (2 tablespoons) light rum over ice in a tall glass, and top up with Açai Super Soda.

antioxidant explosion

Everyday cellular processes occurring in your body throw off free radicals (atoms or molecules with an unpaired electron) as by-products. These free radicals scavenge your body in search of stray electrons, thereby altering healthy cells and making them unstable. The damage from free radicals is implicated in the growth of cancerous cells and in cell aging. You cannot stop the formation of free radicals, but antioxidants help neutralize their activity. Chapter 4 offers recipes for several sodas with fruits that have high levels of antioxidants. The recipe here boosts the antioxidant ante by adding two spices rich in antioxidants: clove and cinnamon.

ANTIOXIDANT SYRUP

- ¾ cup water
- ½ cup sugar
- 6 cloves
- 1 large (5-inch) cinnamon stick, broken into pieces
- 1 cup unsweetened blueberry juice, fresh or bottled
- 1 cup unsweetened pomegranate juice, fresh (page 61) or bottled

ENOUGH FOR 3 SERVINGS

Combine the water, sugar, cloves, and cinnamon in a small saucepan and bring to a boil over medium heat. Boil until reduced to about half of its original volume, a little less than ½ cup. Let cool for 10 minutes, and then strain out the spices and stir in the blueberry and pomegranate juices.

This syrup will keep in the refrigerator for up to 7 days.

TO MIX WITH SELTZER

¾ cup antioxidant syrup
1 cup seltzer

1 SERVING

Pour the syrup into a tall glass. Add the seltzer and stir just until blended. Add ice and serve.

 ## TO CARBONATE WITH A SIPHON

1½ cups water
1 batch antioxidant syrup

3 SERVINGS

Combine the water and syrup in a 1-quart soda siphon. Charge with CO_2 according to the manufacturer's directions. Siphon-charged sodas can be stored in the siphon in a refrigerator for up to 5 days. Disperse as desired into tall glasses filled with ice, and serve.

vitamin A tonic

Vitamin A is essential for night vision, skin elasticity, and circulatory and immune system health. Anyone who eats a good variety of fruit and vegetables will probably get plenty, but if you want a boost, this soda is loaded.

APRICOT CARROT JUICE

1 cup apricot or peach nectar

1 cup carrot juice, fresh (below) or bottled

⅛ teaspoon ground cinnamon

ENOUGH FOR 3 SERVINGS

Combine the apricot nectar, carrot juice, and cinnamon, stirring to blend.

This juice will keep in the refrigerator for up to 3 days.

 ## TO MIX WITH SELTZER

⅔ cup apricot carrot juice
⅔ cup seltzer

1 SERVING

Pour the juice into a tall glass. Add the seltzer and stir just until blended. Add ice and serve.

 ## TO CARBONATE WITH A SIPHON

2 cups water
1 batch apricot carrot juice

3 SERVINGS

Combine the water and juice in a 1-quart soda siphon. Charge with CO_2 according to the manufacturer's directions. Siphon-charged sodas can be stored in the siphon in a refrigerator for up to 5 days. Disperse as desired into tall glasses filled with ice, and serve.

Fresh Carrot Juice

TO EXTRACT THE JUICE FROM CARROTS you will need a juice extractor able to grind up tough vegetable fibers. In general, one medium-length carrot will make about 1 ounce (2 tablespoons) of juice. Carrots should be cleaned with a vegetable brush or plastic scrubbie before juicing. There is no need to peel them.

licorice soda

Licorice is recommended in herbal medicine as a treatment for stomach problems, particularly ulcers. It is also valued for its use as a soothing expectorant and in relieving congestion. Recent studies have shown that people with high cholesterol levels achieved reduced triglyceride and LDL cholesterol levels after daily treatment with licorice root extract. It is believed that the active agent in licorice is glycyrrhizin, which reduces inflammation, promotes mucous secretion, and soothes the lining of the intestinal tract.

LICORICE SYRUP

1½ cups water

1 ounce dried licorice root, chopped

2 star anise

1½ cups dark brown sugar

ENOUGH FOR 3 SERVINGS

Combine the water, licorice, and star anise in a medium saucepan. Bring to a simmer over medium heat, stirring occasionally; let simmer, uncovered, for 5 minutes. Add the sugar. Bring the mixture back to a simmer over medium-high heat, stirring occasionally, until the sugar dissolves, about 1 minute. Remove from the heat, let cool, and strain.

This syrup can be stored in the refrigerator for up to 2 months.

 TO MIX WITH SELTZER

⅔ cup licorice syrup
⅔ cup seltzer

1 SERVING

Pour the syrup into a tall glass. Add the seltzer and stir just until blended. Add ice and serve.

 TO CARBONATE WITH A SIPHON

2 cups water
1 batch licorice syrup

3 SERVINGS

Combine the water and syrup in a 1-quart soda siphon. Charge with CO_2 according to the manufacturer's directions. Siphon-charged sodas can be stored in the siphon in a refrigerator for up to 5 days. Disperse as desired into tall glasses filled with ice, and serve.

 Also see Mixology recipe on page 137.

naturally sweet coconut palm soda

Coconut palm sugar crystallized from palm tree sap has a glycemic index of 35, about one-third that of cane sugar. For a sweetener it is also remarkably packed with trace nutrients, delivering 400 times the potassium and 20 times the amount of zinc and iron as unrefined cane sugar. This soda is mild, sweet, and refreshingly creamy from the beneficial fats in coconut milk.

COCONUT SYRUP

- ½ cup water
- ¾ cup evaporated coconut palm sugar
- 1 tablespoon finely grated lime zest
- 1 cup light coconut milk
- ½ teaspoon vanilla extract

ENOUGH FOR 4 SERVINGS

Combine the water, palm sugar, and lime zest in a small saucepan. Bring to a boil, then remove from the heat and let cool to room temperature. Strain. Stir in the coconut milk and vanilla.

This syrup can be stored in the refrigerator for up to 2 months.

TO MIX WITH SELTZER

- ½ cup coconut syrup
- 1 cup seltzer

1 SERVING

Pour the syrup into a tall glass. Add the seltzer and stir just until blended. Add ice and serve.

TO CARBONATE WITH A SIPHON

- 2 cups water
- 1 batch coconut syrup

4 SERVINGS

Combine the water and syrup in a 1-quart soda siphon. Charge with CO_2 according to the manufacturer's directions. Siphon-charged sodas can be stored in the siphon in a refrigerator for up to 5 days. Disperse as desired into tall glasses filled with ice, and serve.

Herbal Soda

MIXOLOGY

sparkling piña colada

Prepare the coconut syrup as described at left, then carbonate as desired.

Combine 1½ ounces (3 tablespoons) light rum, 2 ounces (¼ cup) pineapple juice, 4 ounces (½ cup) Naturally Sweet Coconut Palm Soda, and 1 cup crushed ice in a blender. Blend, and pour the mixture into a tall glass rimmed with evaporated coconut palm sugar.

forget paris

Prepare the licorice syrup as described on page 135, then carbonate as desired.

Pour 1 ounce (2 tablespoons) Pernod (or another licorice liqueur) into a champagne flute. Fill the glass with chilled Licorice Soda (page 135).

herbal screwdriver

Prepare the rosemary syrup as described on page 142, then carbonate as desired.

Mix 1½ ounces (3 tablespoons) vodka and 2 ounces (¼ cup) orange juice in a tall glass. Add ice and fill the glass with Orange Rosemary Crush (page 142). Stir and garnish with a rosemary sprig.

cold toddy

Prepare the chamomile kava syrup as described on page 143, then carbonate as desired.

Pour 1 ounce (2 tablespoons) brandy into a brandy snifter and top with 4 ounces (½ cup) Calming Waters (page 143) and an ice cube.

sparkling mint julep

Prepare the peppermint syrup as described on page 146, then carbonate as desired.

Pour 2 ounces (¼ cup) bourbon over ½ cup crushed ice in a tall glass. Fill the glass with Peppermint Tummy Tamer (page 146); stir briefly and garnish with a mint sprig.

ancho chile explosion

This slow burn of a soft drink is infused with the magical powers of capsaicin, the active chemical in chile peppers. Ancho chiles, which are dried mature poblano peppers, are in the low range of hotness (about 2,000 Scoville units) and have a wonderful fruity flavor and a vegetal sweetness, both of which are brought out by the use of agave syrup. Don't be turned off by the notion of hot pepper in a soda. The heat is gentle and very sexy. Just sit back, sip, and sigh.

ANCHO SYRUP

1²⁄₃ cups water

   1 or 2 dried ancho chiles, stem and seeds discarded, coarsely chopped

       Finely grated zest and juice of 1 large lime

 ²⁄₃ cup agave syrup or simple syrup (page 15)

ENOUGH FOR 3 SERVINGS

Combine the water, ancho, and lime zest in a medium saucepan. Bring to a simmer over medium heat, stirring occasionally; let simmer, uncovered, for 3 minutes. Then remove from the heat and add the lime juice and agave syrup, stirring until the syrup dissolves. Let cool to room temperature, and then strain.

This syrup will keep in the refrigerator for up to 2 weeks.

TO MIX WITH SELTZER

 ²⁄₃ cup ancho syrup
 ²⁄₃ cup seltzer

1 SERVING

Pour the syrup into a tall glass. Add the seltzer and stir just until blended. Add ice and serve.

TO CARBONATE WITH A SIPHON

2 cups water
1 batch ancho syrup

3 SERVINGS

Combine the water and syrup in a 1-quart soda siphon. Charge with CO_2 according to the manufacturer's directions. Siphon-charged sodas can be stored in the siphon in a refrigerator for up to 5 days. Disperse as desired into tall glasses filled with ice, and serve.

 ### *Mixology*

Prepare the ancho syrup as described at left, then carbonate as desired.

chile margarita fizz

Mix 1 ounce (2 tablespoons) tequila and 4 ounces (½ cup) Ancho Chile Explosion, and pour over crushed ice in a large margarita glass. Serve with a lime wedge and coarse sea salt, if desired.

 ### *Chile Pepper Health*

CAPSAICIN, THE ACTIVE CHEMICAL IN CHILES, makes your skin and mouth feel hot. It does this by binding to nerve receptors that register heat and pain, causing those nerves to become sensitive, producing the sensation you would get if you were being burned. Even though the chile isn't really burning your skin, the feeling triggers the release of pain-relieving endorphins in the brain, which produce a mild anesthetized feeling of well-being. Because the body responds to capsaicin by desensitizing affected areas, capsaicin is effective as a pain-relieving component in muscle creams and other pharmaceuticals. Capsaicin also has antibacterial properties.

sparkling lemongrass lemonade

Lemongrass, a perennial herb from central Asia, has high levels of citral, the pungent aromatic component in lemon peel. It gives this sparkling lemonade a deep, rich citrus-oil flavor, reminiscent of lemon drop candy.

LEMONGRASS SYRUP

3 large stalks lemongrass, untrimmed and thinly sliced

1⅔ cups water

¾ cup sugar

Finely grated zest and juice of 1 large lemon

ENOUGH FOR 4 SERVINGS

Bruise the sliced lemongrass by pounding it on a sturdy surface with a meat mallet or a heavy skillet. Combine the water and bruised lemongrass in a small saucepan. Bring to a simmer over medium heat, stirring occasionally; let simmer, uncovered, for 5 minutes. Add the sugar, stirring until it dissolves, and then add the lemon zest and juice. Bring the mixture back to a simmer over medium-high heat, and let simmer for 5 minutes. Then remove from the heat, let cool for 30 minutes, and strain.

This syrup can be stored in the refrigerator for up to 2 weeks.

 TO MIX WITH SELTZER

⅓ cup lemongrass syrup

2 tablespoons lemon juice

1½ cups seltzer

1 SERVING

Combine the syrup and lemon juice in a tall glass. Add the seltzer and stir just until blended. Add ice and serve.

 Mixology

Prepare the lemongrass syrup as described above, then carbonate with seltzer.

sparkling lemon campari

Combine 3 ounces (6 tablespoons) Campari and 6 ounces (¾ cup) Sparkling Lemongrass Lemonade in a tall glass and fill with ice.

black lemon beer

Combine equal parts ice-cold porter and chilled Sparkling Lemongrass Lemonade.

bedtime chamomile soda

Of all the herbal sedatives, chamomile is one of the most soothing, and by far the most pleasant-tasting. In this bedtime beverage sweetened chamomile tea is mixed with a little milk before it is carbonated. Calcium, the most plentiful mineral in milk, is a natural tranquilizer.

CHAMOMILE MILK

½ cup water

¼ cup sugar

1 chamomile tea bag

½ cup milk

ENOUGH FOR 1 SERVING

Combine the water and sugar in a small saucepan. Bring to a boil, then remove from the heat, add the tea bag, and let steep for 5 minutes. Remove the tea bag and let the syrup cool to room temperature. Stir in the milk.

 TO MIX WITH SELTZER

1 batch chamomile milk

1 cup seltzer

1 SERVING

Pour the milk into a tall glass. Add the seltzer and stir just until blended. Add ice and serve.

orange rosemary crush

Palate prejudice tells us that cinnamon is for spice cake and rosemary is for chicken, but there is nothing in either the spice or herb that predetermines their affinity to sweetness or savoriness. Italians make a fragrant tea cake flavored with rosemary and seasoned with orange that is the inspiration for this soda. Rosemary has high levels of vitamins A and C (both antioxidants), iron, and calcium.

ROSEMARY SYRUP

1²/₃ cups orange juice

2 tablespoons fresh rosemary leaves

¹/₃ cup honey

ENOUGH FOR 3 SERVINGS

Combine the orange juice and rosemary in a medium saucepan; bring to a simmer over medium heat, stirring occasionally. As soon as the mixture begins to simmer, remove it from the heat and add the honey, stirring until it dissolves. Let cool to room temperature, and strain.

This syrup can be stored in the refrigerator for up to 2 days.

TO MIX WITH SELTZER

²/₃ cup rosemary syrup
²/₃ cup seltzer

1 SERVING

Pour the syrup into a tall glass. Add the seltzer and stir just until blended. Add ice and serve.

TO CARBONATE WITH A SIPHON

3 cups water
1 batch rosemary syrup

3 SERVINGS

Combine the water and syrup in a 1-quart soda siphon. Charge with CO_2 according to the manufacturer's directions. Siphon-charged sodas can be stored in the siphon in a refrigerator for up to 5 days. Disperse as desired into tall glasses filled with ice, and serve.

Also see Mixology recipe on page 137.

calming waters

Chamomile blossoms were used for their mild sedative effect by early European herbalists, and kava root was used for the same purpose in the South Pacific. In this mollifying soda, East meets West to relaxing effect. Neither kava nor chamomile is strongly flavored, although the former is slightly more pungent, so I have added mint leaves for brightness. Mint has a marked calming effect on the digestive system and has been shown to be relaxing to the nerves as well.

CHAMOMILE KAVA SYRUP

1 cup sugar

1 cup water

2 chamomile tea bags

2 kava tea bags

¼ cup finely chopped fresh mint leaves

ENOUGH FOR 3 SERVINGS

Combine the sugar and water in a small saucepan and bring to a boil. Remove from the heat, add the chamomile tea bags, kava tea bags, and mint, and let steep for 5 minutes. Remove the tea bags and let the syrup cool to room temperature. Strain to remove the mint leaves.

This syrup will keep in the refrigerator for up to 2 months.

 TO MIX WITH SELTZER

½ cup chamomile kava syrup

1 cup seltzer

1 SERVING

Pour the syrup into a tall glass. Add the seltzer and stir just until blended. Add ice and serve.

 TO CARBONATE WITH A SIPHON

2½ cups water

1 batch chamomile kava syrup

3 SERVINGS

Combine the water and syrup in a 1-quart soda siphon. Charge with CO_2 according to the manufacturer's directions. Siphon-charged sodas can be stored in the siphon in a refrigerator for up to 5 days. Disperse as desired into tall glasses filled with ice, and serve.

 *Also see **Mixology** recipe on page 137.*

sports recovery soda

Sports drinks are designed to replace the electrolytes (particularly sodium) the body loses during exercise, mainly through perspiration. Hyponatremia, or an insufficient concentration of sodium in the blood, can cause nausea, muscle spasms, and weakness, and is not uncommon in hardcore athletes. Sugar and salt help the body absorb and retain water, so sports drinks help athletes maintain hydration as well as a proper electrolyte balance and energy levels.

CITRUS SPORTS JUICE

¼ cup orange juice

2 teaspoons lime juice

1 teaspoon lemon juice

3 tablespoons agave syrup or simple syrup (page 15)

⅛ teaspoon fine sea salt

ENOUGH FOR 1 (20-OUNCE) SERVING

Combine the orange juice, lime juice, lemon juice, agave syrup, and salt, stirring to blend.

 TO MIX WITH SELTZER

1 batch citrus sports juice
2 cups seltzer

20 OUNCES, enough for 1 sports bottle

Pour the citrus juice into a 20-ounce sports bottle. Add the seltzer, seal the top, and shake to mix. Release excess pressure by carefully opening the top.

joint juice

Joint pain, regardless of its origin — injury, tendonitis, or arthritis — is caused by inflammation, and its relief is a question of reducing swelling throughout the body, specifically in affected joints. Turmeric has long been used in Chinese medicine as an anti-inflammatory; its active agent is curcumin, which has been shown in animal studies to help the body fight infection and shrink tumors and inflamed tissue. Pineapple juice has also demonstrated anti-inflammatory results in controlled studies. Its active agent is an enzyme, bromelain, which also helps in the digestion of proteins.

TURMERIC PINEAPPLE JUICE

1 cup water

2 tablespoons ground turmeric

3 cups pineapple juice

1 tablespoon sugar or agave syrup (optional)

ENOUGH FOR 3 SERVINGS

Bring the water to a boil. Add the turmeric and remove from the heat. Let cool, and then strain through a damp coffee filter. Mix the turmeric water with the pineapple juice. Add the sugar if a sweeter drink is desired.

This juice will keep in the refrigerator for up to 2 weeks.

TO MIX WITH SELTZER

1 cup turmeric pineapple juice

½ cup seltzer

1 SERVING

Pour the juice into a tall glass. Add the seltzer and stir just until blended. Add ice and serve.

TO CARBONATE WITH A SIPHON

1 batch turmeric pineapple juice

3 SERVINGS

Pour the juice into a 1-quart soda siphon (add water to fill if necessary). Charge with CO_2 according to the manufacturer's directions. Siphon-charged sodas can be stored in the siphon in a refrigerator for up to 5 days. Disperse as desired into tall glasses filled with ice, and serve.

peppermint tummy tamer

Mint has been a folk cure for stomach distress since Roman times. The main active agent in mint is menthol, which refreshes the lower parts of the gastrointestinal tract as well as the breath. Peppermint is the variety used most often for medicinal purposes. It is analgesic, antiemetic, anti-inflammatory, antimicrobial, and antispasmodic, which means there isn't much that can go wrong digestively that a little peppermint can't help.

PEPPERMINT SYRUP

1 cup sugar

1 cup water

3 peppermint tea bags

⅓ cup finely chopped fresh peppermint leaves

ENOUGH FOR 3 SERVINGS

Combine the sugar and water in a small saucepan. Bring to a boil, then remove from the heat, add the tea bags and mint leaves, and let steep for 5 minutes. Remove the tea bags and let the syrup cool to room temperature. Strain to remove the mint leaves.

This syrup will keep in the refrigerator for up to 2 months.

TO MIX WITH SELTZER

½ cup peppermint syrup
1 cup seltzer

1 SERVING

Pour the syrup into a tall glass. Add the seltzer and stir just until blended. Add ice and serve.

TO CARBONATE WITH A SIPHON

2½ cups water
1 batch peppermint syrup

3 SERVINGS

Combine the water and syrup in a 1-quart soda siphon. Charge with CO_2 according to the manufacturer's directions. Siphon-charged sodas can be stored in the siphon in a refrigerator for up to 5 days. Disperse as desired into tall glasses filled with ice, and serve.

Also see Mixology recipe on page 137.

going green sparkling herb water

Chlorophyll, the green pigment in plants that metabolizes carbon dioxide and sunlight into sugar and oxygen, also acts as a potent antioxidant and anti-inflammatory in the human body. Studies have shown that it has the potential to support the body's fight against cancer and anemia — and it wipes out bad breath too.

CHLOROPHYLL SYRUP

1 cup sugar

1 cup water

⅓ cup finely chopped fresh mint leaves

¼ cup finely chopped fresh basil leaves

1 tablespoon fresh rosemary leaves

ENOUGH FOR 3 SERVINGS

Combine the sugar and water in a small saucepan. Bring to a boil, add the mint, basil, and rosemary leaves, and remove from the heat; let cool to room temperature. Strain to remove the leaves.

This syrup will keep in the refrigerator for up to 2 months.

Note: It is possible to purchase liquid chlorophyll, but I prefer the tastier path of starting with a tea brewed from green leafy aromatic herbs.

TO MIX WITH SELTZER

½ cup chlorophyll syrup

1 cup seltzer

1 SERVING

Pour the syrup into a tall glass. Add the seltzer and stir just until blended. Add ice and serve.

TO CARBONATE WITH A SIPHON

2½ cups water

1 batch chlorophyll syrup

3 SERVINGS

Combine the water and syrup in a 1-quart soda siphon. Charge with CO_2 according to the manufacturer's directions. Siphon-charged sodas can be stored in the siphon in a refrigerator for up to 5 days. Disperse as desired into tall glasses filled with ice, and serve.

immunity solution

Preserve good health by strengthening your immune system. Nutrients that help boost the immune system are vitamin A (plentiful in blueberries) vitamin C (in lemons), beta-carotene (in carrots), and bioflavonoids and polyphenols (in blueberries and grapes). This potent soda has them all.

IMMUNITY SYRUP

1 pint blueberries or elder-
berries

½ cup carrot juice, preferably
fresh (page 134)

½ cup unsweetened purple
grape juice

Juice of ½ lemon

¼ cup honey

1 cinnamon stick, broken into
small pieces

1 (1-inch) length of fresh
gingerroot, coarsely chopped

ENOUGH FOR 3 SERVINGS

Combine the berries, carrot juice, grape juice, lemon juice, and honey in a small saucepan. Mash the mixture with a vegetable masher, and then stir in the cinnamon and ginger. Heat over low heat, stirring often, until the berries have released their liquid. Let cool to room temperature, and strain. You should have about 2 cups of syrup.

This syrup can be stored in the refrigerator for up to 2 days.

 ## TO MIX WITH SELTZER

⅔ cup immunity syrup
⅔ cup seltzer

1 SERVING

Pour the syrup into a tall glass. Add the seltzer and stir just until blended. Add ice and serve.

 ## TO CARBONATE WITH
A SIPHON

2 cups water
1 batch immunity syrup

3 SERVINGS

Combine the water and syrup in a 1-quart soda siphon. Charge with CO_2 according to the manufacturer's directions. Siphon-charged sodas can be stored in the siphon in a refrigerator for up to 5 days. Disperse as desired into tall glasses filled with ice, and serve.

lavender grape migraine mitigator

Lavender is an analgesic that has been shown to halt the onset of or mitigate the symptoms of migraine headaches. Although traditional uses of lavender for migraine relief involve topical application of lavender or oil or inhaling the lavender scent through a pillow or sachet, this aromatic soda is just as soothing, and it tastes delicious too.

LAVENDER GRAPE SYRUP

1 cup water

½ cup sugar

2 tablespoons dried lavender blossoms

2 tablespoons finely grated lemon zest

1 cup unsweetened white grape juice

ENOUGH FOR 3 SERVINGS

Combine the water and sugar in a small saucepan. Bring to a boil, then remove from the heat, add the lavender and lemon zest, and let steep for 5 minutes. Cool the syrup to room temperature. Strain to remove the lavender and zest and stir in the grape juice.

This syrup will keep in the refrigerator for up to 2 months.

TO MIX WITH SELTZER

⅔ cup lavender grape syrup

⅔ cup seltzer

1 SERVING

Pour the syrup into a tall glass. Add the seltzer and stir just until blended. Add ice and serve.

TO CARBONATE WITH A SIPHON

2 cups water

1 batch lavender grape syrup

3 SERVINGS

Combine the water and syrup in a 1-quart soda siphon. Charge with CO_2 according to the manufacturer's directions. Siphon-charged sodas can be stored in the siphon in a refrigerator for up to 5 days. Disperse as desired into tall glasses filled with ice, and serve.

chamomile lavender kombucha

The reputed health benefits of kombucha (page 119) are legion, and I would be remiss if did not include one kombucha recipe in this chapter on healing beverages. Kombucha must be made with tea leaves, as opposed to herbs, because volatile oils in many herbs suppress the kombucha culture. I have found that an addition of chamomile and lavender moderates kombucha's austere tartness without inhibiting fermentation.

This recipe does not begin with a flavor base. Follow the complete brewing instructions to make three servings of Chamomile Lavender Kombucha.

Note: Before you make you first batch of kombucha, see Kombucha Tips (page 119) to familiarize yourself with some important background concepts.

 TO BREW

Distilled white vinegar
for rinsing equipment
5   cups spring water or
filtered water
¼   cup sugar
4   green tea bags
2   tablespoons chamomile
blossoms
1   tablespoon lavender
blossoms
½   cup kombucha starter
green tea (see Kom-
bucha Tips, page 119)

ingredients continued on next page

1 Rinse out a medium stainless-steel saucepan with distilled vinegar. Add 4 cups of the spring water to the pan and bring to a boil over medium-high heat. As soon as the water boils, add the sugar and stir to dissolve. Remove from the heat, add the green tea bags, chamomile blossoms, and lavender blossoms, cover, and let sit for 20 minutes.

Rinse a strainer and a large (at least 1½-quart) glass jar with distilled vinegar. Pour the tea mixture through the strainer and into the glass jar, discarding the tea bags. Let the liquid cool to room temperature, about 2 hours.

2 Stir the starter tea into the sweet tea and add the starter culture ("mother"). Cover the jar with a coffee filter, cheesecloth, or other material that will keep out debris but allow air to circulate. Secure with a rubber band. Set in a warm, dark place to ferment for 8 to 12 days (a spot in the basement near a water heater works well).

TO BREW (CONTINUED)

1 kombucha starter
   culture (called
   "mother"; see Kom-
   bucha Tips, page 119)
½ cup distilled white
   vinegar
1 tablespoon honey
1 mint tea bag

3 SERVINGS

3 As the kombucha ferments a new starter culture (called a "baby") will form on the surface, while the mother will either float beneath it or sink to the bottom of the jar. Strings may extend between the two cultures. When the new baby culture is almost as big as its mother, it's time to taste-test the kombucha. Stick a straw partway into the liquid, cover the end still in the air with a finger, and withdraw the straw from the liquid, thereby removing a dropperful. Taste the kombucha you've captured in the straw. If it is refreshingly tart, it's ready. If not, let the kombucha ferment longer.

4 When the kombucha is fully fermented, preserve the starter culture and starter tea for your next batch of kombucha. Rinse your hands with distilled vinegar, and then lift the mother and baby to a clean glass bowl or glass jar that has been rinsed with vinegar. Pour about ½ cup of the unfiltered kombucha over the culture, and add ½ cup distilled white vinegar. This liquid is starter tea. Cover tightly and store in the refrigerator for up to 1 to 2 months. (If you're using a jar for storage instead and it has a metal lid, cover the jar with a layer of plastic wrap first, before putting on the lid, to keep the contents from coming into contact with metal.)

Bring the remaining 1 cup of water to a boil. Stir in the honey, and let the mixture boil until it is reduced to about ½ cup. Remove from the heat, add the mint tea bag, and let sit for 5 minutes; then remove the tea bag.

5 Filter the remaining kombucha through a damp coffee filter or several layers of damp cheesecloth into a clean glass jar. Stir in the mint tea and seal the jar with a plastic or plastic-wrap-lined lid. Let sit at room temperature for 2 to 5 days, until the kombucha is bubbly, and then chill for 24 hours. Serve over ice.

Sour Cherriade, page 162

CHAPTER FIVE

Fizzy Juices

*J*uice is drinkable health food. Whether from fruit or root, leaf or stem, when you drink juice you ingest all of the flavor, nutrients, and substance that a plant has to give. The main thing missing is cellulose, which is indigestible and therefore nonnutritious (I don't mean you don't need it — we all know what it's for).

Because juice is liquid, all of the nutrients it contains are instantly available to your body. Unfortunately, that same ready access is enjoyed by bacteria, yeasts, and molds, microbes that damage the quality and sometimes the wholesomeness of juices in no time flat. Purchased juices are either chilled, frozen, heat treated, or loaded up with preservatives to give them a shelf life. If you extract a juice yourself you must use it as quickly as possible, and definitely with 24 hours.

To extract the juices from a solid fruit or vegetable you must crush the fibers that contain them. How you crush them depends on the structure of the ingredient in question. Soft, wet fruits, like citrus and berries, can be squeezed or pressed. The force of your hand or a vegetable masher is usually enough to do the trick.

Fibrous, wet vegetables, like celery, spinach, carrots, and peppers, can be ground in a juice extractor, which pulverizes the vegetable fiber and centrifugally separates the juices from the fiber, ejecting them through separate spouts. Or they can be puréed and forced through a strainer, a process that does the same thing as a juice extractor (albeit more coarsely) without special equipment.

Soda making provides a third option for juicing. Because almost all juices used for sodas are going to be sweetened, and because sugars are hydrophilic, meaning they attract moisture, chopping a fruit or vegetable finely and cooking it with a bit of sugar will cause it to weep a good deal of its juices, which can easily be extracted through a strainer.

sparkling apple juice

There are two separate ways to make this soda, and like most important things in life, separate is not equal. Fortunately the easiest method is also the best, but unfortunately it requires a soda siphon. If you don't have a siphon you can make a reasonable facsimile of the real thing by concentrating the juice through boiling and then diluting it back to its original volume with seltzer. The flavor is not as good, both oddly intense and watered down. I think the sugars in the juice caramelize. My advice is to get a siphon.

This recipe does not begin with a flavor base. Follow the complete carbonating instructions to make three servings of Sparkling Apple Juice.

 ## TO MIX WITH SELTZER

1 quart apple juice
3 cups seltzer

3 SERVINGS

Bring the apple juice to a boil in a large saucepan over medium heat; let simmer, uncovered, until the juice is reduced to ¾ cup. Remove from the heat and let cool.

For each serving, mix ¼ cup reduced apple juice and 1 cup seltzer in a tall glass, stirring just enough to combine. Fill with ice and serve.

 ## TO CARBONATE WITH A SIPHON

1 quart apple juice

3 SERVINGS

Pour the apple juice into a 1-quart soda siphon. Charge with CO_2 according to the manufacturer's directions. Siphon-charged sodas can be stored in the siphon in a refrigerator for up to 5 days. Disperse as desired into tall glasses filled with ice, and serve.

 ### Mixology

Prepare the Sparkling Apple Juice as described above.

sparkling apple brandy

Pour 1½ ounces (3 tablespoons) brandy or calvados (apple brandy) into a large snifter. Top with 3 ounces (6 tablespoons) of Sparkling Apple Juice.

applale

If you are looking for the nuanced flavor of a fermented soda but don't want to go to the hassle of bottling, try this recipe. The flavor base is mixed with yeast and set aside to ferment at room temperature for a couple of days. During that time the yeast will digest some of the sugar and start to build some savory flavors into the juice. As soon as it tastes right, the mixture is heated, which kills the carbonation and the yeast, thus setting the fermented flavor. The flavor base is then stored, ready to be carbonated whenever the mood strikes.

FERMENTED APPLE JUICE

- 1 quart unsweetened apple juice
- ½ cup turbinado or light brown sugar
- 2 medium (3-inch) cinnamon sticks
- Finely grated zest and juice of ½ lime
- Pinch of champagne yeast (*Saccharomyces bayanus*)

ENOUGH FOR 6 SERVINGS

Combine the apple juice, sugar, and cinnamon in a large saucepan over medium heat. Bring to a simmer, stirring occasionally until the sugar dissolves, and then remove from the heat and stir in the lime zest and juice. Let cool to a warm room temperature, from 75 to 80°F, then strain out the cinnamon and lime zest.

Add the yeast and stir until it is completely dissolved. Pour the mixture into a clean jar or other sealable container, cover, and let sit at room temperature until very bubbly, about 3 days.

Carefully decant the liquid into a large saucepan, leaving behind any sediment that has fallen to the bottom of the fermenting container. Heat to a simmer to stop the fermentation, and then remove from the heat and let cool.

The flavored juice will keep in the refrigerator for up to 2 weeks.

TO MIX WITH SELTZER

⅔ cup fermented apple
juice
⅔ cup seltzer

1 SERVING

Pour the juice into a tall glass. Add the seltzer and stir just until blended. Add ice and serve.

 ## TO CARBONATE WITH A SIPHON

2 cups water
2 cups (½ batch)
fermented apple juice

3 SERVINGS

Combine the water and juice in a 1-quart soda siphon. Charge with CO_2 according to the manufacturer's directions. Siphon-charged sodas can be stored in the siphon in a refrigerator for up to 5 days. Disperse as desired into tall glasses filled with ice, and serve.

vanilla pear sparkler

Vanilla and pear is one of the great flavor pairings of all time. Vanilla lends its floral fragrance seamlessly to pear. Think poached pear transformed into velvet refreshment. After the purée is mixed with seltzer do not let it sit; the creamy consistency will begin to break down after as little as 30 minutes. It can be refreshed by stirring briefly with a whisk. If you have a juice extractor, you can substitute the juice of three or four pears for the chunked pears. You still must heat the juice to boiling to prevent browning.

PEAR PURÉE

- 2 ripe pears, stemmed, peeled, cored, and cut into chunks
- ⅓ cup sugar
- 2 tablespoons lime juice
- 1 vanilla bean, split lengthwise, seeds scraped and removed

ENOUGH FOR 3 SERVINGS

Toss the pear chunks and sugar into a small saucepan. Add the lime juice and scraped vanilla bean. Cover and cook over medium heat until the pears are very soft, stirring often, about 10 minutes. Remove the vanilla bean. Mash the mixture with a vegetable masher or fork until smooth. Strain and cool.

The purée will keep in the refrigerator for up to 2 days, but it is best if used immediately.

 ## TO MIX WITH SELTZER

- ½ cup pear purée
- 1 cup seltzer

1 SERVING

Pour the purée into a tall glass. Add the seltzer and stir just until blended. Add ice and serve.

 ## TO CARBONATE WITH A SIPHON

- 2½ cups water
- 1 batch pear purée

3 SERVINGS

Combine the water and purée in a 1-quart soda siphon. Charge with CO_2 according to the manufacturer's directions. Siphon-charged sodas can be stored in the siphon in a refrigerator for up to 5 days. Disperse as desired into tall glasses filled with ice, and serve.

sparkling pear berry juice

Pear juice is placid and pale. Berry juice is bright and vibrant. Together, they are delicious. The problem is that they both need to be heated to prevent oxidation and enzymatic browning and they cook at radically different rates. My solution is to cook and purée the berries, then mix them with bottled pear nectar. (Of course you could also cook the fruits in separate pots. If you prefer that route, divide the recipe's sugar between the two, using two pears — stemmed, peeled, cored, and cut into chunks — in place of the pear nectar.)

PEAR BERRY PURÉE

- ½ pint strawberries or raspberries, stemmed and, if strawberries, cut into chunks
- ⅓ cup sugar
- 1 tablespoon lime juice
- 2 cups pear nectar

ENOUGH FOR 3 SERVINGS

Toss the berries and sugar into a small saucepan. Add the lime juice, cover, and cook over medium heat until the strawberries are soft, stirring often, about 5 minutes. Mash with a vegetable masher or a fork until smooth. Strain and let cool. Stir in the pear nectar.

The purée will keep in the refrigerator for up to 24 hours, but it is best if used immediately.

 ## TO MIX WITH SELTZER

- 1 cup pear berry purée
- ½ cup seltzer

1 SERVING

Pour the purée into a tall glass. Add the seltzer and stir just until blended. Add ice and serve.

 ## TO CARBONATE WITH A SIPHON

- 1 cup water
- 1 batch pear berry purée

3 SERVINGS

Combine the water and purée in a 1-quart soda siphon. Charge with CO_2 according to the manufacturer's directions. Siphon-charged sodas can be stored in the siphon in a refrigerator for up to 5 days. Disperse as desired into tall glasses filled with ice, and serve.

papaya punch

Papaya is a great source of antioxidants, especially beta-carotene. But the fruit's flesh is fibrous, and unless the fruit is very ripe the ratio of juice to pulp is disappointing. For that reason I advise puréeing the flesh or buying frozen papaya purée (available at any Hispanic market) for this easy and delicious sparkling juice.

PAPAYA PURÉE

- 1 ripe papaya, peeled, seeded, and puréed, or 2 cups frozen papaya purée, thawed
- 1 cup orange juice
- 3–4 tablespoons agave syrup or honey, depending on the sweetness of the papaya
- 1 tablespoon lime juice
- ½ teaspoon vanilla extract

ENOUGH FOR 3 SERVINGS

Combine the papaya purée, orange juice, agave syrup, lime juice, and vanilla, stirring to blend.

The purée will keep in the refrigerator for up to 2 days, but it is best if used immediately.

 ## TO MIX WITH SELTZER

- ⅔ cup papaya purée
- ⅔ cup seltzer

1 SERVING

Pour the purée into a tall glass. Add the seltzer and stir just until blended. Add ice and serve.

 ## TO CARBONATE WITH A SIPHON

- 2 cups water
- 1 batch papaya purée

3 SERVINGS

Combine the water and syrup in a 1-quart soda siphon. Charge with CO_2 according to the manufacturer's directions. Siphon-charged sodas can be stored in the siphon in a refrigerator for up to 5 days. Disperse as desired into tall glasses filled with ice, and serve.

Fizzy Juice

papaya rum punch

Prepare the papaya purée as described at left, then carbonate as desired.

Mix 1 ounce (2 tablespoons) golden rum with 4 ounces (½ cup) Papaya Punch, and serve over ice in a punch glass.

pineapple slush

Prepare the ginger pineapple juice as described on page 163, then carbonate as desired.

Combine 1 cup chilled pineapple chunks and 1 ounce (2 tablespoons) golden rum in a blender or food processor, and purée. Add 6 ounces (¾ cup) Pineapple Ginger Ale (page 163), pulsing to combine. Serve in a tall chilled glass.

antioxidant daiquiri

Prepare the blueberry grape juice as described on page 172, then carbonate as desired.

Combine 1 cup ice, 1 ounce (2 tablespoons) golden rum, and 1 cup Blueberry Concord Refresher (page 172) in a blender and blend until puréed. Serve in a chilled martini glass.

sour cherriade

Sour cherries don't pull punches. Pop one and puckering your puss is involuntary as your rattled taste buds try to grasp the onslaught. Yes, they're tart, but more impressively, sour cherries are a cherry bomb of flavor exploded in the mouth. Most sour cherries are processed by the food industry, and not many ever arrive fresh to market. For that reason I have concocted this soda using sweet cherries, which are dark red rather than cherry red and far less intense than sour varieties, and I've heightened their flavor with a hefty hit of vinegar and a little almond extract.

CHERRY PURÉE

1 quart fresh cherries, stems and pits removed

¼ cup sugar

3 tablespoons red wine vinegar

⅛ teaspoon almond extract

ENOUGH FOR 3 SERVINGS

Combine the cherries and sugar in a small saucepan and cook over medium heat, stirring often, until the cherries are soft and have released their juice. Purée in a blender or food processor, and then strain; you should have about 2 cups of smooth purée. Stir in the vinegar and almond extract.

The purée will keep in the refrigerator for up to 2 days, but it is best if used immediately.

 TO MIX WITH SELTZER

⅔ cup cherry purée
⅔ cup seltzer

1 SERVING

Pour the purée into a tall glass. Add the seltzer and stir just until blended. Add ice and serve.

 TO CARBONATE WITH A SIPHON

2 cups water
1 batch cherry purée

3 SERVINGS

Combine the water and purée in a 1-quart soda siphon. Charge with CO_2 according to the manufacturer's directions. Siphon-charged sodas can be stored in the siphon in a refrigerator for up to 5 days. Disperse as desired into tall glasses filled with ice, and serve.

pineapple ginger ale

Buy a good-quality unsweetened pineapple juice for this ginger soda. Juice pineapples are processed in factories set up next to the fields, so the fruits do not need to withstand the hardships of transport and therefore enter the juicer fully tree-ripened, ready to give their all. In this spiced-up soda the sweet-tart juice is punctuated by a pronounced exclamation of fresh ginger.

GINGER PINEAPPLE JUICE

- ½ cup water
- 1 (2-inch) length of fresh gingerroot, peeled and finely chopped
- 2 cups pineapple juice

ENOUGH FOR 3 SERVINGS

Bring the water to a boil. Add the ginger and remove from the heat. Let cool, then strain. Stir in the pineapple juice.

The juice will keep in the refrigerator for up to 2 days.

 ## TO MIX WITH SELTZER

- 1 cup ginger pineapple juice
- ½ cup seltzer

1 SERVING

Pour the juice into a tall glass. Add the seltzer and stir just until blended. Add ice and serve.

 ## TO CARBONATE WITH A SIPHON

- 1 batch ginger pineapple juice
- 1½ cups water

3 SERVINGS

Combine the juice and water in a 1-quart soda siphon. Charge with CO_2 according to the manufacturer's directions. Siphon-charged sodas can be stored in the siphon in a refrigerator for up to 5 days. Disperse as desired into tall glasses filled with ice, and serve.

 Also see Mixology recipe on page 161.

pomegranate cranberry crush

Cranberries and pomegranates have much in common: vibrant cardinal color rouged with plum, a dynamic palate-popping flavor seared by titillating tartness, and a reputation for unadulterated healthfulness against which a fortified fruit juice can't compete. Although they are far from deficient in sweetness, their overt acidity makes adding some sugar unavoidable. In this recipe, though, the sugar adds more than just sweetness: because sugar is hydrophilic, it helps extract the juice from the cranberries quickly.

POMEGRANATE CRANBERRY PURÉE

- 2 cups unsweetened pomegranate juice, fresh (page 61) or bottled

- 1 cup fresh or frozen cranberries

- ½ cup sugar

- ¼ cup orange juice

ENOUGH FOR 3 SERVINGS

Combine 1 cup of the pomegranate juice, the cranberries, and the sugar in a small saucepan. Cook over medium heat, stirring often, until the cranberries are soft and the sugar has dissolved, about 5 minutes. Mash the cranberries with a vegetable masher and pass through a strainer to remove seeds and bits of cranberry skin. Stir in the remaining 1 cup pomegranate juice and the orange juice.

The purée will keep in the refrigerator for up to 5 days.

 TO MIX WITH SELTZER

- ⅔ cup pomegranate cranberry purée
- ¾ cup seltzer

1 SERVING

Pour the purée into a tall glass. Add the seltzer and stir just until blended. Add ice and serve.

 ## TO CARBONATE WITH A SIPHON

1 batch pomegranate
  cranberry purée
2 cups water

3 SERVINGS

Combine the purée and water in a 1-quart soda siphon. Charge with CO_2 according to the manufacturer's directions. Siphon-charged sodas can be stored in the siphon in a refrigerator for up to 5 days. Disperse as desired into tall glasses filled with ice, and serve.

homemade tonic

This beautiful artisanal tonic recipe was developed by a friend of a friend, Dave Ewald. It is insanely good and insanely labor-intensive. Some of the ingredients are hard to come by. Cinchona bark is essential; it is what gives the tonic its quinine. You can order it from various herb shops (see Resources). Other items like cassia buds, bitter orange peel, and blackberry leaf are available from homebrew stores and herb shops.

Tonic can be used without carbonation in flavor bases or it can be carbonated in a siphon and used as a bubbly mixer.

TONIC

- 22 grams cinchona bark
- 4 grams dried hawthorn berries
- 8 grams dried sumac berries
- 2 grams cassia buds
- 3 cloves
- 1 small (2-inch) cinnamon stick, preferably Ceylon cinnamon
- 1 star anise
- 12 grams dried bitter orange peel
- 4 grams blackberry leaf
- 5¼ cups spring water
- 50 grams citric acid
- 2 teaspoons sea salt
- 1 stalk lemongrass, cut into ½-inch sections

  Finely grated zest and juice of 2 limes

  Finely grated zest and juice of 1 lemon
- ½ cup agave syrup

3 CUPS TONIC

Combine the cinchona bark, hawthorn berries, sumac berries, cassia buds, cloves, cinnamon, and star anise in a spice mill or mortar and pestle and crush into a coarse powder. Add the orange peel and blackberry leaf, divide the mixture among three large tea baskets or tea bags, and put a few pie weights in each.

Bring the water to a boil in a large stainless-steel saucepan. Add the tea baskets, citric acid, and salt. Let simmer for 5 minutes. Add the lemongrass, cover partially, and let simmer 15 minutes longer. Add the lime and lemon zests and juices and let simmer, uncovered, until the liquid is reduced by a little less than half, making about 3 cups. Remove from the heat and remove the tea balls.

Pour the agave syrup into a bowl. Set a fine-mesh strainer over the bowl and strain the tonic into the syrup. You will need to work in batches and to dump out the strainer after each pour. If the tonic is cloudy, strain again.

Pour into a clean bottle and seal. Store in the refrigerator for up to 1 year.

TO CARBONATE WITH A SIPHON

3 cups tonic

3 CUPS

Pour tonic into a siphon and charge with CO_2 according to the manufacturer's directions. Siphon-charged tonic can be stored in the siphon in a refrigerator for up to 5 days.

grapefruit tonic

¾ cup grapefruit juice, preferably fresh squeezed

¾ cup carbonated Homemade Tonic (page 166) or purchased tonic water

¼ teaspoon agave syrup or simple syrup (page 15)

Hefty pinch of sea salt

1 SERVING

Combine the grapefruit juice, tonic, agave syrup, and salt in a tall drinking glass, and stir just to blend. Fill the glass with ice and serve.

Mixology

Prepare the Grapefruit Tonic as described above.

salty dog

Combine 12 ounces (1½ cups) Grapefruit Tonic with 2 ounces (¼ cup) vodka. Serve over lots of ice.

grapefruit margarita

Shake together 8 ounces (1 cup) Grapefruit Tonic and 2 ounces (¼ cup) tequila. Serve over lots of crushed ice in a salt-rimmed glass.

sparkling lemon drop

If the sweet-tart intensity of old-fashioned lemon drop candies were lique-fied and fizzified, the result would be this invigorating soda. Less sweet but richer than lemonade, it gets a good deal of its punch from the lemon oil in lemon zest. The oil is infused into honey, blended with fresh lemon juice, and carbonated.

LEMON SYRUP

Freshly grated zest and juice of ½ lemon

1 tablespoon honey

ENOUGH FOR 1 SERVING

Combine the lemon zest and honey in a small bowl and let sit for 10 minutes. Strain out the zest with a fine strainer, add the lemon juice to the liquid, and stir to combine.

  TO MIX WITH SELTZER

1 batch lemon syrup
¾ cup seltzer

1 SERVING

Pour the syrup into a tall glass. Add the seltzer and stir briefly to combine. Add ice and serve.

Mixology

Prepare the lemon syrup as described above, then carbonate with seltzer.

limoncello drop

Mix 2 ounces (¼ cup) limoncello liqueur and 4 ounces (½ cup) chilled Sparkling Lemon Drop. Serve over ice.

spiked strawberry lemonade

Combine four strawberries, 1 ounce (2 table-spoons) vodka, 1 ounce (2 tablespoons) rum, and 1 cup ice in a blender, and purée. Stir in 4 ounces (½ cup) Sparkling Lemon Drop and serve in a tall glass.

four-citrus bubbly

All citrus fruits have a similar anatomy, which puts them on more or less equal culinary footing. The thin, waxy, colored outer layer of the peel, the zest, is impregnated with citrus oils, which are used for flavoring sodas, candies, and liqueurs. Underneath the zest lies the pulpy white pith, which contains the bitter phenols and pectin that give citrus marmalades texture and bitter-sweet flavor. The pulp underneath the peel consists largely of juice sacs held in a fibrous membrane. When citrus is squeezed, the membranes and sacs break open, releasing the juice.

MIXED CITRUS JUICE

- ½ cup orange juice
- ⅓ cup grapefruit juice
- 2 tablespoons lime juice
- 1 tablepoon lemon juice
- ¼ cup agave syrup, simple syrup (page 15), or honey

ENOUGH FOR 3 SERVINGS

Combine the orange, grapefruit, lime, and lemon juices with the agave syrup, stirring to blend.

The juice will keep in the refrigerator for up to 2 days, but is best used immediately.

TO MIX WITH SELTZER

- ½ cup mixed citrus juice
- 1 cup seltzer

1 SERVING

Pour the juice into a tall glass. Add the seltzer and stir just until blended. Add ice and serve.

TO CARBONATE WITH A SIPHON

- 2½ cups water
- 1 batch mixed citrus juice

3 SERVINGS

Combine the water and juice in a 1-quart soda siphon. Charge with CO_2 according to the manufacturer's directions. Siphon-charged sodas can be stored in the siphon in a refrigerator for up to 5 days. Disperse as desired into tall glasses filled with ice, and serve.

chocolate prune pop

I have always found the combination of dark chocolate and prune sublime. Prune is not the most popular of fruits, but its sullied reputation can be attributed more to prune jokes than to any real sensorial factors. Like the more commonplace combinations of chocolate and cherries or chocolate and raisins, prune and chocolate are both super-rich, and together they create an interplay of all the flavors vibrating against one another: sweet, savory, acid, bitter, and salt. Delicious and sensuous — no joke.

CHOCOLATE PRUNE JUICE

1½ cups prune juice

½ cup chocolate syrup

¼ teaspoon ground cinnamon

ENOUGH FOR 3 SERVINGS

Combine the prune juice, chocolate syrup, and cinnamon, stirring to blend.

The juice will keep in the refrigerator for up to 5 days.

TO MIX WITH SELTZER

⅔ cup chocolate prune juice

⅔ cup seltzer

1 SERVING

Pour the juice into a tall glass. Add the seltzer and stir just until blended. Add ice and serve.

TO CARBONATE WITH A SIPHON

1 batch chocolate prune juice

2 cups water

3 SERVINGS

Combine the water and juice in a 1-quart soda siphon. Charge with CO_2 according to the manufacturer's directions. Siphon-charged sodas can be stored in the siphon in a refrigerator for up to 5 days. Disperse as desired into tall glasses filled with ice, and serve.

cantaloupe clementine soda

Cantaloupe is one of the most fragrant of melons, harboring a musky, sweaty redolence beneath its light and sweet floral top notes. Its mammalian nuance makes cantaloupe a grateful candidate for a splash of citrus: suddenly light shines into the darkest corners of its fragrance, and it comes out smelling like a, well, cantaloupe.

CANTALOUPE CLEMENTINE JUICE

1 cup fresh cantaloupe chunks

½ cup freshly squeezed clementine juice (or tangerine or orange)

Pinch of sea salt

ENOUGH FOR 1 SERVING

Combine the cantaloupe, clementine juice, and salt in a blender or food processor, and purée. Set a strainer over a large bowl and pass the purée through the strainer, stirring the loose purée gently as it strains to get as much liquid through without forcing any solids into the strained liquid. Discard the solids.

Alternatively, juice 1½ cups of cantaloupe chunks in a juice extractor, and mix the juice with the clementine juice and salt.

 TO MIX WITH SELTZER

1 batch cantaloupe clementine juice

1 cup seltzer

1 SERVING

Pour the juice into a tall glass. Add the seltzer and stir just until blended. Add ice and serve.

blueberry concord refresher

The antioxidant power of any fruit juice is easily measured by color: the darker the hue, the more free radicals the juice will detoxify. Given that criteria, blueberries and purple grapes are a potent combination.

BLUEBERRY GRAPE JUICE

- 1 cup unsweetened blueberry juice, fresh or bottled
- 1 cup unsweetened Concord grape juice
- ¼ teaspoon ground cinnamon
- 2 tablespoons agave syrup, simple syrup (page 15), or honey

ENOUGH FOR 3 SERVINGS

Combine the blueberry juice, grape juice, cinnamon, and agave syrup, stirring to blend.

The juice will keep in the refrigerator for up to 2 days, but is best used immediately.

 TO MIX WITH SELTZER

- ⅔ cup blueberry grape juice
- ⅔ cup seltzer

1 SERVING

Pour the juice into a tall glass. Add the seltzer and stir just until blended. Add ice and serve.

 TO CARBONATE WITH A SIPHON

- 2 cups water
- 1 batch blueberry grape juice

3 SERVINGS

Combine the water and juice in a 1-quart soda siphon. Charge with CO_2 according to the manufacturer's directions. Siphon-charged sodas can be stored in the siphon in a refrigerator for up to 5 days. Disperse as desired into tall glasses filled with ice, and serve.

 Also see Mixology recipe on page 161.

cherry basil juice

I know this one sounds strange, but trust me, the pairing of cherries and basil is as natural as chocolate and mint, or apples and cinnamon, or oranges and nutmeg, or any other fruit and spice combination with which you might be more familiar. There's nothing overtly savory about basil's character. It is floral, with subtle notes of anise, and a hint of mint thrown in. All of these traits emerge with full force when tasted against the sweet-tart almond-scented juice of fresh cherries.

CHERRY PURÉE

- 1 quart fresh cherries, stems and pits removed
- ¼ cup sugar
- ⅛ teaspoon sea salt
- ¼ cup chopped fresh basil leaves
- 1 teaspoon lemon juice

ENOUGH FOR 3 SERVINGS

Combine the cherries, sugar, and salt in a small saucepan. Cook over medium heat, stirring often, until the cherries are soft and have released their juice.

Purée the mixture in a blender or food processor. Then stir in the basil and let cool. Once the mixture is cool, strain it; you should have about 2 cups of juice. Stir in the lemon juice.

The purée will keep in the refrigerator for up to 2 days, but is best used immediately.

TO MIX WITH SELTZER

- ⅔ cup cherry purée
- ⅔ cup seltzer

1 SERVING

Pour the purée into a tall glass. Add the seltzer and stir just until blended. Add ice and serve.

TO CARBONATE WITH A SIPHON

- 2 cups water
- 1 batch cherry purée

3 SERVINGS

Combine the water and purée in a 1-quart soda siphon. Charge with CO_2 according to the manufacturer's directions. Siphon-charged sodas can be stored in the siphon in a refrigerator for up to 5 days. Disperse as desired into tall glasses filled with ice, and serve.

sparkling homemade apricot nectar

The intense sweet-tart perfume of ripe apricots is completely intoxicating. The one drawback is that by the time apricots develop that unbelievable aroma, their flesh has turned mealy. The solution is to juice them. You get all of the sensual charm with none of the overblown pulp.

APRICOT PURÉE

8 ripe fresh apricots, pitted and cut in eighths

⅓ cup sugar

1 cup water

ENOUGH FOR 3 SERVINGS

Toss the apricots and sugar in a small saucepan. Add the water, cover, and cook over medium heat until the apricots are very soft, stirring often, about 8 minutes.

Mash with a vegetable masher or a fork until smooth. Strain and let cool.

The purée will keep in the refrigerator for up to 3 days, but is best used immediately.

 TO MIX WITH SELTZER

⅔ cup apricot purée
⅔ cup seltzer

1 SERVING

Pour the purée into a tall glass. Add the seltzer and stir just until blended. Add ice and serve.

 TO CARBONATE WITH A SIPHON

2 cups water
1 batch apricot purée

3 SERVINGS

Combine the water and purée in a 1-quart soda siphon. Charge with CO_2 according to the manufacturer's directions. Siphon-charged sodas can be stored in the siphon in a refrigerator for up to 5 days. Disperse as desired into tall glasses filled with ice, and serve.

peach habanero tongue twister

The burn of chiles and the sweetness of fruit combine their flavors in an exciting soda. Specific fruits pair best with specific peppers. Cherry and chipotle has become a classic hot sauce blend, as has jalapeño with green apple. One of my favorites is peach and habañero. Habaneros are very fiery peppers (100,000 to 500,000 Scoville units), so all you need is a touch.

PEACH PURÉE

2 ripe peaches, peeled, pitted, and cut into chunks

½ cup sugar

2 tablespoons lime juice

¼ fresh habanero chile, seeds and interior membranes removed

ENOUGH FOR 3 SERVINGS

Toss the peach chunks and sugar in a small saucepan. Add the lime juice and chile, cover, and cook over medium heat until the peaches are very soft, stirring often, about 10 minutes. Remove the chile.

Mash the peaches with a vegetable masher or a fork until smooth. Strain and let cool.

The purée will keep in the refrigerator for up to 3 days, but is best used immediately.

Note: This soda is purposely sweeter than others in this chapter to balance the intensity of the chile.

TO MIX WITH SELTZER

⅔ cup peach purée

⅔ cup seltzer

1 SERVING

Pour the purée into a tall glass. Add the seltzer and stir just until blended. Add ice and serve.

TO CARBONATE WITH A SIPHON

2 cups water

1 batch peach purée

3 SERVINGS

Combine the water and purée in a 1-quart soda siphon. Charge with CO_2 according to the manufacturer's directions. Siphon-charged sodas can be stored in the siphon in a refrigerator for up to 5 days. Disperse as desired into tall glasses filled with ice, and serve.

mango carrot bubbly

This highly nutritious drink (it has lots of beta-carotene) can be made with fresh juices, if you have a juice extractor, or with convenience, by using bottled juice. A word about processed carrot juice: frozen products are much closer to fresh than bottled. The heat processing needed for bottling juice does a real number on carrot juice.

MANGO CARROT JUICE

1 cup carrot juice, fresh (page 134) or frozen

1 cup mango juice, fresh or bottled

1 tablespoon lime juice

1 tablespoon honey

ENOUGH FOR 3 SERVINGS

Combine the carrot juice, mango juice, lime juice, and honey, stirring to blend.

The juice will keep in the refrigerator for up to 2 days, but is best used immediately.

TO MIX WITH SELTZER

⅔ cup mango carrot juice

⅔ cup seltzer

1 SERVING

Pour the juice into a tall glass. Add the seltzer and stir just until blended. Add ice and serve.

TO CARBONATE WITH A SIPHON

2 cups water

1 batch mango carrot juice

3 SERVINGS

Combine the water and juice in a 1-quart soda siphon. Charge with CO_2 according to the manufacturer's directions. Siphon-charged sodas can be stored in the siphon in a refrigerator for up to 5 days. Disperse as desired into tall glasses filled with ice, and serve.

carrot ginger soda

Ginger is frequently paired with carrots in both savory and sweet recipes. This spicy vegetable juice is ever so slightly on the sweet side. If your carrots are thick or woody you might want to add a bit more sugar and a pinch of salt to bring out more of their vegetal flavors. Carrot juice is, of course, rich in beta-carotene, and ginger has long been used in Eastern medicine as a digestive aid and to counter inflammation of soft tissue.

GINGER CARROT JUICE

- ½ cup water
- 2 tablespoons sugar
- 1 (2-inch) length of fresh gingerroot, peeled and finely chopped
- 3 cups fresh carrot juice, fresh (page 134) or frozen

ENOUGH FOR 3 SERVINGS

Bring the water and sugar to a boil in a small saucepan. Add the ginger, remove from the heat, and let cool. Strain, and stir in the carrot juice.

The juice will keep in the refrigerator for up to 2 days, but is best used immediately.

TO MIX WITH SELTZER

- 1 cup ginger carrot juice
- ½ cup seltzer

1 SERVING

Pour the juice into a tall glass. Add the seltzer and stir just until blended. Add ice and serve.

TO CARBONATE WITH A SIPHON

- 1 batch ginger carrot juice
- 1 cup water

3 SERVINGS

Combine the juice and water in a 1-quart soda siphon. Charge with CO_2 according to the manufacturer's directions. Siphon-charged sodas can be stored in the siphon in a refrigerator for up to 5 days. Disperse as desired into tall glasses filled with ice, and serve.

carrot cinnamon slush

This carrot slush, a liquefied vegetable on the verge of returning to solidity, contains the nutrition of more than a dozen carrots, and because it is both icy and bubbly, it is amazingly refreshing. The infusion of cinnamon into the syrup that sweetens the drink is a good source of antioxidants.

SPICED CARROT JUICE

1 cup water

¼ cup sugar

1 large (5-inch) cinnamon stick, broken into pieces

2 cups carrot juice, fresh (page 134) or frozen

ENOUGH FOR 4 SERVINGS

Combine the water, sugar, and cinnamon in a small saucepan. Bring to a boil, then reduce the heat and let simmer uncovered for 2 minutes. Remove from the heat, let cool, and then refrigerate until well chilled, about 1 hour.

Strain out the cinnamon. Stir the carrot juice into the the cinnamon syrup, and pour the mixture into a shallow pan. Freeze until semisolid, about 2 hours, stirring occasionally.

If the slush should freeze solid, cut it into cubes and purée in a food processor.

 TO MIX WITH SELTZER

1 batch spiced carrot juice
2 cups crushed ice
1 cup seltzer

4 SERVINGS

Combine the slush in a blender with the crushed ice, and blend until the mixture is uniformly slushy. Stir the seltzer into the slush, pour into glasses, and serve.

cucumber mint cooler

Cucumbers are destined for juice. They're more than 90 percent water, and that fluid is fairly nutritious, containing about 10 mg of vitamin C per cup, as well as some silica, which helps keep your soft tissues supple, and caffeic acid, which helps prevent water retention and swelling. Cucumber's flavor is refreshing and so mild that it meshes easily with other flavors, particularly herbs. In this soda the addition of mint helps the cucumber bridge the gastronomic divide between savory and sweet.

CUCUMBER PURÉE

- 1 cup water
- ½ cup sugar
- ¼ cup chopped fresh mint leaves
- ¼ teaspoon fine sea salt
- 1 large cucumber, trimmed, peeled, and cut into chunks

ENOUGH FOR 3 SERVINGS

Combine the water, sugar, mint, and salt in a small saucepan. Bring to a simmer, stirring until the sugar dissolves, and then remove from the heat, let cool, and strain.

Combine the syrup and cucumber in a blender or food processor, and purée until smooth. Pass the purée through a strainer to remove any chunks.

The purée will keep in the refrigerator for up to 24 hours, but is best used immediately.

 TO MIX WITH SELTZER

- ⅔ cup cucumber purée
- ⅔ cup seltzer

1 SERVING

Pour the purée into a tall glass. Add the seltzer and stir just until blended. Add ice and serve.

CHAPTER SIX

Sparkling Teas,

Coffees & Chocolates

On any given day, about one-half of the U.S. population drinks tea, and about half drinks coffee, according to the Tea Association of the USA and the Coffee Research Institute. I'm not sure where that leaves all us Scotch drinkers, but aside from water, tea and coffee are the most popular still beverages in the country. Although most of the coffee is consumed hot (less than 1 percent is consumed iced), about 85 percent of the tea drunk in the United States is iced. It's my mission to add some sparkle to those figures.

To make tea-flavored sodas, you simply steep tea leaves in sugar syrup, often with other spices and herbs. You then carbonate the syrup in the same way as other sodas. Coffee sodas are made similarly to tea sodas, with ground coffee substituted for the tea leaves. You also can add sugar to already-brewed coffee and cook that mixture down into a syrup.

The third member of our intensely flavored, caffeinated beverage trio is chocolate. Though most of us tend to think of chocolate as a creamy rich solid bar, for most of history chocolate was sipped, not chewed. The Aztecs drank chocolate (unsweetened, mixed with ground chiles) as a medicinal to fortify themselves physically and mentally, and when the Spanish brought chocolate from the New World to the Old World, the fashion for drinking chocolate spread quickly through Europe, right around the same time that coffee was moving in from the Middle East and tea from China.

To turn cocoa powder into soda, you must first hydrate and sweeten it, in much the same way that tea and coffee syrups are made. You simply mix the cocoa with sugar, water, and other flavorings, and then simmer the mixture until the sugar and ground cocoa dissolve. Once the syrup is made, you can dilute it with carbonated water whenever you desire a chocolaty beverage, which for most people is any time.

sparkling green tea with a hint of coconut

This fragrant soda enriches the green vegetal flavor of green tea with a floral note from honey and the creamy nuttiness of coconut milk. For cooking I prefer full-fat coconut milk, but in this soda defatted coconut milk is better, since coconut oils congeal when chilled. Green tea contains moderate levels of antioxidant phenols that can help protect artery walls, prevent cell damage, and reduce the risk of heart disease and cancer.

COCONUT TEA SYRUP

1 cup water

½ cup honey

4 green tea bags

¾ cup canned light coconut milk

ENOUGH FOR 3 SERVINGS

Combine the water and honey in a small saucepan. Bring to a boil, then remove from the heat, add the tea bags, and let steep for 5 minutes. Remove the tea bags and let the syrup cool to room temperature. Stir in the coconut milk.

This syrup will keep in the refrigerator for up to 2 months.

 ## TO MIX WITH SELTZER

⅔ cup coconut tea syrup
⅔ cup seltzer

1 SERVING

Pour the syrup into a tall glass. Add the seltzer and stir just until blended. Add ice and serve.

 ## TO CARBONATE WITH A SIPHON

1 batch coconut tea syrup
2 cups water

3 SERVINGS

Pour the syrup into a 1-quart siphon. Add the water. Charge with CO_2 according to the manufacturer's directions. Siphon-charged sodas can be stored in the siphon in a refrigerator for up to 5 days. Disperse as desired into tall glasses filled with ice, and serve.

chai fizz

Chai, the spiced tea from South Asia, can have more than half a dozen spices in its blend. Cardamom, cinnamon, cloves, ginger, nutmeg, peppercorns, and star anise are common. You can mix up your own blend, or you can use any of the plentiful good-quality commercial chai tea blends. Because chai is typically served hot, it has a reputation for being soothing and calming. But chilling it and adding carbonation changes the chai experience dramatically. Chai spiced soda spurs the passions and is more sultry than sedating.

CHAI SYRUP

1 cup water

1 cup raw sugar, such as turbinado, or evaporated coconut palm sugar

4 chai tea bags, or 2 black tea bags and 2 tablespoons Basic Chai Spice Blend (page 185)

ENOUGH FOR 3 SERVINGS

Combine the water and sugar in a small saucepan. Bring to a boil, stirring occasionally until the sugar dissolves.

Remove from the heat, add the chai tea bags, and let steep for 5 minutes. Remove the tea bags (or strain out the spices if using black tea and spice blend). Let the syrup cool to room temperature.

This syrup will keep in the refrigerator for up to 2 months.

 TO MIX WITH SELTZER

¼ cup chai syrup
1¼ cups seltzer

1 SERVING

Pour the syrup into a tall glass. Add the seltzer and stir just until blended. Add ice and serve.

Note: If you prefer your chai latte-style, replace ½ cup of the seltzer with milk.

 TO CARBONATE WITH A SIPHON

1 batch chai syrup
3 cups water

3 SERVINGS

Pour the syrup into a 1-quart siphon. Add the water. Charge with CO_2 according to the manufacturer's directions. Siphon-charged sodas can be stored in the siphon in a refrigerator for up to 5 days. Disperse as desired into tall glasses filled with ice, and serve.

Note: If you prefer your chai latte-style, replace ½ cup of the water with milk.

basic chai spice blend

8 green cardamom pods, cracked

1 star anise

12 cloves

1 medium-large (4-inch) cinnamon stick

¼-inch-thick slice of fresh gingerroot

¼ teaspoon black peppercorns

ENOUGH FOR 1 QUART OF CHAI

Combine the spices. For best flavor, use immediately; for good flavor, store in a sealed container away from light and heat, and use within 1 month.

///////////////////////

Tea Facts

TEAS ARE INFUSIONS made from the leaves of the tea plant (*Camellia sinensis*). The leaves are processed into four main types: green, black, oolong, and white.

GREEN TEA comes from young leaves that are steamed to kill enzymes that would darken them. The leaves are flattened, dried to 3 percent moisture, and sorted by size, from gunpowder (small) to hyson (large). Green teas are light green in color and have a fresh, grassy flavor.

BLACK TEA is made from mature leaves that are allowed to wither and blacken after being picked. Then they are flattened and held for several hours at high humidity to ferment, during which time tannins in the leaves oxidize and develop the characteristic tea flavor and a brown-red color. The leaves are then oven-dried and sorted by size from orange pekoe (small) to souchong (large).

OOLONG TEA falls between green and black. It's made from mature leaves that are flattened right after being picking and then fermented, creating a tea that is grassy like green tea, mildly astringent like black tea, and pale brown in color. Oolong teas can be roasted, in which case they develop a subtle smokiness.

WHITE TEA comes from young leaves that are barely processed. The leaves are not flattened and are only very lightly fermented. White tea leaves are often silver-gray in color and produce a brew that is colorless and subtly sweet, with a fresh, grassy aroma.

effervescent raspberry white tea

Of all forms of tea, white tea has the highest levels of antioxidants. White tea leaves are the least processed. They are gently heated only enough to stop enzymatic activity that could cause them to ferment, and then they are dried naturally. That's all. The result is tea that is exceptionally mild, without a trace of the astringency that characterizes fermented teas. When carbonated, white teas can taste washed out, so I usually boost their flavor with fruit. Citrus and tropical fruits are good complements, but my favorite is raspberry, for its tartness, flowery aroma, and beautiful color.

RASPBERRY TEA SYRUP

- 1 cup water
- ¾ cup sugar
- 4 white tea bags
- ½ cup fresh or frozen raspberries

ENOUGH FOR 3 SERVINGS

Combine the water and sugar in a small saucepan. Bring to a boil, then remove from the heat, add the tea bags and the raspberries, and let steep for 5 minutes.

Remove the tea bags and mash the raspberries with a vegetable masher or the back of a fork. Let the syrup cool to room temperature, and strain to remove bits of raspberry.

This syrup will keep in the refrigerator for up to 2 weeks.

 TO MIX WITH SELTZER

- ⅔ cup raspberry tea syrup
- ⅔ cup seltzer

1 SERVING

Pour the syrup into a tall glass. Add the seltzer and stir just until blended. Add ice and serve.

 ## TO CARBONATE WITH A SIPHON

   1 batch raspberry tea syrup
   2 cups water

3 SERVINGS

Pour the syrup into a 1-quart siphon. Add the water. Charge with CO_2 according to the manufacturer's directions. Siphon-charged sodas can be stored in the siphon in a refrigerator for up to 5 days. Disperse as desired into tall glasses filled with ice, and serve.

POP CULTURE

Tea Bags

THE FIRST CUP-SIZE SILK TEA BAGS were patented in 1903 and marketed commercially starting in 1904 by Thomas Sullivan of New York City. Sullivan intended for his customers to remove the loose tea from the bags before brewing, but people found it convenient to brew cups of tea using the bags, and tea bags quickly replaced loose tea as the principal method of brewing tea in the States. The rectangular paper tea bag was introduced in 1944.

sparkling tamarind tea

Extracted from the pulp inside the seedpods of the African tamarind tree, tamarind paste is sold in Indian groceries and sometimes in the Asian section of supermarkets. Tamarind pulp is quite sour, being about 20 percent acid (mostly tartaric), but it is also somewhat sweet and savory, with a complex roasted underpinning. In much of Asia, tamarind is used to acidify sauces, soups, preserves, and beverages. If you can't find it, you could substitute a combination of lime juice and Marmite and come close. Tamarind paste will keep almost indefinitely in the refrigerator in a tightly closed container.

TAMARIND TEA SYRUP

1 cup water

¾ cup sugar

3 black tea bags

1 tablespoon tamarind paste

ENOUGH FOR 3 SERVINGS

Combine the water and sugar in a small saucepan. Bring to a boil, then remove from the heat, add the tea bags, and let steep for 5 minutes.

Remove the tea bags, and pour ⅓ cup of the hot tea into a separate bowl. Add the tamarind paste, stir to dissolve, and then strain the mixture back into the tea. Let the syrup cool to room temperature.

This syrup will keep in the refrigerator for up to 2 months.

 TO MIX WITH SELTZER

⅓ cup tamarind tea syrup

1 cup seltzer

1 SERVING

Pour the syrup into a tall glass. Add the seltzer and stir just until blended. Add ice and serve.

TO CARBONATE WITH A SIPHON

1 batch tamarind tea
   syrup
3 cups water

3 SERVINGS

Pour the syrup into a 1-quart siphon. Add the water. Charge with CO_2 according to the manufacturer's directions. Siphon-charged sodas can be stored in the siphon in a refrigerator for up to 5 days. Disperse as desired into tall glasses filled with ice, and serve.

POP CULTURE

Snapple: The Rise of Bottled Iced Tea

SNAPPLE BEGAN BOTTLING JUICES "made from the best stuff on Earth" in 1972. The company, founded by Arnold Greenburg, who ran a health food store on the Lower East Side of New York City, his boyhood friend Leonard Marsh, and Marsh's brother-in-law Hyman Golden, began by selling unusual fruit juice blends with quirky names to health food stores.

The company grew slowly, adding a new product about once a year, until 1987 when it launched a bottled brewed iced tea made without preservatives as a summertime beverage. By the end of 1988, Snapple's yearly sales had increased to over $13 million, and its line of noncarbonated beverages, increasingly tea, had grown to include 53 flavors. In the first six months of 1989 the company's revenues grew by 600 percent. Today it is the largest retailer of single-serve bottled iced tea in the United States and the second largest seller of fruit drinks. The three founders are given credit for fueling the movement in the beverage industry toward noncarbonated beverages.

pomegranate rose-hip cooler

When roses are left on the bush long enough to be fertilized, the spherical fruit that forms behind them is a rose hip. Rose hips have a fruity, astringent flavor, not unlike that of pomegranate, and they are exceptionally potent in vitamin C. Like other dark-pigmented vegetation they contain a good amount of anti-oxidant flavonoids. Although it is possible to buy rose hip syrup and dried or ground rose hips, the most common and cost-effective form is tea bags.

POMEGRANATE SYRUP

- 1 cup unsweetened pomegranate juice, fresh (page 61) or bottled
- ¾ cup sugar
- 4 rose hip tea bags
- 1 tablespoon finely grated lime zest (optional)

ENOUGH FOR 3 SERVINGS

Combine the pomegranate juice and sugar in a small saucepan. Bring to a boil, then remove from the heat, add the tea bags and the lime zest (if using), and let steep for 5 minutes. Remove the tea bags and let the syrup cool to room temperature. If you've used lime zest, strain the syrup.

This syrup will keep in the refrigerator for up to 2 months.

TO MIX WITH SELTZER

- ⅓ cup pomegranate syrup
- 1 cup seltzer

1 SERVING

Pour the syrup into a tall glass. Add the seltzer and stir just until blended. Add ice and serve.

TO CARBONATE WITH A SIPHON

- 1 batch pomegranate syrup
- 3 cups water

3 SERVINGS

Pour the syrup into a 1-quart siphon. Add the water. Charge with CO_2 according to the manufacturer's directions. Siphon-charged sodas can be stored in the siphon in a refrigerator for up to 5 days. Disperse as desired into tall glasses filled with ice, and serve.

effervescent jasmine honey tea

Jasmine's scent is sweet and delicate, like honeyed baby powder. The best jasmine teas are made by mating the blossoms and tea leaves under controlled humidity and temperature until the tea leaves absorb the scent of the blossoms. Cheap jasmine teas are made by mixing dried tea leaves with jasmine oil. For this soda I underscore the jasmine's floral fragrance with honey and a splash of vanilla.

JASMINE TEA SYRUP

1¼ cups water

⅓ cup honey

4 jasmine green tea bags or
5 tablespoons loose jasmine green tea

⅛ teaspoon vanilla extract

ENOUGH FOR 3 SERVINGS

Combine the water and honey in a small saucepan. Bring to a boil, then remove from the heat, add the tea bags, and let steep for 5 minutes. Remove the tea bags (or strain out the loose tea), and let the syrup cool to room temperature. Stir in the vanilla.

This syrup will keep in the refrigerator for up to 2 months.

TO MIX WITH SELTZER

½ cup jasmine tea syrup
1 cup seltzer

1 SERVING

Pour the syrup into a tall glass. Add the seltzer and stir just until blended. Add ice and serve.

TO CARBONATE WITH A SIPHON

1 batch jasmine tea syrup
2½ cups water

3 SERVINGS

Pour the syrup into a 1-quart siphon. Add the water. Charge with CO_2 according to the manufacturer's directions. Siphon-charged sodas can be stored in the siphon in a refrigerator for up to 5 days. Disperse as desired into tall glasses filled with ice, and serve.

sweet sparkling moroccan tea

Green tea infused with mint is served several times a day in Moroccan homes. Moroccans tend to like their tea sweet, which makes it the perfect base for a cool, refreshing soda. All you have to do is make a pot of superstrong tea and cool it with some carbonated water.

MINT GREEN TEA SYRUP

- 1 cup sugar
- 1 cup water
- 3 green tea bags or 3 tablespoons loose green tea leaves
- ½ cup finely chopped fresh mint leaves

ENOUGH FOR 3 SERVINGS

Combine the sugar and water in a small saucepan. Bring to a boil, then remove from the heat, add the tea and mint leaves, and let steep for 5 minutes. Strain the syrup and let it cool to room temperature.

This syrup will keep in the refrigerator for up to 2 months.

TO MIX WITH SELTZER

- ⅓ cup mint green tea syrup
- 1 cup seltzer

1 SERVING

Pour the syrup into a tall glass. Add the seltzer and stir just until blended. Add ice and serve.

TO CARBONATE WITH A SIPHON

- 1 batch mint green tea syrup
- 3 cups water

3 SERVINGS

Pour the syrup into a 1-quart siphon. Add the water. Charge with CO_2 according to the manufacturer's directions. Siphon-charged sodas can be stored in the siphon in a refrigerator for up to 5 days. Disperse as desired into tall glasses filled with ice, and serve.

sparkling iced tea lemonade

A triumvirate of summer thirst quenchers — iced tea, lemonade, and soda — join forces in this all-purpose soft drink. Use this recipe as a base formula, and by switching the type of tea you use, substituting lime or orange for lemon, and switching out the sugar for honey or agave syrup, you can parlay this easy beverage into an entire summer's worth of refreshment.

LEMON TEA SYRUP

1 cup sugar

1 cup water

3 tea bags, any variety

Finely grated zest and juice of 2 lemons

ENOUGH FOR 3 SERVINGS

Combine the sugar and water in a small saucepan. Bring to a boil, then remove from the heat, add the tea bags, and let steep for 5 minutes. Remove the tea bags and stir in the lemon zest and juice. Let the syrup cool to room temperature, then strain to remove the lemon zest.

This syrup will keep in the refrigerator for up to 2 months.

TO MIX WITH SELTZER

½ cup lemon tea syrup

1 cup seltzer

1 SERVING

Pour the syrup into a tall glass. Add the seltzer and stir just until blended. Add ice and serve.

TO CARBONATE WITH A SIPHON

1 batch lemon tea syrup

2½ cups water

3 SERVINGS

Pour the syrup into a 1-quart siphon. Add the water. Charge with CO_2 according to the manufacturer's directions. Siphon-charged sodas can be stored in the siphon in a refrigerator for up to 5 days. Disperse as desired into tall glasses filled with ice, and serve.

black tea cola

The astringent tannins that bloom during the fermentation of black tea leaves are so compatible with the savory flavors that develop in the formulation of colas that joining the two in a glass seems more redundant than inspired. But inspirational it proves to be. This manly beverage has the look and stature of Guinness or stout and the complex satiety of being both filling and refreshing all at once.

COLA TEA SYRUP

1 cup Natural Cola syrup (page 104)
3 black tea bags

ENOUGH FOR 3 SERVINGS

Bring the cola syrup to a boil, then remove from the heat, add the tea bags, and let steep for 5 minutes. Remove the tea bags and let the syrup cool to room temperature.

This syrup will keep in the refrigerator for up to 2 months.

 ## TO MIX WITH SELTZER

⅓ cup cola tea syrup
1 cup seltzer

1 SERVING

Pour the syrup into a tall glass. Add the seltzer and stir just until blended. Add ice and serve.

 ## TO CARBONATE WITH A SIPHON

1 batch cola tea syrup
3 cups water

3 SERVINGS

Pour the syrup into a 1-quart siphon. Add the water. Charge with CO_2 according to the manufacturer's directions. Siphon-charged sodas can be stored in the siphon in a refrigerator for up to 5 days. Disperse as desired into tall glasses filled with ice, and serve.

sparkling latte

Ice cream sodas are sinful snacks: rich, sweet, effervescent, and available in any cloying flavor you could wish for. If they didn't make you fat and lazy, we all might be indulging 'round the clock. Sparkling latte to the rescue: not too rich, mildly sweet, and just as effervescent as the naughty stuff, it is the guiltless ice cream soda.

LATTE SYRUP

- 2 cups water
- 1 cup sugar
- 1 medium (3-inch) cinnamon stick
- ⅓ cup finely ground coffee

ENOUGH FOR 3 SERVINGS

Combine the water and sugar in a small saucepan; add the cinnamon stick. Bring to a boil, then reduce the heat and let simmer until reduced to 1 cup (about half of the original volume).

Add the coffee and return to a boil. As soon as the mixture boils, remove it from the heat; set aside until the coffee settles to the bottom of the pot. Remove the cinnamon stick, and decant the liquid into a small bowl through a coffee filter to trap any stray coffee. Let cool to room temperature.

This syrup will keep in the refrigerator for up to 1 week.

TO MIX WITH SELTZER

- ⅓ cup latte syrup
- ¼ cup milk
- 1 cup seltzer

1 SERVING

Combine the syrup and the milk in a tall glass, stirring to blend. Add the seltzer, and stir just until blended. Add ice and serve.

TO CARBONATE WITH A SIPHON

- 1 batch latte syrup
- ¾ cup milk
- 2¼ cups water

3 SERVINGS

Pour the syrup and milk into a 1-quart siphon. Add the water. Charge with CO_2 according to the manufacturer's directions. Siphon-charged sodas can be stored in the siphon in a refrigerator for up to 5 days. Disperse as desired into tall glasses filled with ice, and serve.

espresso jolt

In making espresso, water is forced through coffee grounds under pressure in order to extract the most coffee flavor with the least amount of fluid. Espresso is not just strong, it is concentrated. I make a point out of this because starting with real espresso, though not essential, results in a huge difference in the mouthfeel and flavor of this soda. If you don't have an espresso machine, you can replace the espresso with strong coffee and combine 1½ teaspoons maltodextrin or ¼ teaspoon gum arabic with the sugar to mimic the consistency of pressure-drawn espresso.

ESPRESSO SYRUP

1½ cups brewed espresso, hot

1 cup sugar

ENOUGH FOR 3 SERVINGS

Combine the espresso and sugar in a small saucepan. Cook over low heat, stirring constantly, until the sugar dissolves. Remove from the heat and let cool to room temperature.

This syrup will keep in the refrigerator for up to 1 week.

 TO MIX WITH SELTZER

⅔ cup espresso syrup
⅔ cup seltzer

1 SERVING

Pour the syrup into a tall glass. Add the seltzer and stir just until blended. Add ice and serve.

 TO CARBONATE WITH A SIPHON

1 batch espresso syrup
2 cups water

3 SERVINGS

Pour the syrup into a 1-quart siphon. Add the water. Charge with CO_2 according to the manufacturer's directions. Siphon-charged sodas can be stored in the siphon in a refrigerator for up to 5 days. Disperse as desired into tall glasses filled with ice, and serve.

 Also see Mixology recipe on page 199.

BEFORE RED BULL DEFINED THE MARKET for energy drinks, there was Jolt Cola. Jolt stimulated the soft drink market in 1985, claiming to deliver "all the sugar and twice the caffeine" of regular cola. Jolt later changed its slogan to "All the Flavor and Twice the Caffeine" when the price of cane sugar forced the company to switch to using high-fructose corn syrup in its formula.

Coffee Facts

THE FLAVOR OF COFFEE, and that of the soda brewed from it, will be affected by a few factors:

THE TYPE OF COFFEE BEAN. The two primary species of coffee are *Coffea arabica* and *Coffea canephora*, also called robusta. Arabica beans account for about 70 percent of the world's crop. They have a complex aroma owing to their high sugar content. Robusta beans are more bitter and overt in flavor.

WHERE THE COFFEE GROWS. Coffee grows best at high elevations and has different characteristics depending upon its growing conditions. Coffee trees were traditionally grown in the shade of taller trees. Today most coffee is grown in full sun, which makes for higher yields but puts more wear and tear on the environment. Shade-grown coffee beans are smaller and more flavorful; also, since they don't require the clear-cutting of tropical forest, they are more eco-friendly than beans from full-sun trees.

HOW THE COFFEE IS ROASTED. Coffee beans are roasted at high temperatures until they brown, ranging from lightly roasted (about 375°F) to dark roasted (up to 425°F). As the beans brown, they develop the rich caramelized flavors we associate with coffee. Lighter roasted beans will be fruitier and more acidic. A darker roast emphasizes richer, more pungent flavors, such as chocolate, dried fruit, and tobacco. When the beans reach 400°F, the oils in the beans work their way to the surface, which is an indication that dark-roasted flavors have started to develop.

HOW THE COFFEE IS GROUND AND BREWED. The more finely coffee beans are ground, the more contact each particle makes with the water and the stronger the resulting coffee will be. The grind, along with how long the ground coffee is steeped, determines the finished coffee's strength. Espresso coffee is brewed under pressure, so even though the grounds have very little contact with water, their volatile flavors are forced from them by the intense pressure of the water flow.

iced café brûlot

The pyrotechnics involved in presenting café brûlot in New Orleans restaurants is spectacular: a spiral of flaming orange peel held aloft above a cup of brandied coffee. But this showmanship is hardly essential in the privacy of your own home. It does nothing to flavor the beverage itself. In this recipe for soda inspired by café brûlot, you get all the flavor of the original (coffee, spices, orange, and brandy) plus some bubbles.

CAFÉ BRÛLOT SYRUP

2⅓ cups brewed coffee

1 cup sugar

1 medium (3-inch) cinnamon stick

3 cloves

Zest of 1 orange

1 tablespoon brandy (optional)

ENOUGH FOR 3 SERVINGS

Combine the coffee and sugar in a small saucepan; add the cinnamon stick and cloves. Bring to a boil, then reduce the heat to a simmer. Add the orange zest and let simmer until the mixture is reduced to 1½ cups. Remove from the heat and let cool to room temperature. Remove the cinnamon stick, cloves, and orange zest. Stir in the brandy (if using).

This syrup will keep in the refrigerator for up to 1 month.

 TO MIX WITH SELTZER

½ cup café brûlot syrup
1 cup seltzer

1 SERVING

Pour the syrup into a tall glass. Add the seltzer and stir just until blended. Add ice and serve.

 TO CARBONATE WITH A SIPHON

1 batch café brûlot syrup
2½ cups water

3 SERVINGS

Pour the syrup into a 1-quart siphon. Add the water. Charge with CO_2 according to the manufacturer's directions. Siphon-charged sodas can be stored in the siphon in a refrigerator for up to 5 days. Disperse as desired into tall glasses filled with ice, and serve.

Coffee

MIXOLOGY

southern comfortable

Prepare the café brûlot syrup as described at left, then carbonate as desired.

Pour 2 ounces (¼ cup) Southern Comfort over a few ice cubes in a tall glass. Fill with Iced Café Brûlot.

black black russian

Prepare the espresso syrup as described on page 196, then carbonate as desired.

Mix 1 ounce (2 tablespoons) Kahlua and 1 ounce (2 tablespoons) vodka in a rocks glass. Add a few ice cubes and fill with Espresso Jolt (page 196).

irish hazelnut cream

Prepare the hazelnut coffee syrup as described on page 202, then carbonate as desired.

Pour 1 ounce (2 tablespoons) Irish whiskey into a rocks glass. Add a few ice cubes and top with Hazelnut Coffee Creamery (page 202).

coffee coconut daiquiri

Prepare the Kona syrup as described on page 204, then carbonate as desired.

Blend 1½ ounces (3 tablespoons) golden rum with 1 cup crushed ice. Mix in 1 cup Kona Coconut Latte (page 204) and pour into a tall glass.

cinnamon coffee gulp

For this cinnamon-scented coffee I prefer to use Vietnamese cinnamon, which is most often sold as Saigon cinnamon. It is a Southeast Asian variety that is overtly sweet and aromatic. In the recipe, the cinnamon stick is simmered with water and sugar into a syrup and then combined with coffee, since long simmering would diminish the aromatics in the coffee.

CINNAMON COFFEE SYRUP

2 cups water

1 cup sugar

1 large (5-inch) cinnamon stick, preferably Saigon cinnamon

⅓ cup finely ground coffee

ENOUGH FOR 3 SERVINGS

Combine the water and sugar in a small saucepan; add the cinnamon stick. Bring to a boil, then reduce the heat and let simmer until reduced to 1½ cups (about three-quarters of the original volume).

Add the coffee and return to a boil. As soon as the mixture boils, remove it from the heat; set aside until the coffee settles to the bottom of the pot. Remove the cinnamon stick, and decant the liquid into a small bowl through a coffee filter to trap any stray coffee. Let cool to room temperature.

This syrup will keep in the refrigerator for up to 1 week.

TO MIX WITH SELTZER

½ cup cinnamon coffee syrup

1 cup seltzer

1 SERVING

Pour the syrup into a tall glass. Add the seltzer and stir just until blended. Add ice and serve.

TO CARBONATE WITH A SIPHON

1 batch cinnamon coffee syrup

2½ cups water

3 SERVINGS

Pour the syrup into a 1-quart siphon. Add the water. Charge with CO_2 according to the manufacturer's directions. Siphon-charged sodas can be stored in the siphon in a refrigerator for up to 5 days. Disperse as desired into tall glasses filled with ice, and serve.

turkish java mud

Turkish coffee, made from coffee ground baby-powder fine, is boiled with sugar, rather than dripped or expressed, into a beverage that is the consistency of wet mud. It is sweet enough on its own to qualify for a soft drink. In this recipe I have just gone the extra step and added carbonation. Because the base is naturally thick, the finished soda has a slightly powdery mouthfeel.

TURKISH COFFEE SYRUP

- 1½ cups water
- 1½ cups sugar
- ¼ cup very finely ground (powdery) coffee
- ½ teaspoon ground cardamom

ENOUGH FOR 3 SERVINGS

Combine the water, sugar, coffee, and cardamom in a small saucepan. Bring to a boil, then remove from the heat and let cool to room temperature. Strain.

    This syrup will keep in the refrigerator for up to 1 week.

 ## TO MIX WITH SELTZER

- ⅔ cup Turkish coffee syrup
- ⅔ cup seltzer

1 SERVING

Pour the syrup into a tall glass. Add the seltzer and stir just until blended. Add ice and serve.

 ## TO CARBONATE WITH A SIPHON

- 1 batch Turkish coffee syrup
- 2 cups water

3 SERVINGS

Pour the syrup into a 1-quart siphon. Add the water. Charge with CO_2 according to the manufacturer's directions. Siphon-charged sodas can be stored in the siphon in a refrigerator for up to 5 days. Disperse as desired into tall glasses filled with ice, and serve.

hazelnut coffee creamery

The flavor of hazelnut comes from a compound, heptenone (a.k.a. filbertone), that is present in minute quantities in raw hazelnuts but increases 600 to 800 times when the nuts are roasted. Because it is nearly impossible to infuse nut flavors into watery beverages like coffee, this soda is flavored with hazelnut syrup. Syrups for flavoring coffees are sold in most supermarkets.

HAZELNUT COFFEE SYRUP

2⅓ cups brewed coffee

1 cup sugar

2 tablespoons hazelnut syrup

¾ cup cream, half-and-half, or whole milk

ENOUGH FOR 3 SERVINGS

Combine the coffee and sugar in a small saucepan. Bring to a boil, then reduce the heat and let simmer until the mixture is reduced to ¾ cup (about one-third of its original volume). Let cool to room temperature. Stir in the hazelnut syrup and cream.

This syrup will keep in the refrigerator for up to 1 week.

TO MIX WITH SELTZER

½ cup hazelnut coffee syrup

1 cup seltzer

1 SERVING

Pour the syrup into a tall glass. Add the seltzer and stir just until blended. Add ice and serve.

TO CARBONATE WITH A SIPHON

1 batch hazelnut coffee syrup

2½ cups water

3 SERVINGS

Pour the syrup into a 1-quart siphon. Add the water. Charge with CO_2 according to the manufacturer's directions. Siphon-charged sodas can be stored in the siphon in a refrigerator for up to 5 days. Disperse as desired into tall glasses filled with ice, and serve.

Also see Mixology recipe on page 199.

Caffeine

IN ADDITION TO THE INTENSITY OF THEIR FLAVOR, tea, coffee, and chocolate all share a common characteristic: they are all sources for caffeine, the most common mood-altering drug in the world. This chemical affects several types of cells in the human body. Its most marked effect is on the central nervous system, which it stimulates, diminishing fatigue and quickening reaction time. It increases the ability of muscle cells to produce energy. Too much causes nervousness, jittery muscle reactions, insomnia, and an abnormally fast heartbeat. One thing it does not do is add flavor or texture to beverages, and because of that I have not included caffeine extract as an ingredient for any of the sodas in this book. The only caffeine you will find in these pages is in preparations that use flavorings that naturally contain caffeine, most notably coffee, chocolate, and tea.

CAFFEINE CONTENT OF COMMON BEVERAGES

Beverage	Serving Size (fluid ounces)	Caffeine (mg) per Serving	Caffeine (mg) per fluid ounce
Chai	16	100	4.7
Chocolate milk or cocoa	8	5	0.6
Cola, diet	12	36 to 45	3 to 3.8
Cola, regular	12	35 to 38	2.9 to 3.2
Coffee, brewed	8	108	13.4
Coffee, drip	8	145	18.1
Coffee, espresso	1.5	77	51.3
Coffee, instant	8	57	7.1
Energy drinks	8	80	9.5
Energy shots	2 to 2.5	80 to 220	40 to 110*
Lemon-lime sodas	12	0	0
Mountain Dew	12	55	4.6
Orange soda	12	36 to 41	3 to 3.4
Tea, black	8	47	5.9
Tea, green	8	25	3.1
Tea, herbal	8	0	0
Tea, white	8	15	1.9

*A few highly concentrated energy shots that are sold in extremely small serving sizes (less than 5 grams) have more than 2,000 mg of caffeine for every fluid ounce of product.

kona coconut latte

Kona is the premium coffee bean grown in a narrow strip of mineral-rich volcanic soil in the Kona districts of the Big Island of Hawaii. Kona coffee is rare and expensive because the growing region is tiny. It is a great coffee, but I cannot say that it is worth twice the price of other premium coffees. I chose it in this soda because its island origin pairs aesthetically with coconut milk, but any good-quality coffee will work as well. The coconut milk adds creaminess without dairy and a sweet nuttiness similar to that of hazelnut syrup.

KONA SYRUP

- 1 cup double-strength brewed Kona coffee, or any good-quality coffee
- ⅔ cup sugar
- ½ cup light coconut milk

ENOUGH FOR 3 SERVINGS

Combine the coffee and sugar in a small saucepan. Cook over low heat, stirring often, until the sugar dissolves. Remove from the heat and let cool to room temperature. Stir in the coconut milk.

This syrup will keep in the refrigerator for up to 1 week.

 ## TO MIX WITH SELTZER

- ½ cup Kona syrup
- 1 cup seltzer

1 SERVING

Pour the syrup into a tall glass. Add the seltzer and stir just until blended. Add ice and serve.

 ## TO CARBONATE WITH A SIPHON

- 1 batch Kona syrup
- 2½ cups water

3 SERVINGS

Pour the syrup into a 1-quart siphon. Add the water. Charge with CO_2 according to the manufacturer's directions. Siphon-charged sodas can be stored in the siphon in a refrigerator for up to 5 days. Disperse as desired into tall glasses filled with ice, and serve.

 Also see Mixology recipe on page 199.

brown sugar mocha soda

This soda is all about brown: browned roasted coffee, brown fermented cocoa, brown sugar, and brown cinnamon. Brown tastes rich, roasted, meaty, spicy, and sweet. Brown is substantial. Brown is delicious. Because of the savory and slightly bitter character of some of the ingredients, the sweetness of this soda is restrained, making it a bit more adult than your average soft drink.

MOCHA SYRUP

- 1 cup dark brown sugar
- 1 cup brewed coffee
- ¼ cup unsweetened cocoa powder
- 1 large (5-inch) cinnamon stick

ENOUGH FOR 3 SERVINGS

Mix the brown sugar, coffee, and cocoa powder together in a small saucepan; add the cinnamon stick. Bring to a boil, stirring until the sugar and cocoa dissolve, and then remove from the heat and let cool to room temperature. Remove and discard the cinnamon stick.

This syrup will keep in the refrigerator for up to 2 months.

 TO MIX WITH SELTZER

- ½ cup mocha syrup
- 1 cup seltzer

1 SERVING

Pour the syrup into a tall glass. Add the seltzer and stir just until blended. Add ice and serve.

 TO CARBONATE WITH A SIPHON

- 1 batch mocha syrup
- 2½ cups water

3 SERVINGS

Pour the syrup into a 1-quart siphon. Add the water. Charge with CO_2 according to the manufacturer's directions. Siphon-charged sodas can be stored in the siphon in a refrigerator for up to 5 days. Disperse as desired into tall glasses filled with ice, and serve.

cold fudge soda

The rich, sugary decadence of hot fudge sauce is the inspiration for this cold fudge soda. Fudge is a kind of chocolate caramel; when warmed it liquefies, becoming fudge sauce. You can make the fudge syrup for this soda ahead of time and refrigerate it, but it will solidify. To regain its saucy persona so it can be made into a beverage, it must first be softened to room temperature.

FUDGE SYRUP

- ¾ cup unsweetened cocoa powder
- ⅔ cup sugar
- ⅔ cup cold water
- ⅔ cup milk
- 1 tablespoon unsalted butter

ENOUGH FOR 3 SERVINGS

Combine the cocoa and sugar in a small saucepan; add the water and stir with a small whisk until smooth. Stir in the milk, and bring to a boil over medium heat, stirring often to keep the syrup smooth; let simmer for 2 minutes, stirring frequently. Remove from the heat and add the butter, stirring until it is melted and blended. Then let cool to room temperature.

This syrup will keep in the refrigerator for up to 1 week. Bring back to room temperature before mixing into soda.

TO MIX WITH SELTZER

- ⅔ cup fudge syrup
- ⅔ cup seltzer

1 SERVING

Pour the syrup into a tall glass. Add the seltzer and stir just until blended. Add ice and serve.

TO CARBONATE WITH A SIPHON

- 1 batch fudge syrup
- 2 cups water

3 SERVINGS

Pour the syrup into a 1-quart siphon. Add the water. Charge with CO_2 according to the manufacturer's directions. Siphon-charged sodas can be stored in the siphon in a refrigerator for up to 5 days. Disperse as desired into tall glasses filled with ice, and serve.

cocoa chile taste-bud tingler

The bite of chiles and soothing caress of chocolate dance in a playful paso doble *in this sexy Latin-style soda. You can use any chile that you desire, but I would steer you toward ground ancho chiles. With their mild fruity flavor, they deliver just enough heat to ignite, but not enough to really burn. Under no circumstances should you use commercial chili powder, which includes cumin and oregano in its blend.*

COCOA CHILE SYRUP

¾ cup unsweetened cocoa powder

⅔ cup sugar

½ teaspoon ground chiles, preferably ancho

½ teaspoon ground cinnamon

1⅓ cups cold water

1 tablespoon unsalted butter

ENOUGH FOR 3 SERVINGS

Combine the cocoa, sugar, chiles, and cinnamon in a small saucepan; add the water and stir with a small whisk until smooth. Bring to a boil, stirring often to keep the syrup smooth; let simmer for 2 minutes, stirring frequently. Remove from the heat and add the butter, stirring until it is melted and blended. Then let the syrup cool to room temperature.

This syrup will keep in the refrigerator for up to 2 months. Bring back to room temperature before mixing into soda.

TO MIX WITH SELTZER

⅔ cup cocoa chile syrup

⅔ cup seltzer

1 SERVING

Pour the syrup into a tall glass. Add the seltzer and stir just until blended. Add ice and serve.

TO CARBONATE WITH A SIPHON

1 batch cocoa chile syrup

2 cups water

3 SERVINGS

Pour the syrup into a 1-quart siphon. Add the water. Charge with CO_2 according to the manufacturer's directions. Siphon-charged sodas can be stored in the siphon in a refrigerator for up to 5 days. Disperse as desired into tall glasses filled with ice, and serve.

chocolate ginger ale

The mating of chocolate and ginger possesses a spicy titillation. Gingerol, the active flavoring agent in ginger, is cousin to capsaicin, the compound that gives chile peppers their heat. Dried ginger is spicier than fresh ginger-root, and cooking it into the chocolate syrup encourages some of its hotter properties. If you are familiar with Jamaican ginger beer, this soda has a comparable intensity.

CHOCOLATE GINGER SYRUP

¾ cup unsweetened cocoa powder

⅔ cup sugar

2 teaspoons ground ginger

1⅓ cups cold water

1 tablespoon unsalted butter

ENOUGH FOR 3 SERVINGS

Combine the cocoa, sugar, and ginger in a small saucepan; add the water and stir with a small whisk until smooth. Bring to a boil, stirring often to keep the syrup smooth; let simmer for 2 minutes, stirring frequently. Remove from the heat and add the butter, stirring until melted and blended. Let cool to room temperature.

This syrup will keep in the refrigerator for up to 2 months. Bring back to room temperature before mixing into soda.

TO MIX WITH SELTZER

⅔ cup chocolate ginger syrup

⅔ cup seltzer

1 SERVING

Pour the syrup into a tall glass. Add the seltzer and stir just until blended. Add ice and serve.

TO CARBONATE WITH A SIPHON

1 batch chocolate ginger syrup

2 cups water

3 SERVINGS

Pour the syrup into a 1-quart siphon. Add the water. Charge with CO_2 according to the manufacturer's directions. Siphon-charged sodas can be stored in the siphon in a refrigerator for up to 5 days. Disperse as desired into tall glasses filled with ice, and serve.

pumped-up chocolate milk

If chocolate syrup mixed into a glass of milk is the cold beer of childhood, then this is the champagne. The only thing that trumps a squirt bottle of chocolate syrup is this homemade version, reinforced with a melted lozenge of pure chocolate. You can make the syrup anytime for an instant hit of chocolate soda. Just warm it up to room temperature before squirting; it sets up like a block of fudge when it gets cold.

CHOCOLATE SYRUP

- ¾ cup unsweetened cocoa powder
- ⅔ cup sugar
- 1⅓ cups cold milk
- 1 ounce semisweet chocolate

ENOUGH FOR 3 SERVINGS

Combine the cocoa and sugar in a small saucepan; add the milk and stir with a small whisk until smooth. Bring to a simmer, stirring often to keep the syrup smooth; let simmer for 2 minutes, stirring frequently. Remove from the heat and add the chocolate, stirring until melted and blended. Let cool to room temperature.

This syrup will keep in the refrigerator for up to 1 week. Bring back to room temperature before mixing into soda.

 ## TO MIX WITH SELTZER

- ⅔ cup chocolate syrup
- ⅔ cup seltzer

1 SERVING

Pour the syrup into a tall glass. Add the seltzer and stir just until blended. Add ice and serve.

 ## TO CARBONATE WITH A SIPHON

- 1 batch chocolate syrup
- 2 cups water

3 SERVINGS

Pour the syrup into a 1-quart siphon. Add the water. Charge with CO_2 according to the manufacturer's directions. Siphon-charged sodas can be stored in the siphon in a refrigerator for up to 5 days. Disperse as desired into tall glasses filled with ice, and serve.

Chocolate Facts

LIKE COFFEE, COCOA IS BREWED FROM BEANS, in this case the beans of the cacao tree (*Theobroma cacao*). Chocolate is made from roasted cacao beans that are ground into a thick paste, composed of 30 percent cocoa solids and 55 percent cocoa butter; during processing the solids and fat are separated from one another. Chocolate bars are made by recombining the two in various ratios. Cocoa powder, made by drying and pulverizing chocolate solids, is the most concentrated and chocolaty form of chocolate, and the one that is most commonly used for making chocolate sodas.

POP CULTURE

Yoo-hoo Chocolate Soda

NATALE OLIVIERI PRODUCED TRU-FRUIT SODAS from his store in northern New Jersey in the 1920s. He wanted to add a milk chocolate drink to the line but didn't know how to package it so that it would not spoil. After watching his wife putting up tomato sauce, he tried heat-processing the soda after it was in the bottle, and with a little trial and error it worked. Yoo-hoo became the first milk-based soda to be bottled and sold commercially.

CHAPTER SEVEN

Cream Egg Creams

Sodas, & Floats

*C*ream sodas, egg creams, and floats bubble with nostalgia for the good old days before bottled sodas, when carbonated beverages were dispensed from the local soda fountain, usually located at the corner pharmacy.

The term *soda fountain* originally referred to the tap that dispersed sparkling mineral waters from underground springs, and it was adopted by Samuel Fahnestock in 1819 when he patented the first commercial man-made carbonation machine. In 1825 the first commercial soda fountain opened in a pharmacy in Philadelphia, thereby establishing the connection between the dispensing of sparkling water and drugstores, and in 1832 John Matthews, a British immigrant living in New York, built a small carbonating machine for pharmacies that would bring the soda fountain to every corner drugstore in the country.

The healthy attributes of sparking spring water made the connection between carbonation and health a natural for pharmacies. But the soda fountain became such a popular section of the pharmacy that it soon evolved from a place to get healthful waters to a center for social gathering. With that shift, it was only a short step from carbonated water to flavored carbonated water. One of the first and most popular flavors was vanilla, which became known as vanilla cream soda, probably because of the creamy head that developed when carbonated bubbles became coated with the natural oils in vanilla syrup. Some pharmacists added milk for extra richness.

The story of the first ice cream soda has been so oft repeated it is hard to know which part of it is history and which part pure delight. The story is told that in 1874 entrepreneur Robert Green was selling cream soda, a mixture of vanilla, milk, and carbonated water, at the celebration of the semi-centennial of the Franklin Institute in Philadelphia. Sales were okay. One day, when he ran out of milk, he substituted vanilla ice cream (this sounds so suspicious), and a classic was born. Who knows if this is true? There are several others who claim to have invented the pairing of ice cream and flavored carbonated water under similarly dubious circumstances. At any rate, all the claims stem from the same time period, and it was around that time that ice cream sodas became popular.

Sparkling Orange Creamsicle, page 221

The Cream in Cream Soda

JUST AS THERE IS NO EGG IN A NEW YORK EGG CREAM (see page 228), there is no dairy in a cream soda. Or is there? One of the earliest fountain sodas (introduced in 1854), cream soda originally was carbonated water flavored with sweetened vanilla syrup. Some historical sources say that the "cream" moniker came about because vanilla-flavored soda was the fizzy beverage of choice for an ice cream soda. However, the ice cream soda wasn't introduced until almost 20 years after cream soda, so that seems unlikely. Today, bottled cream sodas are vanilla-flavored and often have ingredients added to give them a silky mouthfeel, but no cream.

plain delicious cream soda

Some soda fountain cream sodas and many home recipes for cream soda include the addition of half-and-half or cream, but the classic cream soda recipe includes only carbonated water and sweetened vanilla syrup. When it comes to cream soda, I'm a purist; I do not add dairy, or any additional ingredients to change the texture, and I use vanilla bean, not vanilla extract. When a preparation is this spare, the type and quality of every ingredient is important.

VANILLA SYRUP

½ cup water

¾ cup sugar

1 large vanilla bean, thinly sliced

ENOUGH FOR 3 SERVINGS

Combine the water, sugar, and vanilla bean in a small saucepan. Bring to a boil, stirring occasionally, and then remove from the heat and let cool to room temperature. Strain out the vanilla bean.

This syrup will keep in the refrigerator for up to 2 months.

TO MIX WITH SELTZER

¼ cup vanilla syrup

1¼ cups seltzer

1 SERVING

Pour the syrup into a tall glass. Add the seltzer and stir just until blended. Add ice and serve.

TO CARBONATE WITH A SIPHON

1 batch vanilla syrup

3 cups water

3 SERVINGS

Pour the syrup into a 1-quart siphon. Add the water. Charge with CO_2 according to the manufacturer's directions. Siphon-charged sodas can be stored in the siphon in a refrigerator for up to 5 days. Disperse as desired into tall glasses filled with ice, and serve.

strawberry cream soda

When I'm using a flavor other than or in addition to vanilla, I often add milk to cream sodas. Not only does milk add protein to the drink, but its natural sweetness allows you to reduce or eliminate the sugar in your recipes. If you're thirsting for something closer to an ice cream soda, you can substitute half-and-half for the milk.

STRAWBERRY PURÉE

- 1 pint strawberries, hulled
- ½ cup whole milk
- 1 tablespoon honey or agave syrup
- 1 teaspoon vanilla extract

ENOUGH FOR 4 SERVINGS

Combine the strawberries, milk, honey, and vanilla in a blender or food processor and purée. Strain to remove the strawberry seeds.

This purée will keep in the refrigerator for up to 24 hours, but is best used immediately.

TO MIX WITH SELTZER

- ⅓ cup strawberry purée
- 1 cup seltzer

1 SERVING

Pour the purée into a tall glass. Add the seltzer and stir just until blended. Add ice and serve.

almond honey cream soda

To my palate, the combination of honey, vanilla, and a little almond is completely sublime: floral, fruity, musky, and sweet. It takes the flavor elements of vanilla, which is the soul of cream soda, and ignites them into a beverage that is both simple and spectacular, like the quiet librarian who takes off her wire rims and unpins her bun, setting free the siren inside.

HONEY MILK

¾ cup honey

¼ cup milk

1 teaspoon almond extract

1 teaspoon vanilla extract

ENOUGH FOR 3 SERVINGS

Combine the honey, milk, almond extract, and vanilla, and stir until smooth.

This syrup will keep in the refrigerator for up to 3 days.

 ## TO MIX WITH SELTZER

⅓ cup honey milk
1 cup seltzer

1 SERVING

Pour the syrup into a tall glass. Add the seltzer and stir just until blended. Add ice and serve.

 ## TO CARBONATE WITH A SIPHON

1 batch honey milk
3 cups water

3 SERVINGS

Pour the syrup into a 1-quart siphon. Add the water. Charge with CO_2 according to the manufacturer's directions. Siphon-charged sodas can be stored in the siphon in a refrigerator for up to 5 days. Disperse as desired into tall glasses filled with ice, and serve.

banana cream soda

Think of sipping the essence of banana cream pie (minus the crust) through a straw and you have an inkling of the creamy rich satiety of this soda. The way the soda foams and filters through the honeyed banana purée is similar to how it behaves in an ice cream soda, giving you the sensual pleasure of an ice cream treat with a fraction of the calories and a lot more nutrition. Note: The banana purée does not keep, so gather some friends for a treat and finish it all off right away.

BANANA PURÉE

⅓ cup honey

¼ cup milk

1 ripe medium banana, peeled and cut in chunks

1 teaspoon vanilla extract

ENOUGH FOR 3 SERVINGS

Combine the honey, milk, banana, and vanilla in a blender or food processor, and purée until smooth.

 ## TO MIX WITH SELTZER

1 batch banana purée
3 cups seltzer

3 SERVINGS

Divide the purée among 3 tall glasses. Add 1 cup of seltzer to each glass and stir just until blended. Add ice and serve.

 ## TO CARBONATE WITH A SIPHON

1 batch banana purée
3 cups water

3 SERVINGS

Pour the purée into a 1-quart siphon. Add the water. Charge with CO_2 according to the manufacturer's directions. Disperse as desired into tall glasses filled with ice, and serve.

lemon cream soda

In this drink, the richness of cream soda and the refreshment of lemon join forces. The fragrant oils in the lemon zest emulsify throughout the soda, giving it a creamy mouthfeel that is reinforced by the scent of vanilla. I don't use lemon juice because its tartness might interfere with the creamy sensation.

LEMON SYRUP

¾ cup sugar

½ cup water

Finely grated zest of 1 lemon

½ teaspoon vanilla extract

ENOUGH FOR 3 SERVINGS

Combine the sugar, water, and lemon zest in a small saucepan. Bring to a boil, then remove from the heat and let cool to room temperature. Strain out zest and stir in the vanilla.

This syrup will keep in the refrigerator for up to 2 months.

 TO MIX WITH SELTZER

¼ cup lemon syrup

1¼ cups seltzer

1 SERVING

Pour the syrup into a tall glass. Add the seltzer and stir just until blended. Add ice and serve.

 TO CARBONATE WITH A SIPHON

1 batch lemon syrup

3¼ cups water

3 SERVINGS

Pour the syrup into a 1-quart siphon. Add enough water to fill the siphon. Charge with CO_2 according to the manufacturer's directions. Siphon-charged sodas can be stored in the siphon in a refrigerator for up to 5 days. Disperse as desired into tall glasses filled with ice, and serve.

sparkling orange creamsicle

The Creamsicle has been an inspiration for countless beverages, alcoholic and otherwise, so I guess I might as well get in line. My version is a little bit nutritious (half the dairy is yogurt), a little bit rich (the other half is ice cream), very flavorful (equal parts orange and vanilla), and ultimately refreshing (carbonation titillates every time). This is one of the most filling sodas in the book, and it's best served as a snack or a dessert.

VANILLA ORANGE PURÉE

1 cup cold orange juice

1 cup cold vanilla yogurt

1 cup vanilla ice cream

ENOUGH FOR 4 SERVINGS

Combine the orange juice, yogurt, and ice cream in a blender or food processor, and purée.

This purée will keep in the refrigerator for up to 2 days, but it is best if used immediately.

TO MIX WITH SELTZER

¾ cup vanilla orange purée

¾ cup chilled seltzer

1 SERVING

Pour the purée into a tall glass. Add the seltzer, stir just until blended, and serve.

crème brûlée soda

Imagine the flavors of a crème brûlée — toasted caramel, slight bitterness, and a touch of sweetness, washed with a lush flood of cream and the innocent scent of vanilla. That's what you get in this sippable caramel custard.

CARAMEL SYRUP

½ cup granulated sugar

½ cup light brown sugar

⅓ cup water

1½ cups whole milk

1 teaspoon vanilla extract

ENOUGH FOR 4 SERVINGS

Combine the granulated sugar, brown sugar, and water in a small heavy saucepan. Cook over medium-high heat until the mixture turns dark amber, washing away any sugar crystals clinging to the inside of the pan with a damp pastry brush. (See next page for more detail on making this liquid caramel.)

While the sugar is caramelizing, heat the milk to a simmer in another saucepan or in the microwave. When the sugar is fully caramelized, stir the warm milk into it. The sugar will immediately crystallize, and the milk will vigorously bubble and steam. Stand back so you don't get burned. Then, as the bubbling subsides, stir the caramel until it becomes smooth and fluid again. Remove from the heat, stir in the vanilla, and let cool for 5 minutes.

This syrup will keep in the refrigerator for up to 2 days, but must be warmed until liquid before using to make a soda.

 ## TO MIX WITH SELTZER

1 batch caramel syrup

4 cups seltzer

4 SERVINGS

Divide the liquid caramel among four tall glasses. Stir 1 cup seltzer into each. Fill the glasses with ice and serve.

Liquid Caramel

CARAMELIZING SUGAR IS A LITTLE TRICKY. If you're not careful the caramel can crystallize, becoming grainy. This usually happens right when the caramel is almost finished. At that point the concentration of sugar in the liquid caramel is so close to saturated that a single grain of sugar falling into the caramel can trigger a chain of crystallization. To prevent this from happening, it is advisable to wash any stray sugar grains clinging to the side of the pot into the caramel with a wet pastry brush as soon as they appear. When the sugar is melted and caramelized, you'll add the milk, which will bubble and steam angrily at first. At the same time the caramel will turn rock hard. But within a minute or two the bubbling will subside and the caramel will return to a liquid state, and you will have the most delicious soda base imaginable.

coconut milk fizz

This completely nondairy creamy soda is enriched with canned coconut milk. The fat content of coconut milk is similar to that of whole milk, but coconut fat contains a good amount of omega-3 and omega-6 fatty acids, as well as some monounsaturated fat, so it's pretty heart-healthy. The rich coconut flavor and texture are seasoned with a sprinkling of cinnamon and a bit of vanilla.

COCONUT MILK SYRUP

¾ cup sugar

½ cup water

¼ teaspoon ground cinnamon

1 cup light coconut milk

½ teaspoon vanilla extract

ENOUGH FOR 3 SERVINGS

Combine the sugar, water, and cinnamon in a small saucepan. Bring to a boil, then remove from the heat and let cool to room temperature. Stir in the coconut milk and vanilla.

This syrup will keep in the refrigerator for up to 2 months.

 ## TO MIX WITH SELTZER

½ cup coconut milk syrup
1 cup seltzer

1 SERVING

Pour the syrup into a tall glass. Add the seltzer and stir just until blended. Add ice and serve.

 ## TO CARBONATE WITH A SIPHON

1 batch coconut milk syrup
2½ cups water

3 SERVINGS

Pour the syrup into a 1-quart siphon. Add the water. Charge with CO_2 according to the manufacturer's directions. Siphon-charged sodas can be stored in the siphon in a refrigerator for up to 5 days. Disperse as desired into tall glasses filled with ice, and serve.

peanut cream soda

Creamy peanut butter sweetened with sugar syrup and blended with half-and-half is not unlike peanut butter ice cream, which is one of the great ice cream inventions of recent decades. Adding carbonation transforms it into the closest thing to a peanut butter ice cream soda, which could be the confectionery claim to fame of the decade to come. It's got my vote!

PEANUT BUTTER SYRUP

- ¾ cup sugar
- ½ cup water
- ¾ cup half-and-half
- ¼ cup smooth natural peanut butter
- ½ teaspoon vanilla extract

ENOUGH FOR 3 SERVINGS

Combine the sugar and water in a small saucepan. Bring to a boil, then remove from the heat and stir in the half-and-half and peanut butter. Let cool to room temperature. Stir in the vanilla.

This syrup will keep in the refrigerator for up to 2 months.

TO MIX WITH SELTZER

- ½ cup peanut butter syrup
- 1 cup seltzer

1 SERVING

Pour the syrup into a tall glass. Add the seltzer and stir just until blended. Add ice and serve.

TO CARBONATE WITH A SIPHON

- 1 batch peanut butter syrup
- 2½ cups water

3 SERVINGS

Pour the syrup into a 1-quart siphon and add the water. Charge with CO_2 according to the manufacturer's directions. Siphon-charged sodas can be stored in the siphon in a refrigerator for up to 5 days. Disperse as desired into tall glasses filled with ice, and serve.

root beer cream soda

This potentially fat-free (depending on the fat content of the milk you use) facsimile of a root beer float has all the tangy-sweet dairy flavors of the soda fountain classic without its diet-busting downside.

ROOT BEER CREAM SYRUP

¾ cup sugar

½ cup water

1 cup milk or half-and-half

1 tablespoon Rooty Toot Root Beer syrup (page 88) or purchased root beer syrup

ENOUGH FOR 4 SERVINGS

Combine the sugar and water in a small saucepan. Bring to a boil, then remove from the heat and stir in the milk and root beer syrup. Let cool to room temperature.

This syrup will keep in the refrigerator for up to 2 days.

TO MIX WITH SELTZER

⅓ cup root beer cream syrup

1 cup seltzer

1 SERVING

Pour the syrup into a tall glass. Add the seltzer and stir just until blended. Add ice and serve.

TO CARBONATE WITH A SIPHON

1 batch root beer cream syrup

2½ cups water

4 SERVINGS

Pour the syrup into a 1-quart siphon. Add the water. Charge with CO_2 according to the manufacturer's directions. Siphon-charged sodas can be stored in the siphon in a refrigerator for up to 5 days. Disperse as desired into tall glasses filled with ice, and serve.

bubbling dulce de leche

Dulce de leche (caramelized sweetened condensed milk), the ubiquitous sweetener in Latin American desserts, is the base for this effortless carbonated beverage. Dulce de leche soda is so naturally delicious that it is remarkable to me that no one has thought yet to bottle it. If you want to cut some of the calories, and all of the fat, it is fine to use fat-free condensed milk.

DULCE DE LECHE SYRUP

2½ cups sweetened condensed milk

1 medium (3-inch) cinnamon stick

1 teaspoon vanilla extract

ENOUGH FOR 4 SERVINGS

Combine the condensed milk and cinnamon in a small saucepan. Cook over medium-high heat until the mixture turns pale amber, stirring often. Let cool to room temperature, then remove the cinnamon and stir in the vanilla.

This syrup will keep in the refrigerator for up to 2 days, but must be warmed until liquid before using it to make a soda.

TO MIX WITH SELTZER

½ cup dulce de leche syrup
1 cup seltzer

1 SERVING

Pour the syrup into a tall glass. Add the seltzer and stir just until blended. Add ice and serve.

TO CARBONATE WITH A SIPHON

1 batch dulce de leche syrup
2 cups water

4 SERVINGS

Pour the syrup into a 1-quart siphon. Add the water. Charge with CO_2 according to the manufacturer's directions. Siphon-charged sodas can be stored in the siphon in a refrigerator for up to 5 days. Disperse as desired into tall glasses filled with ice, and serve.

dark chocolate egg cream

Just as cream sodas have no dairy products, egg creams don't actually contain egg. The name refers to the foam generated when milk and carbonated water are mixed together. The bubbles of CO_2 get trapped in milk protein, causing it to expand in the same way that the protein of egg whites can be inflated by beating it with a whisk. In this dark chocolate creamy Fudgsicle of a soda, the bubbles take on a luxurious silken consistency.

CHOCOLATE EGG CREAM SYRUP

- ¾ cup sugar
- ½ cup unsweetened cocoa powder
- ½ cup water
- 1 cup milk
- 1 teaspoon vanilla extract

ENOUGH FOR 3 SERVINGS

Combine the sugar, cocoa powder, and water in a small saucepan, and whisk together until smooth. Bring to a boil, then remove from the heat and stir in the milk and vanilla. Let cool to room temperature, then chill.

This syrup will keep in the refrigerator for up to 2 days.

 TO MIX WITH SELTZER

- ½ cup ice-cold chocolate egg cream syrup
- ¼ cup crushed ice
- ¾ cup seltzer, preferably from a siphon

1 SERVING

Combine the syrup and crushed ice in a tall glass. Add the seltzer, aiming it toward the side of the glass to encourage a large white head of foam to rise to the top.

New York Egg Creams

THOUGH THE TERM *EGG CREAM* did not appear in print until 1954, these sweet soft drinks became popular soda fountain treats in New York City in the 1930s and have continued to weave their mythology ever since. The first egg creams were chocolate, made from chocolate syrup mixed with ice-cold milk and carbonated with seltzer. Soda jerks in New York practiced in the art of the egg cream were known for their technique. To make a proper egg cream, the milk must be so cold that it is flecked with shards of ice, and the soda must be added under pressure to create a bulging white head of foam.

french vanilla egg cream

For this gourmet version of the vanilla egg cream, a split vanilla bean is simmered in milk and sugar until the seeds from the vanilla pod scatter into the milk, making a sweet custardlike base speckled with real vanilla. When combined with carbonated water, a typical egg cream foam cascades skyward, launching jets of vanilla-scented spray.

VANILLA MILK SYRUP

2 cups milk

1 cup sugar

1 vanilla bean, split lengthwise

ENOUGH FOR 3 SERVINGS

Combine the milk, sugar, and vanilla bean in a small saucepan. Cook over medium-high heat, stirring occasionally, until the sugar dissolves. Remove from the heat and let cool to room temperature. Remove the vanilla bean, and scrape the seeds from the beans back into the milk for a little more flavor. Chill.

This syrup will keep in the refrigerator for up to 2 days.

 ## TO MIX WITH SELTZER

¾ cup ice-cold vanilla milk syrup

¼ cup crushed ice

¾ cup seltzer, preferably from a siphon

1 SERVING

Combine the syrup and crushed ice in a tall glass. Add the seltzer, aiming it toward the side of the glass to encourage a large white head of foam to rise to the top.

salted caramel egg cream

In this subtly sweet, richly caramelized soda, browned sugar syrup is enriched with milk into liquid candy. Simply add seltzer and a pinch of fleur de sel, and you've got the effervescent equivalent of a salted caramel.

CARAMEL SYRUP

½ cup sugar

¼ cup water

1 cup whole milk

¼ teaspoon fleur de sel

ENOUGH FOR 2 SERVINGS

Combine the sugar and water in a small heavy saucepan. Cook over medium-high heat until the mixture turns pale amber, washing away any sugar crystals clinging to the inside of the pan with a damp pastry brush. (See page 223 for more detail on caramelizing sugar.)

While the sugar is caramelizing, heat the milk to a simmer in another saucepan or in the microwave. When the sugar is pale amber, stir the milk into the pan. The sugar will immediately crystallize, and the milk will vigorously bubble and steam. Stand back so you don't get burned. When the foaming subsides in a few seconds, stir until the caramel becomes smooth again. Remove from the heat and stir in the salt.

This syrup will keep in the refrigerator for up to 2 days, but must be warmed until liquid before using to make a soda.

 TO MIX WITH SELTZER

½ cup caramel syrup

1 cup seltzer, preferably from a siphon

½ cup crushed ice

1 SERVING

Pour the syrup into a tall glass. Add the seltzer, aiming it toward the side of the glass to encourage a large white head of foam to rise to the top. Add the crushed ice to the glass and stir briefly.

sparkling egg nog

Real egg nog always includes some booze (nog is Old English for ale), but this family-friendly version has all the flavor of the real thing, but with carbonation taking the place of inebriation. Egg nog is a stovetop custard sauce that is traditionally thinned to drinking consistency with rum. In this recipe, rum extract provides the flavor and carbonated water the drinkability.

EGG NOG SYRUP

¾ cup sugar

½ cup water

¼ cup milk

1 teaspoon rum extract

⅛ teaspoon freshly grated nutmeg

1 egg yolk

ENOUGH FOR 3 SERVINGS

Combine the sugar and water in a small saucepan and bring to a boil. While the sugar syrup is heating, combine the milk, rum extract, nutmeg, and egg yolk in a small bowl, and whisk together. When the sugar syrup reaches a boil, remove it from the heat and slowly pour it into the milk mixture, whisking continuously until the mixture thickens lightly. Let cool to room temperature.

This syrup will keep in the refrigerator for up to 2 days, but it is best used immediately.

 ## TO MIX WITH SELTZER

⅓ cup egg nog syrup
1 cup seltzer

1 SERVING

Pour the syrup into a tall glass. Add the seltzer and stir just until blended. Add ice and serve.

 ## TO CARBONATE WITH A SIPHON

1 batch egg nog syrup
3 cups water

3 SERVINGS

Pour the syrup into a 1-quart siphon. Add the water. Charge with CO_2 according to the manufacturer's directions. Siphon-charged sodas can be stored in the siphon in a refrigerator for up to 5 days. Disperse as desired into tall glasses filled with ice, and serve.

sparkling cinnamon latte

The latte is the New York egg cream of the twenty-first century, hiding its simplicity behind a complex mythology of barista technique and professional equipment. It seemed only fitting to merge the two, and the technique that wins out is that of the 1930 Brooklyn soda jerk, not the coffee geek pulling shots and scooping foam.

CINNAMON LATTE SYRUP

1 cup brewed coffee, preferably espresso

¾ cup sugar

1 large (5-inch) cinnamon stick,
   broken into three pieces

ENOUGH FOR 4 SERVINGS

Combine the coffee, sugar, and cinnamon in a small saucepan. Bring to a boil, then remove from the heat and let cool to room temperature. Remove the cinnamon stick. Chill.

This syrup will keep in the refrigerator for up to 2 weeks.

 TO MIX WITH SELTZER

⅓ cup cinnamon latte
   syrup
⅓ cup ice-cold milk
¼ cup crushed ice
¾ cup seltzer, preferably
   from a siphon

1 SERVING

Combine the syrup and milk in a tall drinking glass, stirring to blend. Add the crushed ice. Add the seltzer, aiming it toward the side of the glass to encourage a large white head of foam to rise to the top.

chocolate raspberry cream pop

Because raspberries have to be seeded, sweetened, and cooked before they can be liquefied and drunk, I have streamlined their preparation by using raspberry jelly, which is nothing more than fresh raspberries that are already seeded, sweetened, and cooked. I love when an ingredient meets you halfway.

CHOCOLATE RASPBERRY CREAM SYRUP

- ½ cup sugar
- ½ cup unsweetened cocoa powder
- ½ cup water
- ¼ cup raspberry jelly
- ¼ cup half-and-half
- ½ teaspoon vanilla extract

ENOUGH FOR 4 SERVINGS

Combine the sugar, cocoa powder, water, and jelly in a small saucepan, and whisk together until smooth. Bring to a boil, then remove from the heat and stir in the half-and-half and vanilla. Let cool to room temperature.

This syrup will keep in the refrigerator for up to 2 weeks.

TO MIX WITH SELTZER

- ⅓ cup chocolate raspberry cream syrup
- 1 cup seltzer

1 SERVING

Pour the syrup into a tall glass. Add the seltzer and stir just until blended. Add ice and serve.

TO CARBONATE WITH A SIPHON

- 1 batch chocolate raspberry cream syrup
- 2⅔ cups water

4 SERVINGS

Combine the syrup and water in a 1-quart siphon. Charge with CO_2 according to the manufacturer's directions. Siphon-charged sodas can be stored in the siphon in a refrigerator for up to 5 days. Disperse as desired into tall glasses filled with ice, and serve.

ginger pineapple coconut-cream float

In addition to being fairly acidic, pineapple contains bromelain, an enzyme that breaks down protein, which means that it is tricky to pair it with fresh dairy products. That is why the cream that would normally enrich this float has been replaced with double-rich coconut milk, called coconut cream. If you add the soda slowly to the glass, you can encourage the foam from the coconut cream to rise to the top in a bulbous head, making the float look like it was made with ice cream.

PINEAPPLE COCONUT SYRUP

- 1 cup pineapple juice
- ¾ cup sugar
- 1 cup coconut cream
- ½ teaspoon vanilla extract

ENOUGH FOR 6 SERVINGS

Combine the pineapple juice and sugar in a small saucepan. Bring to a boil, then reduce the heat and let simmer uncovered for 5 minutes. Remove from the heat and let cool to room temperature. Stir in the coconut cream and vanilla. Chill.

This syrup will keep in the refrigerator for up to 2 weeks.

TO MIX WITH GINGER BEER

- ⅓ cup pineapple coconut syrup
- 1 cup Szechuan Ginger Beer (page 109) or purchased ginger beer

1 SERVING

Pour the syrup into a tall glass. Slowly add the ginger beer, carefully pouring it down the side of the glass to mix it as little as possible with the coconut milk. The coconut cream should rise to the top. Serve with a spoon for eating the sweet cream.

start-the-day-right breakfast cocktail

Want to make tomorrow a better day? Start it with soda. I know it sounds slacker-ish and sort of debauched, but what if the soda were made from puréed fruit, a container of yogurt, and some carbonated water — sort of a fizzy smoothie? It's nutritious. It tastes great. It's ready in minutes. What are you waiting for?

FRUIT PURÉE

¼ pint strawberries, hulled

½ of a ripe banana, peeled and cut into chunks

¼ cup vanilla yogurt

ENOUGH FOR 1 SERVING

Combine the strawberries, bananas, and yogurt in a blender or food processor, and purée. Use immediately.

 TO MIX WITH SELTZER

1 batch fruit purée

¾ cup seltzer

1 SERVING

Pour the purée into a tall glass. Add the seltzer and stir just until blended. Add ice and serve.

sparkling fruit lassi

The very popular yogurt drink from South Asia is the inspiration for this healthful sparkling beverage. It is made with fresh mango, which is a traditional fruit for lassi, but you can replace the mango with a pint of berries or a banana with equal success. It is an easy and delicious drinkable breakfast.

MANGO PURÉE

- 1 mango, peeled, pitted, and chopped
- 1 cup vanilla yogurt
- ⅔ cup orange juice

ENOUGH FOR 4 SERVINGS

Combine the mango, yogurt, and orange juice in a blender or food processor, and purée.

This purée will keep in the refrigerator for up to 24 hours, but it is best if used immediately.

TO MIX WITH SELTZER

- ½ cup mango purée
- ¾ cup seltzer

1 SERVING

Pour the purée into a tall glass. Add the seltzer and stir just until blended. Add ice and serve.

CHAPTER EIGHT

Shrubs, & Vinegar

Switchels & Other Drinks

Shrubs and switchels are soft drinks spiked with vinegar. They were developed as temperance beverages in the eighteenth and nineteenth centuries, with vinegar taking the place of alcohol, which is fitting given that vinegar and alcohol production are interdependent.

Vinegar (from the French for wine, *vin*, and sour, *aigre*) results when oxygen gets into a vat of fermenting alcohol. As a result, in alcohol production it is vital to make sure no air gets into the system. When you let in oxygen, you are making vinegar, not wine.

Because fermenting fruit juice naturally turns sour and alcoholic, early peoples experienced wine and vinegar together, and had an appreciation for both. Babylonians made vinegar from date wine and beer as early as 4000 BCE. Ancient Romans drank *posca*, a mixture of vinegar and water, and seasoned their food with a sweet-and-sour condiment made from vinegar and honey.

For thousands of years vinegar was made simply by leaving wine and other alcoholic beverages out in the air to sour, a process that took weeks or months, depending on conditions, and had unpredictable results. Eventually the circumstances necessary for turning alcohol into vinegar were isolated, and by World War II, modern methods produced vinegars of consistent quality in a day or two.

Three things are necessary to make vinegar: alcohol, oxygen, and *Acetobacter* bacteria, a genus of bacteria that is among the few that can metabolize energy from alcohol. Because acetic acid bacteria require oxygen, they live on the surface of fermenting liquids, where they can form into thick mats of "mother," so called because the mother from one batch of vinegar is used to inoculate the next, and so on. The method for making kombucha (page 119) is similar.

Vinegar drinks are delicious, refreshing, and healthful. Like salt, sourness elevates our sense of taste, which is why tart beverages taste clean and fresh. In addition, the molecular structure of vinegars helps them transfer other flavor molecules into the nose, so an addition of vinegar elevates our perception of all the aromatics in a beverage. In recent years detoxifying health benefits have been attributed to vinegar drinks and consequently they have become trendy, appearing increasingly on the drink menus of high-end restaurants.

apricot raspberry shrub

The allure of both apricots and raspberries lies in a delicate balance between sweetness, tartness, and aroma. When fruit is liquefied, these qualities tend to get watered down. The sweet-and-sour flavor system of vinegar drinks powers up the game while keeping the players in balance. By definition and by their nature, fresh fruit vinegar drinks should be "fresh," so although this fruit mixture can be made ahead and refrigerated for up to a day, it is best prepared right before it is served.

APRICOT RASPBERRY PURÉE

- 1 cup fresh or frozen raspberries
- 1 cup apricot nectar
- ¼ cup agave syrup or simple syrup (page 15)
- ¼ cup raspberry or white wine vinegar

ENOUGH FOR 2 SERVINGS

Mash the berries in a medium bowl with the back of a fork. Mix in the apricot nectar a little bit at a time, until thoroughly incorporated. Pour the mixture into a strainer set over a small bowl. Gently lift and stir the mixture to help the liquid pass through, without forcing any solids through the strainer. Discard the solids. Stir the agave syrup and vinegar into the strained purée.

 TO MIX WITH SELTZER

- ¾ cup apricot raspberry purée
- ¾ cup seltzer

1 SERVING

Pour the purée into a tall glass. Add the seltzer and stir just enough to blend. Fill the glass with ice and serve.

honey shrub

The notion of drinking vinegar may seem odd, but think again. Sure, vinegar is sour, but it is also bright and fruity, secretly sweet, bracing and tangy. Like lemonade, sweetened vinegar drinks are some of the best thirst quenchers on a hot summer day. This one is made simply from honey, sherry vinegar, and sparkling water, and can be mixed up in a minute.

HONEY VINEGAR SYRUP

¼ cup honey

3 tablespoons sherry vinegar

ENOUGH FOR 2 SERVINGS

Combine the honey and vinegar in a small bowl, and stir with a whisk until combined.

 TO MIX WITH SELTZER

¼ cup honey vinegar syrup

1½ cups seltzer

1 SERVING

Pour the syrup into a tall glass. Add the seltzer and stir just enough to blend. Fill the glass with ice and serve.

 Mixology

Prepare the honey vinegar syrup as described above, then carbonate with seltzer.

mead-iation

Add 3 ounces (6 tablespoons) brandy to 1 serving Honey Shrub.

sangria shrub

Sangria is the only punch that never gets tired. Fresh, fruit-filled, a little sweet, a little tart, and ever so slightly buzzy — what could be wrong? This temperate vinegared version trades the buzz for an acceleration of flavor. The addition of vinegar punches up all the other ingredients.

SANGRIA SHRUB

1 orange

1 lime

4 teaspoons sugar

1⅓ cups unsweetened purple grape juice

¼ cup red wine vinegar

ENOUGH FOR 4 SERVINGS

Cut the orange and lime in half crosswise. Squeeze together the juice from half of each. Slice the tip from each remaining citrus half, and cut each half into four slices. Put a slice of orange and a slice of lime into each of four tall glasses. Add 1 teaspoon sugar to each glass, and muddle the fruit and sugar with the back of a spoon. Add ⅓ cup grape juice, about 2 tablespoons of the orange-lime juice, and 1 tablespoon vinegar to each glass. Stir to combine.

TO MIX WITH SELTZER

1 quart seltzer

4 SERVINGS

Add 1 cup seltzer to each glass, and stir just enough to blend. Fill the glasses with ice and serve.

Mixology

kiss-me-quick sangria

Follow the recipe for Sangria Shrub, substituting a fruity red wine, like Tempranillo, for the grape juice.

vanilla pear shrub

Pears can taste timid, which is why pear preparations are frequently goosed up with something sweet and something tart. Poached pears have wine; pear tarts, sugar and lemon. In this perfumed shrub, the secret ingredients are white wine vinegar and vanilla. Mashing the pear with vinegar and cooking it with sugar prevents it from browning, a problem with any pale low-acid fruit.

PEAR PURÉE

1 large ripe Bartlett or Anjou pear, coarsely chopped

¼ cup white wine vinegar

½ cup sugar

1 teaspoon vanilla extract

ENOUGH FOR 2 SERVINGS

Mash the pear and vinegar into a purée in a medium saucepan using a vegetable masher. Cook over medium-low heat, gradually stirring in the sugar, until the mixture is very moist and bubbling and all of the sugar has dissolved. Stir in the vanilla. Pour the mixture into a strainer set over a small bowl to remove the solid pieces. Gently lift and stir the mixture to help the liquid pass through, without forcing any solids through the strainer. Discard the solids. Let the strained liquid cool.

 TO MIX WITH SELTZER

¼ cup pear purée

1½ cups seltzer

1 SERVING

Combine the purée and seltzer in a tall glass and stir just enough to blend. Fill the glass with ice and serve.

 Mixology

Prepare the pear purée as described above.

pear flower

Follow the instructions for mixing the pear purée with seltzer, adding 3 ounces (6 tablespoons) vodka to the pear mixture before adding the soda.

orchard orchid

Follow the instructions for mixing the pear purée with seltzer, adding 3 ounces (6 tablespoons) golden rum to the pear mixture before adding the soda.

root beery sherry vinegar shrub

Like balsamic vinegar, good-quality sherry vinegar is aged for years in wooden barrels. Made from young sherry wine with very low concentrations of sugar, it develops high concentrations of savory amino acids from the long contact with wood, which gives it a powerful affinity to the savory, tangy qualities in root beer.

ROOT BEER VINEGAR SYRUP

- ¼ cup Rooty Toot Root Beer syrup (page 88) or purchased root beer syrup (see Resources)
- 3 tablespoons sherry vinegar, preferably Spanish solera

ENOUGH FOR 2 SERVINGS

Combine the syrup and vinegar in a small bowl and stir with a whisk until blended.

 TO MIX WITH SELTZER

- ¼ cup root beer vinegar syrup
- 1½ cups seltzer

1 SERVING

Combine the syrup and seltzer in a tall glass, and stir just enough to blend. Fill the glass with ice and serve.

spiced balsamic fig sparkler

While wine vinegar goes from wine to vinegar in about 24 hours, a good grade of balsamic vinegar concentrates and ages for a minimum of 12 years, and the best balsamics can be scores of years old. The nice thing about this shrub is that you don't need the best-quality balsamic vinegar to make a fabulous beverage. The intense syrupy sweetness of dried figs is the perfect foil for the delicious pungency of aged balsamic. I add some spice to the blend by steeping chai tea bags in the syrup.

FIG PURÉE

- 6 ripe Turkish or Calimyrna figs, coarsely chopped
- 5 tablespoons moderately aged balsamic vinegar

  Contents of 2 chai tea bags
- ⅔ cup sugar

  Pinch of sea salt

ENOUGH FOR 4 SERVINGS

Combine the figs and and vinegar in a medium saucepan, and mash into a purée using a vegetable masher. Add the chai tea leaves. Cook over medium-low heat, gradually stirring in the sugar, until the mixture is very moist and bubbling and all of the sugar has dissolved. Stir in the salt.

Pour the mixture into a strainer set over a small bowl to remove the solid pieces. Gently lift and stir the mixture to help the liquid pass through, without forcing any solids through the strainer. Discard the solids, and let the strained liquid cool.

 ## TO MIX WITH SELTZER

- ¼ cup fig purée
- ¾ cup seltzer

1 SERVING

Combine the purée and seltzer in a tall glass, and stir just enough to blend. Fill the glass with ice and serve.

sweet-and-sour apple cider

This novel beverage leverages the browned, concentrated sweetness of apple cider with the tart spark of a fresh green apple. Its expansiveness is underscored by a hefty hit of apple cider vinegar and a little sugar for sweetness. Because apple cider vinegar is a fermented product, it develops some of the same malolactic savoriness of hard apple cider, adding yet another dimension of apple to the glass.

APPLE VINEGAR SYRUP

- 1 large tart apple, such as Granny Smith, coarsely shredded
- ¼ cup apple cider
- ⅓ cup apple cider vinegar
- ½ cup sugar

ENOUGH FOR 2 SERVINGS

Combine the shredded apple and apple cider in a medium saucepan. Bring to a boil over medium heat, add the vinegar, and return to a boil. Cook over medium-low heat, gradually stirring in the sugar, until the mixture is bubbling and all of the sugar has dissolved.

Pour the mixture into a strainer set over a small bowl to remove the solid pieces. Gently lift and stir the mixture to help the liquid pass through, without forcing any solids through the strainer. Discard the solids, and let the strained liquid cool.

 TO MIX WITH SELTZER

- ¼ cup apple vinegar syrup
- 1½ cups seltzer

1 SERVING

Combine the syrup and seltzer in a tall glass, and stir just enough to blend. Fill the glass with ice and serve.

malted molasses switchel

Etymologists surmise that the word switchel *derives from the same root that gave us* swizzle stick, *connecting this temperance beverage to the realm of alcoholic potables. The original switchels were alcoholic, sweet-and-sour mixtures of rum, molasses, vinegar, and water. This one is a nonalcoholic version of the original. It is extremely easy to assemble.*

MALTED MOLASSES

¼ cup mild (Barbados) molasses

3 tablespoons malt vinegar

ENOUGH FOR 2 SERVINGS

Combine the molasses and vinegar in a small bowl, and stir with a whisk until blended.

 TO MIX WITH SELTZER

¼ cup malted molasses

1½ cups seltzer

1 SERVING

Combine the molasses and seltzer in a tall glass, and stir just until blended. Fill the glass with ice and serve.

 Mixology

Prepare the malted molasses as described above.

colonial switchel

Follow the instructions for mixing the malted molasses with seltzer, adding 3 ounces (6 tablespoons) dark rum to the malted molasses before adding the soda.

lemon honey switchel

This pale, mild rendition of switchel is lighter and fruitier that the traditional molasses version. Its combination of lemon and honey gives it a good hit of vitamin C and makes it a soothing drink during cold season.

LEMON HONEY SYRUP

¼ cup honey

3 tablespoons freshly squeezed lemon juice

ENOUGH FOR 2 SERVINGS

Combine the honey and lemon juice in a small bowl, and stir with a whisk until blended.

 ## TO MIX WITH SELTZER

¼ cup lemon honey syrup

1½ cups seltzer

1 SERVING

Combine the syrup and seltzer in a tall glass, and stir just enough to blend. Fill the glass with ice and serve.

black vinegar water

Dark vinegars are aged for a long time, and that aging produces complex, rich, savory flavors. It also concentrates nutrients, which gives dark vinegars like balsamic and Chinese black vinegar widespread anecdotal reputations for healthfulness. Balsamic vinegar starts out as fresh grape juice, rather than wine, so by the time it is fully fermented (at least 12 years) it still retains a good deal of residual sugar, which is why it is much sweeter and more syrupy than wine vinegar.

This recipe does not begin with a flavor base. Follow the complete mixing instructions to make one serving of Black Vinegar Water.

 TO MIX WITH SELTZER

2 tablespoons aged
     balsamic vinegar
1½ cups seltzer

1 SERVING

Pour the vinegar into a tall glass. Add the seltzer and stir just enough to blend. Fill the glass with ice and serve.

 Mixology

Prepare the Black Vinegar Water as described above.

balsamic sour

Mix 2 ounces (¼ cup) vodka with 8 ounces (1 cup) Black Vinegar Water in a tall glass with a few ice cubes.

pomegranate vinegar ade

Pomegranate juice has a natural balance of sweetness and tartness that lends itself effortlessly to the flavor profile of vinegar drinks. All you really have to do is augment it with a little vinegar. You'll get the cleanest flavor using pomegranate vinegar, but it can be pricey and slightly difficult to find, and red wine vinegar is an adequate substitute.

POMEGRANATE VINEGAR SYRUP

½ cup unsweetened pomegranate juice, fresh (page 61) or bottled

2 tablespoons agave syrup or simple syrup (page 15)

2 tablespoons pomegranate or red wine vinegar

ENOUGH FOR 2 SERVINGS

Combine the pomegranate juice, syrup, and vinegar in a small bowl, and stir with a whisk until blended.

 TO MIX WITH SELTZER

Generous ⅓ cup pomegranate vinegar syrup

1½ cups seltzer

1 SERVING

Combine the syrup and seltzer in a tall glass, and stir just enough to blend. Fill the glass with ice and serve.

green apple winegar

This pale green, clean-tasting cocktail is the very essence of fresh apple. The addition of wine modulates the acidity of the vinegar, making the drink less acidic but no less refreshing. Any white wine will do. Sweeter wines like gewürztraminer will give the finished drink a fuller flavor, but one that travels away from green apple. If you wish to eliminate the wine, you can replace it with water. But note that the wine is cooked in this recipe, so that it retains only about half its alcohol.

GREEN APPLE SYRUP

1 large tart green apple, such as Granny Smith, coarsely shredded

¼ cup white wine

⅓ cup apple cider vinegar

½ cup sugar

Pinch of sea salt

ENOUGH FOR 2 SERVINGS

Combine the shredded apple and wine in a medium saucepan. Bring to a boil over medium heat, add the vinegar, and return to a boil. Cook over medium-low heat, gradually stirring in the sugar, until the mixture is bubbling and all of the sugar has dissolved. Stir in the salt.

Pour the mixture into a strainer set over a small bowl to remove the solid pieces. Gently lift and stir the mixture to help the liquid pass through, without forcing any solids through the strainer. Discard the solids, and let the strained liquid cool.

 ## TO MIX WITH SELTZER

¼ cup green apple syrup

1½ cups seltzer

1 SERVING

Combine the syrup and seltzer in a tall glass, and stir just enough to blend. Fill the glass with ice and serve.

red grape winegar

Though there is wine in this drink, and it contains many of the elements of wine — grapes, fermentation, acid, and sugar — I encourage you to try not to think of wine when you experience it, for fear that you will be disappointed. The clean, spare, sparkling tartaric sweetness of this beverage is completely different from the aromatic roundness you experience with a glass of red wine. It is ultimately refreshing and a great summer pick-me-up, but it isn't cabernet.

GRAPE WINEGAR

- 1 pint red or black seedless grapes
- ¼ cup fruity red wine, such as cabernet or shiraz
- ¼ cup red wine vinegar
- ¼ cup sugar

ENOUGH FOR 2 SERVINGS

Crush the grapes in a medium saucepan with the back of a fork. Add the wine and bring to a boil over medium heat. Add the vinegar and return to a boil. Cook over medium-low heat, gradually stirring in the sugar, until the mixture is bubbling and all of the sugar has dissolved.

Pour the mixture into a strainer set over a small bowl to remove the solid pieces. Gently lift and stir the mixture to help the liquid pass through, without forcing any solids through the strainer. Discard the solids, and let the strained liquid cool.

 TO MIX WITH SELTZER

- ¼ cup grape winegar
- 1½ cups seltzer

1 SERVING

Combine the winegar and seltzer in a tall glass, and stir just enough to combine. Fill the glass with ice and serve.

berry vinegar cordial

Cordials are vinegar drinks that are more highly sweetened, in the same way the liqueurs are sweeter versions of liquors. This one is very colorful and simple. You can make it with any kind of berry, or even grapes.

CORDIAL SYRUP

- 1 pint strawberries, raspberries, blueberries, or a combination, hulled if necessary
- ½ cup sugar
- ¼ cup red wine vinegar

ENOUGH FOR 2 SERVINGS

Crush the berries in a medium saucepan with the back of a fork. Add the sugar and vinegar and cook over medium heat, stirring frequently, until the mixture is bubbling and all the sugar has dissolved.

Pour the mixture into a strainer set over a small bowl to remove the solid pieces. Gently lift and stir the mixture to help the liquid pass through, without forcing any solids through the strainer. Discard the solids, and let the strained liquid cool.

 TO MIX WITH SELTZER

- ¼ cup cordial syrup
- 1½ cups seltzer

1 SERVING

Combine the syrup and seltzer in a tall glass, and stir just enough to combine. Fill the glass with ice and serve.

citrus rice vinegar cordial

Rice vinegar and other Asian grain vinegars are made by breaking down the starch in the grains through the addition of a mold culture, which gives these vinegars a sweet-savory quality that is quite distinctive. Because the grain mash is not usually fermented before it is made into vinegar, rice vinegars tend to retain a good deal of sugar and therefore taste less acidic and sweeter than fruit-based vinegars, even though their acidity level can be quite high. The sweet-tart balance is not dissimilar to the acid-sugar ratio in citrus fruit — hence the pairing in this concoction.

CITRUS VINEGAR SYRUP

- 1 cup orange juice
- ½ cup simple syrup (page 15)
- 3 tablespoons lime juice or lemon juice
- 2 tablespoons unflavored rice vinegar

ENOUGH FOR 2 SERVINGS

Combine the orange juice, simple syrup, lime juice, and vinegar in a small bowl, stirring to blend.

 TO MIX WITH SELTZER

- ¾ cup citrus vinegar syrup
- 1 cup seltzer

1 SERVING

Combine the syrup and seltzer in a tall glass, and stir just enough to combine. Fill the glass with ice and serve.

watermelon mint cordial

Watermelon in its solid state is so loaded with water and sugar that it is little more than a beverage waiting to be released from captivity. This tangy, refreshing drink is the fulfillment of that promise. The addition of a little vinegar does much to expand the aroma of the watermelon, which is barely perceptible when you're eating the fruit. Mint and watermelon are natural BFFs. If you were unaware of that relationship before tasting this recipe, afterward you will try never to serve a slice of watermelon without a mint sprig somewhere nearby.

WATERMELON PURÉE

Big chunk of watermelon, about 1 pound, rind removed, cut into chunks

¼ cup agave syrup or simple syrup (page 15)

¼ cup finely chopped fresh mint leaves

2 tablespoons white wine vinegar

ENOUGH FOR 4 SERVINGS

Combine the watermelon, syrup, mint, and vinegar in a blender or food processor, and purée until smooth (though there still may be watermelon seeds and shards of mint floating around).

Pour the mixture into a strainer set over a small bowl to remove the solid pieces. Gently lift and stir the mixture to help the liquid pass through, without forcing any solids through the strainer.

TO MIX WITH SELTZER

¾ cup watermelon purée
¾ cup seltzer
Mint sprigs (optional)

1 SERVING

Combine the purée and seltzer in a tall glass, and stir just enough to combine. Fill the glass with ice and serve, garnished with mint sprigs, if using.

Recipes for Soda Food

CHAPTER NINE

Savory

Mains
Sides

*T*he trick to cooking savory food with sweet liquids, like sodas, is to add enough savory flavors that the sweetness becomes a backup taste rather than a dominant perception. Sweetness is an essential element in savory cooking. All wholesome foods are somewhat sweet. Think about it. Carrots and onions are loaded with sugar. Fresh meat has a sweet taste; even hot sauce contains a good amount of sugar. In fact, the more savory a food is (especially if it has a lot of heat), the sweeter it needs to be for balance.

Most cuisines use sugar as a seasoning. Think teriyaki, sweet and sour, wine sauce, tomato sauce, Thai peanut sauce, caramelized onions, barbecue, pickles, chutneys, ketchup, sweet potatoes, sauerkraut, baked beans . . . I could go on for a few pages. The challenge with using soda for sweetness is that some sodas are very sweet, so you can use only a small amount.

Soda pop cuisine hit its heyday after World War II, when soda manufacturers found a hidden market for their products in the kitchen. They began creating recipes and issuing cooking pamphlets, and America's sweet tooth bit. Recipes for meatloaf, chili con carne, barbecue, goulash, and sweet-and-sour anything joined the cookbooks of busy homemakers. Particularly in the South (where the largest soft drink companies originated), food cooked with pop became standard fare.

lemonade shrimp cocktail

The flavor of sparkling lemonades comes not only from lemon juice but also, more importantly, from lemon zest, which is filled with flavorful oils that give a rich lemon-drop-type flavor. In this recipe, the lemonade is turned into a pungent sweet-tart vinaigrette for sautéed shrimp. Its flavor is expanded and amended with lemon juice, extra-virgin olive oil, lots of garlic, and a hit of cayenne. Serve these shrimp as a quick hors d'oeuvre or for a special lunch.

4 tablespoons extra-virgin olive oil

2 garlic cloves, thinly sliced

24 jumbo shrimp, shelled and deveined

½ cup Sparkling Lemongrass Lemonade (page 140) or Sparkling Lemon Drop (page 168) or purchased sparkling lemonade

2 tablespoons lemon juice

Pinch of cayenne

Finely ground sea salt

2 scallions, thinly sliced

4 SERVINGS

1. Heat 2 tablespoons of the oil in a large skillet over medium-high heat. Add the garlic and sauté until aromatic, about 30 seconds. Add the shrimp and sauté just until the shrimp color from pale pink to coral (depending on the variety of shrimp), about 1 minute. Add the lemonade and simmer until the shrimp are firm, about 2 minutes. Remove the shrimp with a slotted spoon to a serving bowl.

2. Simmer the liquid in the pan until it is reduced by half, a little more than ¼ cup. Stir in the lemon juice, cayenne, salt to taste, and the remaining 2 tablespoons oil, and return to a boil. Stir in the scallions, then pour the sauce over the shrimp. Let cool. Serve warm or at room temperature with toothpicks.

sweet heat mahogany chicken wings

The flavor palate of Southeast Asia — sweet, sour, salty, and hot — is captured in this one-pot chicken wing orgy. The streamlined method takes about half an hour and results in the gooiest, most pungent, sticky-fingered chicken wings you can imagine. They're the perfect food for tailgating, afternoons watching ballgames, or just hanging out.

1 tablespoon canola oil

2 garlic cloves, minced

1 dried hot chile pepper

1 tablespoon freshly grated gingerroot

1 cup root beer, any type, purchased or homemade

⅓ cup soy sauce

2 pounds chicken wings, sectioned, third joint discarded

1 tablespoon dark sesame oil

6 SERVINGS

1. Heat the oil in a large skillet over medium-high heat. Add the garlic, chile pepper, and ginger, and sauté until fragrant, about 30 seconds. Add the root beer and soy sauce. Bring to a boil, add the wings, cover, and let simmer for 5 minutes.

2. Uncover the skillet and cook at a slow simmer until the liquid reduces enough to glaze the wings, about 20 minutes. Toss gently every few minutes near the end of cooking to prevent scorching, and stir in the sesame oil. Serve hot.

cola chili

Forget about the image of cola as the world's favorite sweet-tooth refreshment and think about what it really is. Cola started out as tonic, a combination of citrus peel and spices, not unlike a formula for bitters. That savory richness underscores the hot peppers, browned beef, caramelized onions, oregano, and cumin that are at the heart of a great chili. When viewed in that light, cola is no longer a quirky addition to this spicy stew, but a neglected aspect of its destiny.

3 tablespoons vegetable oil

3 pounds beef stew meat, cut into bite-size pieces

⅓ cup plus 1 tablespoon flour

1 cup chopped onion

1 green or red bell pepper, stemmed, seeded, and chopped

2 canned or fresh jalapeño peppers, finely chopped

2 garlic cloves, minced

3 tablespoons chili powder

1 tablespoon ground cumin

2 teaspoons dried oregano

1½ cups beef broth

12 ounces (1½ cups) Natural Cola (page 104) or purchased cola

2 tablespoons tomato paste

1 teaspoon apple cider vinegar

Salt and freshly ground black pepper

1 (19-ounce) can pinto beans, drained and rinsed (optional)

¼ cup chopped fresh cilantro

4 TO 6 SERVINGS

1. Heat 2 tablespoons of the oil in a wide, deep pot (such as a Dutch oven) over medium-high heat. Dredge the beef in the ⅓ cup flour. Add the beef to the pot, and cook until it is browned, turning as necessary. Do not crowd the pan; if needed, brown the beef in batches. Remove the beef to a plate and set aside.

2. Add the remaining 1 tablespoon oil to the pan. Add the onion and bell pepper and sauté over medium heat until the vegetables begin to soften, about 4 minutes. Add the jalapeño pepper, garlic, chili powder, cumin, oregano, and the 1 tablespoon flour, and sauté 1 minute.

3. Stir in the beef broth, cola, tomato paste, and cider vinegar, and heat to simmer, stirring often. Stir in the browned beef, cover the pot, reduce the heat, and let simmer until the meat is fork-tender, about 2 hours. Season with salt and black pepper to taste. Add the beans (if using) and the cilantro; heat through and serve.

baked root beer ham

The intense muscularity and salinity of salt-cured ham is mollified by a lacquer of sweet glaze, and this one made from root beer is happy to accommodate. The tangy, woody, herbal flavors of root beer, particularly sarsaparilla, mesh well with the salty, savory taste of ham. Sweet ham glaze, like this one, scorches easily, partly because it sits up on the surface of the meat, and partly because its sugar content makes it prone to burning. For those reasons glazes are added only after a ham is mostly cooked. In this recipe, because the oven is set at a moderate temperature and the ham is not too big, the glaze is given 20 minutes to set and develop a light crust. I love a little bit of char, but if you don't, remove the glazed ham after 15 minutes.

1 boneless smoked, salt-cured ham, about 2 pounds

1 tablespoon canola oil

4 cups root beer, any type, purchased or homemade

⅓ cup apple cider vinegar

1 tablespoon ground coriander

1 teaspoon ground allspice

1 teaspoon ground cinnamon

1 teaspoon coarsely ground black pepper

1 teaspoon coarse salt

¼ cup spicy brown mustard

6 TO 8 SERVINGS

1. Preheat the oven to 375°F.

2. Set the ham on a baking rack in a roasting pan and rub with the oil. Bake for 40 minutes.

3. While the ham is baking, combine the root beer, vinegar, coriander, allspice, cinnamon, pepper, and salt in a saucepan. Bring to a boil, then reduce the heat and let simmer until the mixture is reduced to one third its original volume, about 1⅓ cups. Stir in the mustard.

4. After the ham has baked for 40 minutes, remove it from the oven. Brush half of the root beer glaze over the ham, then return it to the oven and bake 20 minutes longer, until the ham is brown and shiny.

5. Slice to serve, and drizzle with the remaining root beer glaze.

baked sweet potatoes
with root beer rum butter

Sweetness is relative. Root beer is sweet, but it is also tangy and acrid, with woodsy aromas and hints of allspice and pine. Sweet potatoes are sugary too, but their sweetness is modified by plush, creamy starch and the scent of earth nestling just beneath the skin. The two ingredients have a lot in common and in this recipe they join forces, generating a love fest for the mouth. If you are a fan of crusty brown sugar on your sweet potatoes, get ready to taste the X-rated version of an old favorite.

4 sweet potatoes (about 3 pounds total), scrubbed and pricked several times each with a fork

1 tablespoon canola oil

1 cup root beer, any type, purchased or homemade

2 tablespoons dark rum

½ teaspoon ground cinnamon

½ teaspoon kosher salt

3 tablespoons unsalted butter

1 tablespoon finely grated lime zest

4 SERVINGS

1. Preheat the oven to 425°F.

2. Coat the sweet potatoes with the oil. Bake about 45 minutes, until tender.

3. Meanwhile, bring the root beer and rum to a boil in a small saucepan over high heat. Boil until reduced to about ⅓ cup, 10 to 15 minutes. Stir in the cinnamon and salt. Remove from the heat and add the butter, stirring until melted.

4. Remove the sweet potatoes from the oven and let cool a few minutes. Cut each sweet potato in half lengthwise, and mash the flesh of each half with a fork. Drizzle on the root beer rum butter, and scatter the lime zest on top.

pork shoulder
braised with ginger ale

Pork shoulder is a tough, fatty, flavorful cut that can be a leathery piece of gristle if cooked too harshly or a pudgy butterball of succulent porkiness if given time and plenty of TLC. This recipe is heavy on time (it takes about 4 hours), but not on work. Ginger ale helps spice the basting liquid for the meat. I usually serve pork shoulder like a pot roast, sliced in a pool of its cooking juices, but it also makes great pulled pork served on a bun. It's your choice.

2 tablespoons flour

1 tablespoon ground cardamom

1 tablespoon ground ginger

1 tablespoon dried thyme leaves

2 teaspoons coarse salt

1 teaspoon coarsely ground black pepper

Pinch of ground allspice

1 boneless pork shoulder, about 3 pounds

1 tablespoon canola oil

1 onion, coarsely chopped

1 tablespoon minced garlic

1 tablespoon minced gingerroot

2 cups chicken or beef broth

12 ounces (1½ cups) Ginger Ginger Ale (page 108) or purchased ginger ale

Finely grated zest and juice of 1 lime

2 tablespoons finely chopped fresh cilantro

8 SERVINGS

---

1. Combine the flour, cardamom, ginger, thyme, salt, pepper, and allspice, and stir to blend. Rub the blend all over the pork and let sit for 30 minutes.

---

2. Preheat the oven to 325°F.

---

3. Put a braiser or a large, deep, ovenproof skillet over medium-high heat. When the pan is hot, add the oil. Let warm for 30 seconds, then add the pork, and brown the pork on all sides in the hot oil. Transfer to a platter and set aside.

4. Add the onion to the fat in the pan and sauté until it begins to soften, stirring often, about 4 minutes. Add the garlic and ginger and sauté for 30 seconds longer. Add the broth and ginger ale and bring to a boil. Return the pork to the pan and cover. Set the pan in the oven and cook for about 3 hours, until the pork can be easily pierced with a fork, basting the roast with the pan juices every 30 to 45 minutes.

5. Remove the pork to a carving board. If the braising liquid in the pan is thick, add a little water; if it is thin, bring it to a simmer over medium-high heat and cook until it thickens to the consistency of fresh heavy cream.

6. Stir the lime zest, lime juice, and cilantro into the braising liquid. Slice the pork and serve on a platter. Spoon enough of the braising liquid over the top to moisten the pork thoroughly. Serve the remaining liquid at the table as a sauce.

cola can grilled chicken

The sight of a naked chicken perched on a grill with a beer can in its butt is well known to anyone who has used a grill in the last decade. The sight is funny, but the cooking method is nothing but smart. As the chicken cooks, the beer steams, keeping the interior meat moist and the skin crisp. In this recipe all I've done is replace the can of beer with a can of cola and kick up the flavor profile with a handful of seasoning; the resulting cooking liquid, tangy sweet and inundated with spices and chicken drippings, makes a tasty jus to drizzle over the chicken at the table.

1 tablespoon coarsely ground black pepper

1½ teaspoons ground allspice

1½ teaspoons ground ginger

1½ teaspoons grated nutmeg

1½ teaspoons coarse salt

1 chicken (about 4 pounds), washed and patted dry

1 tablespoon canola oil

1 (10- or 12-ounce) can cola

4 SERVINGS

1. Light a grill for indirect medium heat. If you're using a two-burner gas grill, set one side to medium and leave the other side off. If you're using a gas grill with three or more burners, set the outside burners to medium and turn the middle burner(s) off. If you're using a charcoal grill, make a medium-thick bed of coals, banking half on one side of the grill and half on the other, leaving the center section empty. Whatever your setup, if your grill has a thermostat in the hood it should read 325°F.

2. Mix together the pepper, allspice, ginger, nutmeg, and salt. Rub the chicken inside and out with 2 tablespoons of the spice mixture, and rub the outside of the chicken with 2 teaspoons of the oil.

3. Open the can of cola, and pour off ¼ cup (toss it if you don't want to drink it). Stir the remaining spice mixture into the can. Coat the outside of the can with the remaining 1 teaspoon oil, and put the can on an oven-proof plate or sturdy rimmed sheet pan. Lower the chicken onto the can, inserting the can into the cavity of the bird. Position the chicken so that the front legs and the can form a tripod, holding the chicken upright.

4. Set the chicken and can on the grill away from the direct heat, cover the grill, and cook about 1 hour and 10 minutes, until an instant-read thermometer inserted into the inside of a thigh registers about 165°F.

5. Transfer the chicken, still on the can, to a plate or tray. Holding the can with tongs and gripping the chicken with a towel, twist and lift the chicken off the can. You might need an extra set of hands to help you. Transfer to the chicken to a carving board. Let rest for 8 to 10 minutes, then carve and serve, drizzled with some cola au jus.

fruity meatballs

Sweet and sour is the epitome of incompatibility. The two flavors don't combine — they fight, and in the ruckus gustatory sparks start to fly. This very easy recipe for sweet-and-sour meatballs is a case in point. Both sugar and acid are built into the ingredients, so there is no need for any added sugar or vinegar.

¼ cup fresh breadcrumbs

2¼ cups fruit-based cola, such Medjool Cola (page 106) or Fruity Root Beer (page 70) or Dr Pepper

1½ pounds meatloaf/meatball mix (50 percent ground beef, 25 percent ground veal, 25 percent ground pork)

¾ teaspoon salt

½ teaspoon freshly ground black pepper

1 tablespoon canola oil

1 teaspoon chopped garlic

1⅓ cups ketchup

2 tablespoons finely chopped parsley (optional)

4 SERVINGS AS AN ENTRÉE, or 8 as an appetizer

1. Combine the breadcrumbs with just enough cola to moisten them, about 3 tablespoons. Mix with your hands until the breadcrumbs are mushy.

2. Add the ground meat, salt, and ¼ teaspoon of the pepper, and mix with your hands until everything is blended. Form into 1-inch meatballs. You will have about three dozen.

3. Heat the oil in a large skillet over medium-high heat. Add the meatballs and brown on all sides. Add the garlic and cook, stirring, until the garlic is aromatic, about 10 seconds. Add the remaining cola (there should be a little more than 2 cups), the ketchup, and the remaining ¼ teaspoon pepper. Stir until well mixed, cover, and simmer over medium-low heat until the meatballs are cooked through and the sauce is lightly thickened, about 30 minutes. Stir in the parsley (if using). Serve with bread to sop up the sauce, with toothpicks as an appetizer, or spooned into split hoagie rolls as a sandwich.

pork chops with chipotle cherry cola gravy

Chile peppers and fruit seem like odd flavor partners, but I've found that chipotle peppers (smoked jalapeños) have a distinct affinity to tart cherries. There is something about the scent of smoke and the subtle afterburn of chipotle that finds it soulmate in the fragrant savory-sweet-tart fruitiness of cherry cola and sour cherry preserves. Titillating flavors and a mahogany sheen make this dish seem gourmet, but the preparation is almost effortless.

4 (½-inch-thick) pork chops, bone-in

1 teaspoon Italian seasoning

1 tablespoon extra-virgin olive oil

¾ cup Very Cherry Cola (page 72) or purchased cherry cola

¾ cup reduced-sodium chicken broth (see note)

2 tablespoon sour cherry preserves

1 canned chipotle pepper, finely chopped, or 1 teaspoon chipotle hot sauce

4 SERVINGS

Note: Because the broth is reduced to make a sauce, it is important to use a reduced-sodium broth. Otherwise the amount of salt in the broth will become overpowering when it is concentrated through reduction.

1. Season the pork chops with the Italian seasoning on both sides. Heat the oil in a large skillet over medium-high heat. Brown the pork chops on both sides, then remove to a plate. Pour off the excess fat from the pan.

2. Add the cola and broth to the pan. Bring to a boil and let boil until the liquid is reduced to about half of its original volume (about ¾ cup). Reduce the heat to a simmer and return the pork chops to the pan. Simmer, turning once or twice, until they feel resilient to the touch, about 5 minutes. Transfer the chops to a platter.

3. Add the cherry preserves and chipotle to the pan. Bring to a boil over medium-high heat and let boil until the pan liquid thickens slightly. Pour over the pork.

ginger beer chicken curry

Ginger beer, the grown-up version of ginger ale, is usually so loaded with ginger that its spice radiates long after the first gulp is swallowed. It is that intensity that drives the flavors of this sweet-hot coconut curry over the top. If you prefer the flavor of white meat chicken over dark, you can substitute a similar weight of boneless chicken breast for thighs, but if you do, reduce the chicken's simmering time to 10 minutes. But even with the reduction in cooking time, chicken breast will tend to be dry in this kind of preparation.

8 boneless, skinless chicken thighs

Salt and freshly ground black pepper

1 tablespoon canola oil

1 tablespoon brown mustard seed

3 garlic cloves, minced

1 tablespoon curry powder

1 cup diced tomato, fresh or canned and drained

1 cup Szechuan Ginger Beer (page 109) or purchased ginger beer

¼ cup coconut milk

Finely grated zest and juice of 1 lime

4 SERVINGS

1. Season the chicken with salt and pepper. Heat the oil in a large skillet over medium-high heat. Add the chicken, brown on all sides, and then remove to a plate.

2. Add the mustard seed and garlic to the pan and sauté until the seeds pop, about 15 seconds. Add the curry powder, tomato, and ginger beer, and bring to a simmer. Return the chicken to the pan along with any juices that have collected around it. Cover and let simmer until the chicken is fork-tender, about 15 minutes.

3. Remove the cover from the pan. Transfer the chicken to a serving platter. If the juices are thin, boil the mixture until it is reduced enough to lightly coat a spoon. Stir in the coconut milk, lime zest, and lime juice. Pour over the chicken.

root beer baked beans

The natural tang of root beer meshes effortlessly with the tangy sweetness of a vat of baked beans. This traditional method for oven-baked beans is flavored with onions, bacon, mustard, jalapeños, and a little liquid smoke, if you are so inclined.

2   slices bacon

1   medium onion, finely chopped

1   jalapeño pepper, stemmed, seeded, and finely chopped

2   (16-ounce) cans small white beans, drained and rinsed

¾   cup Rooty Toot Root Beer (page 88) or purchased root beer

½   cup barbecue sauce

1   tablespoon spicy brown mustard

1   teaspoon liquid smoke (optional)

4 TO 6 SERVINGS

1. Preheat the oven to 375°F.

2. Cook the bacon in a medium skillet over medium heat until crisp. Remove the bacon from the pan, drain on pepper towels, and crumble.

3. Pour off all but 2 teaspoons of the fat from the skillet. Add the onion and jalapeño and sauté until tender, about 4 minutes.

4. Combine the crumbled bacon, sautéed onion and pepper, beans, root beer, barbecue sauce, mustard, and liquid smoke (if using) in a 1-quart casserole, and stir to blend. Bake about 1 hour, until the sauce has thickened.

sarsaparilla sauerbraten

Sauerbraten can take weeks to pickle and cure. In this recipe I start with an already pickled corned beef to streamline the process. The main difference between sauerbraten and corned beef is the cut of beef (round for sauerbraten, brisket for corned beef) and the curing agent (sauerbraten is pickled with acid, while corned beef is cured in a salt brine). To my palate, the change of cut makes the meat more succulent, but the lack of acid is something that has to be rectified. I do this by simmering the corned beef very slowly in the oven with cider vinegar and sarsaparilla.

1 corned beef, about 4 pounds

1 onion, chopped

1 carrot, peeled and thinly sliced

1½ cups Not-Too-Sweet Sarsaparilla (page 92) or purchased sarsaparilla soda

½ cup cider vinegar

12 gingersnap cookies, crushed

⅓ cup golden raisins

6 SERVINGS

1. Preheat the oven to 325°F.

2. Set the corned beef with its pickling spices in a Dutch oven (or any roasting pan with a cover) just large enough to hold it snugly. Scatter the onion and carrot around the meat. Pour the soda and vinegar over everything, cover the pot, and bake in the oven about 4 hours, until fork-tender.

3. Remove the meat from the pan, and cover with foil to keep warm. Pour the liquid remaining in the pan through a fine-mesh strainer to remove the solids, and return the strained liquid to the pan. Bring to a boil over medium-high heat. Stir in the gingersnaps and let simmer until thickened, stirring often, about 10 minutes. If the sauce is a little lumpy, purée it in a blender or food processor. Then stir in the raisins.

4. Slice the meat and serve with the sauce.

cola meatloaf

A good meatloaf is hard to find. Duped by fears of fat and a reverence for beef, too many recipes ignore the simple truth that the sensual charm of any ground meat mixture is in the filler, not the meat. Once meat is ground, any moisture it previously possessed is gone. Baking it only manages to dry up what's left. To make a meatloaf succulent, you must replenish its moisture from the inside out by adding liquid along with a starch, to absorb the moisture and hold it in the loaf. In this recipe the liquid is cola, which adds a pleasant flavor of fruit and spice to the meat. The starch comes from crumbled fresh bread.

2 slices good-quality bread, crust removed, processed into fine crumbs

¾ cup Natural Cola (page 104) or any type of purchased or homemade cola

½ cup minced onion

¼ cup ketchup

3 tablespoons spicy brown mustard

2 tablespoons Worcestershire sauce

1 egg

1–2 teaspoons salt

½ teaspoon freshly ground black pepper

2½ pounds meatloaf mix (50 percent ground beef, 25 percent ground veal, 25 percent ground pork)

8–10 SERVINGS

1. Preheat the oven to 350°F.

2. Combine the bread crumbs and cola in a large bowl, stir to mix, and set aside until the bread absorbs all the liquid, about 5 minutes.

3. Stir the onion, ketchup, mustard, Worcestershire sauce, egg, salt, and pepper into the bread crumbs. Add the meat and blend with your hands until thoroughly mixed.

4. Form the meat into a mounded loaf on a rimmed sheet pan. Bake about 45 minutes, until browned and firm and a thermometer inserted into the center registers 155°F. Slice and serve.

ginger citrus baked ribs

Spare ribs are always tasty, but they can be tough and dry if they are not moisturized in some way. That moisture can be added by soaking the ribs in brine before cooking them or by simmering the ribs in liquid before browning them. This recipe takes the latter course. The ribs are simmered with a lot of citrus fruit and ginger beer until the meat is ready to fall from the bone. Unlike your typical ketchup-based barbecue-style sauce, the citrus sauce is bright and light with a pronounced ginger kick. After being baked, the ribs are finished under a hot broiler or over a charcoal fire for a few minutes.

1 lemon, cut in half crosswise

1 lime, cut in half crosswise

1 orange, cut in half crosswise

1 cup ketchup

1 teaspoon ground chipotle

1 teaspoon ground cumin

½ teaspoon ground oregano

2 racks baby back ribs, weighing about 1½ pounds each

1 onion, thinly sliced

2 garlic cloves, thinly sliced

3 cups Szechuan Ginger Beer (page 109) or purchased ginger beer

4 SERVINGS

1. Squeeze the juice from half of each lemon, lime, and orange into a small bowl. Add the ketchup, chipotle, cumin, and oregano, and mix well. Set aside ¾ cup of the sauce. Place the ribs in a roasting pan large enough to hold them in a single layer and brush them with the remaining sauce.

2. Cut the remaining citrus into thin slices and scatter them, along with the onion and garlic, over and around the ribs. Pour the ginger beer all around, cover tightly with foil, and bake for about 1½ hours, until very tender.

3. Preheat the broiler or grill. Remove the ribs from the oven and broil (on a broiling pan) or grill until browned, 8 to 10 minutes. While the ribs are finishing, combine ¼ cup of the juice from the roasting pan with the remaining reserved sauce. Serve the ribs with the sauce on the side.

caramelized onions
in sweet jus

Although caramelized garlic products abound, no one, as yet, has manufactured and marketed caramelized onions. One day a savvy produce packager will figure this out and reap the rewards, but until then we will have to make our own. By deglazing the roasting pan with root beer you increase the natural sweetness of the onions and augment their brownness. Caramelized onions can be served as a side dish with roasted meat or poultry or kept on hand to boost the flavors of soups and sauces anytime. They will keep in the refrigerator for about 2 weeks.

2 pounds large yellow onions (about 4)

2 tablespoons extra-virgin olive oil

½ teaspoon coarse salt

¼ teaspoon freshly ground black pepper

6 tablespoons root beer or cola, any type, purchased or home-made

3 tablespoons chopped flat-leaf parsley

6 SERVINGS AS A SIDE DISH

1. Preheat the oven to 400°F.

2. Cut the onions in half lengthwise. Cut off the pointed end of each onion half, and peel off the dry layers. Trim the root ends so that all the roots and dirt are gone but the core holding the onion layers together is still attached. Cut each onion half lengthwise into three wedges.

3. Toss the onions, oil, salt, and pepper on a large rimmed sheet pan and spread out in an even layer. Roast for about 30 minutes, tossing the onions halfway through to help them caramelize evenly, until they are browned on their edges.

4. Remove the pan from the oven and sprinkle the soda and parsley over the top of the onions. Toss to combine, scraping up any brown bits stuck to the bottom of the pan.

root beer barbecue sauce

The sweet, sour, tangy, spicy, smoky amalgamation is very close in complexity to the multidimensionality of good root beer, especially one that is homebrewed. This sauce is lip-smacking, finger-nibbling good. Use it in any way that you would use a tomato-based barbecue sauce. Fair warning: If you're using it on grilled food, add it only in the last few minutes of grilling. It scorches easily.

¼ cup root beer, any type, purchased or homemade

¼ cup tomato paste

3 tablespoons apple cider vinegar

2 tablespoons molasses

2 tablespoons spicy brown mustard

2 tablespoons Tabasco hot pepper sauce

1 teaspoon smoked salt

½ teaspoon freshly ground black pepper

1 CUP

Combine the root beer, tomato paste, vinegar, molasses, mustard, Tabasco, salt, and pepper in a small saucepan. Bring to a simmer over medium heat and let simmer until lightly thickened, about 5 minutes.

sweet-and-sour soda pop brisket

This rendition of a 1960s convenience recipe is invitingly simple and embarrassingly delicious. Nothing this good should take so little effort. The trick is in the cola or root beer. Both are complex formulas blending savory, sweet, and tart elements, and when they are combined with the juices percolating from braising beef, the result is as sweet and savory and nuanced as a recipe that has dozens of ingredients.

1 first-cut brisket, about 3 pounds

Salt and coarsely ground black pepper

2 tablespoons canola oil

2 onions, thinly sliced

12 ounces (1½ cups) cola or root beer, any type, purchased or homemade

1½ cups ketchup

⅓ cup apple cider vinegar

6 SERVINGS

1. Preheat the oven to 325°F.

2. Season the brisket generously with salt and pepper. Heat the oil over medium heat in a Dutch oven (or any roasting pan with a cover) large enough to hold the brisket snugly. Add the brisket and brown on both sides. Remove to a platter.

3. Add the onions to the pan and cook until translucent and tender, about 8 minutes. Add the soda, ketchup, and vinegar, and bring to a boil. Return the brisket to the pan and turn to coat in the hot sauce. Cover the pan tightly and set in the oven. Bake about 3 hours, until very tender.

4. Remove the brisket to a cutting board, let it rest for 30 minutes, then cut into slices.

5. Skim the fat from the cooking liquid. Add the brisket slices to the cooking liquid, and reheat before serving.

roast teriyaki ginger ale turkey breast

Teriyaki is a sweet, salty, tangy sauce used to flavor and glaze grilled meats, poultry, and seafood in Japan. Teri literally translates as "shine" or "luster," referring to the sheen that develops on the surface of grilled (yaki) items when they have been marinated or glazed with teriyaki sauce. Several of the key elements in this teriyaki sauce come from one ingredient: ginger ale, which adds sweetness, tartness, and ginger to the blend. It is mixed with soy sauce, hot pepper sauce, a little brown sugar, and spices to become both a brine and sauce for the roasted turkey breast.

1 cup ginger ale, any type, purchased or homemade

1 cup soy sauce

3 tablespoons light or dark brown sugar

2 teaspoons ground mustard

1 teaspoon hot pepper sauce

1 garlic clove, minced

1 turkey breast (bone-in), about 6 pounds

2 tablespoons peanut or canola oil

6 SERVINGS

1. Combine the ginger ale, soy sauce, brown sugar, mustard, hot pepper sauce, and garlic in a large ziplock plastic bag. Seal the bag and shake until the sugar dissolves. Open the bag, pour half the marinade into another container, cover, and set aside in the refrigerator. Seal the turkey breast in the bag, and refrigerate for at least 6 hours.

2. Preheat the oven to 350°F.

3. Remove the turkey from the marinade, discarding the used marinade. Pat dry and coat with the oil. Set the turkey bone-side down in a roasting pan and roast for about 1½ hours, until a thermometer inserted into a thickest part of the breast registers 165°F, basting with the reserved marinade every 15 minutes for the last hour.

4. Transfer the turkey to a cutting board and let rest for 15 minutes. Carve and serve.

dr pepper corned beef

Dr Pepper has always been pitched as a mystery beverage — not just a secret formula, but a soft drink that defies classification: not a fruit, not a cola, not a root beer, but "a different kind of drink with a unique taste all its own." The overall flavor is not unlike that of a cola with a strong fruit profile, one that is highly adaptable to a variety of recipes: Dr Pepper cakes, Dr Pepper sauces, and this sweet and tangy corned beef, simmered with Dr Pepper and served with mustard, sweetened with a reduction of the famous soda.

1 corned beef, about 4 pounds

1 onion, coarsely chopped

1 carrot, peeled and sliced

1 stalk celery, sliced

24 ounces (3 cups) Dr Pepper or Medjool Cola (page 106)

⅓ cup spicy brown mustard

6 TO 8 SERVINGS

1. Set the corned beef in a large heavy pot with a lid, such as a Dutch oven. Scatter the onion, carrot, and celery around the meat. Add 2 cups of the Dr Pepper and enough water to just cover the meat. Bring the mixture to a boil over high heat, then reduce the heat to a low simmer, cover, and let simmer until very tender, about 3 hours.

2. While the meat is cooking, bring the remaining 1 cup Dr Pepper to a boil in a saucepan, and boil until reduced to ¼ cup and slightly thickened. Let cool, then mix with the mustard.

3. When the corned beef is done, remove it to a cutting board, and let it rest for about 10 minutes before slicing. Cut in slices across the grain and serve with the mustard sauce.

orange coffee cola pork tenderloin

Pork tenderloin, a diminutive boneless cut of pork, is butter-knife tender but has a tendency to dry out during cooking. It benefits greatly from being soaked in brine, a mixture of salt, sweetener, and aromatic ingredients. The salt in the brine denatures some of the protein in the pork, encouraging the protein molecules to open up and latch on to moisture. This increases the moisture content of the meat by as much as 10 percent, and as it takes on moisture the pork also absorbs any flavorful elements in the brine. The flavors in this elegant pork are multilayered — orange and cola in the brine; coffee, cinnamon, and orange zest in the marinade; and bacon, beef broth, coffee, and orange in the sauce.

2 cups cola, any type, purchased or homemade

2 cups orange juice

2 tablespoons kosher salt

3 pork tenderloins, about 1 pound each, trimmed

3 tablespoons finely ground coffee beans

2 tablespoons dark brown sugar

1 tablespoon flour

1 teaspoon ground cinnamon

Finely grated zest of 1 orange

3 strips bacon

1 cup low-sodium beef broth

6 SERVINGS

1. Combine 1 cup of the cola, 1 cup of the orange juice, and the salt in a large ziplock plastic bag. Seal the bag and shake until the salt dissolves. Seal the tenderloins in the bag, and refrigerate for at least 3 hours.

2. Combine the coffee, sugar, flour, cinnamon, and orange zest. Remove the pork from the marinade and pat dry. Coat with the coffee-sugar mixture. Set aside.

3. Cook the bacon in a large skillet over medium heat until crisp. Remove the bacon and drain on paper towels.

4. Increase the heat under the skillet to medium-high. Add the pork and brown on all sides. Then reduce the heat to medium and check the temperature of the thickest tenderloin with an instant-read thermometer inserted into the thickest end. It should register 150°F. Cook a little longer if necessary. Remove the pork to a cutting board and let rest for 5 to 10 minutes.

5. While the meat is resting, add the beef broth and the remaining 1 cup cola and 1 cup orange juice to the pan. Bring to a boil over high heat, and boil until reduced by half and slightly thickened. Crumble the bacon and add to the sauce.

6. Cut the pork into thick slices and serve with the sauce.

ginger glazed carrots and red peppers

This Asian-style vegetable stir-fry can be an accompaniment for fish, white meats, or poultry. The ginger ale delivers a sweetness that underscores the natural sugars in the carrots and peppers, as well as ginger, which seasons the sauce.

2 tablespoons extra-virgin olive oil

1 pound carrots, peeled, trimmed, and thinly sliced

½ cup chopped onion

1 teaspoon minced gingerroot

⅓ cup ginger ale, any type, purchased or homemade

¼ cup diced red bell pepper

1 small garlic clove, minced

1 teaspoon freshly squeezed lemon juice

4 SERVINGS

Heat the oil in a large skillet or wok over medium-high heat. Add the carrots, onion, and ginger, and sauté for 1 minute. Add the ginger ale and red pepper, cover, and cook until the carrots are tender, about 4 minutes. Uncover and boil off the excess liquid. Toss in the garlic and lemon juice. Serve immediately.

soda-raised matzah balls

Dumplings, morsels of steamed or boiled dough, appear in every cooking tradition, and they all pose the same culinary challenge: how can they both be light and fluffy and still hold together against the rigors of boiling liquid? There are many methods, including folding in stiffly beaten egg whites or adding chemical leaveners, but the easiest and cheapest solution is to use a liquid loaded with air to make the dough. Soda-raised dumplings have been a trick of home cooks for at least a hundred years. This recipe for matzah balls, the dumplings essential to Jewish-style chicken soup, is a classic.

½ cup matzah meal

1 egg

3 tablespoons seltzer or ginger ale, any type, purchased or homemade

1 tablespoon minced fresh dillweed

1 teaspoon canola oil

½ teaspoon salt

¼ teaspoon freshly ground white pepper

Pinch of garlic powder

2 egg whites

12 DUMPLINGS

1. Combine the matzah meal, egg, seltzer, dill, oil, salt, pepper, and garlic powder in a bowl, and stir to blend. Beat the egg whites to a soft peak in a separate clean bowl. Fold the whites into the matzah mixture, cover, and refrigerate for 30 minutes.

2. Bring a large pot of salted water to a boil.

3. Wet your hands to keep the dough from sticking to you, and shape the dough into 1-inch balls. Drop into the boiling water, cover, and simmer until they are puffed and tender, about 50 minutes. Remove the dumplings with a slotted spoon. Serve in chicken soup. To store, pack the matzah balls in a freezer-safe container, and ladle enough cooking liquid into the container to cover them. They'll keep in this manner in the freezer for up to 4 months.

Cola Fruit Cupcakes, page 304

CHAPTER TEN

Sweet Desserts

$\mathcal{A}$ nice, tall glass of ice-cold soda is already a sweet, refreshing treat, so turning it into dessert is more a fulfillment than a transformation. Soda pop manufacturers began to publish recipes using their products at the dawn of the twentieth century. But they didn't get into full swing until after World War II. The earliest print references to Coca-Cola cake are from the mid-1950s, and the 7UP Company began publishing recipes for various 7UP cakes in 1957, claiming that the bubbles in their soda made cakes lighter and airier.

In most cake recipes the carbonation in the soda doesn't have a large effect. Soda cakes are by and large delicious, but not really lighter than cakes made with still liquids. The aeration of a cake depends far more on the balance of baking soda and baking powder in the recipe than it does on which type of liquid is used. The one possible exception is pound cake: Traditional pound cakes do not contain any chemical leaveners and are consequently quite dense. Those made with carbonated drinks are lighter, which could be a factor of the carbonation, or it could be that the addition of soda replaces some of the eggs in the recipe, and thereby lightens the result.

The favorite traditions for soft drink cakes centers in the South, probably because several of the most famous commercial soft drinks originated there. In Southern families, soft drink cakes are often talked about fondly as family recipes, taking center stage at special celebrations or for Sunday dinner.

In addition to cakes, soft drinks can be turned into cheesecakes, cream pies, short cakes, biscuits, dessert sauces, frozen desserts, puddings, custards, and candies. I even have a recipe for soda pop soufflé.

ginger ale pound cake

This takeoff of the classic 7UP pound cake is an old standby throughout the South; it is also one of the easiest (no sifting needed) and most delicious pound cakes you are likely to encounter. Subtly scented with ginger and amazingly rich and delicate, it's not as heavy as a traditional pound cake, being slightly lightened by the carbonation of the ginger ale and by the replacement of some egg with soda.

1½ cups (3 sticks) unsalted butter, at room temperature

2½ cups sugar

1 teaspoon vanilla extract

5 eggs

3 cups flour

½ cup finely chopped candied ginger

1 cup ginger ale, any type, purchased or homemade

12 SERVINGS

1. Preheat the oven to 325°F. Coat a nonstick 10-inch Bundt or tube pan with vegetable cooking spray; set aside.

2. Beat the butter and sugar in a large bowl with an electric mixer until fluffy and smooth. Beat in the vanilla. Add the eggs one at a time, beating well after each addition, scraping the bowl as needed. Gradually beat in the flour. The batter will be very thick. Add the candied ginger and ginger ale, stirring just until incorporated.

3. Scrape the batter into the prepared pan and bake about 1 hour 15 minutes, until a tester inserted into the cake comes out with just a few moist crumbs clinging to it. If the cake is browning too much, cover it loosely with foil for the last 30 minutes of baking.

4. Let the cake cool in its pan on a rack until the pan is cool enough to handle. Then invert the cake onto the rack, removing the pan. Let cool to room temperature.

lemon-lime cheesecake

The lightness of this simple cheesecake is guaranteed by an aeration of soda and long, gentle baking that melts the cream cheese into a silken mousse. Cheesecakes are custards made from fresh cheese instead of milk. Like all custards, they can become dry and grainy if overbaked or baked at too high a temperature. If you keep the oven temperature at 200°F, very close to the setting temperature of the custard, no part of this cheesecake can possibly overcook. Its texture is creamy from side to side. It is very rich, so serve in slim slices.

¼ cup cookie crumbs, such as graham cracker, lemon cookies, or vanilla cookies

2 pounds cream cheese, at room temperature

1 cup sugar

½ cup Four-Citrus Bubbly (page 169) or purchased lemon-lime soda

Finely grated zest and juice of 1 lemon

Finely grated zest and juice of 1 lime

2 teaspoons vanilla extract

5 eggs

16 SERVINGS

---

1. Preheat the oven to 200°F. Coat the inside of a 3-quart soufflé dish thoroughly with vegetable cooking spray and dust with the cookie crumbs. Tap out any excess. Set aside.

---

2. Beat the cream cheese in a large bowl with an electric mixer or a heavy wooden spoon until creamy. Add the sugar and continue beating until thoroughly incorporated. Slowly mix in the soda, lemon zest and juice, lime zest and juice, and the vanilla, scraping the sides of the bowl as necessary to make sure that the batter stays absolutely smooth. Add the eggs, and beat just until blended. Do not overmix.

3. Pour the batter into the prepared soufflé dish and bake for 6 to 8 hours (it's fine to bake this cake while you sleep), until the top is set and a tester inserted in the center comes out clean.

4. Let the cake cool to room temperature in its pan on a rack. Cover with a sheet of plastic wrap or wax paper, and set a plate upside down over it. Invert, turning the cake out onto the plate. Remove the pan, and refrigerate the cake upside down for at least 1 hour, and for up 12 hours.

5. Set a serving plate upside down on the cheesecake. Invert, turning the cake right side up onto the serving plate. Remove the top plate and the paper. Cut with a long, sharp knife (dip the knife in warm water to prevent it from sticking). The cake can be stored tightly covered in the refrigerator for up to 5 days.

chocolate root beer cheesecake

I don't get it. Peanut butter and chocolate is an inspired combination, and coffee and chocolate is so commonplace as to warrant its own moniker — any mocha lovers in the house? So why not root beer and chocolate? The flavors are equally dark and complex, tangy and rich, sparkling and creamy. Once you taste them together in this velvety concoction you will be asking the same question. Like the Lemon-Lime Cheesecake (page 200), this cheesecake bakes very slowly, so slowly that you can bake it while you sleep. Stick it in the oven when you are ready to retire, and 6 to 8 hours later you will awake refreshed, with a finished cheesecake ready to do your bidding.

½ cup unsweetened cocoa powder

¾ cup root beer, any type, purchased or homemade

4 ounces semisweet chocolate, broken into pieces

1½ pounds cream cheese, at room temperature

1¼ cups sugar

2 teaspoons vanilla extract

5 eggs

16 SERVINGS

1. Preheat the oven to 200°F. Coat the inside of a 3-quart soufflé dish thoroughly with vegetable cooking spray and dust with ¼ cup of the cocoa powder. Tap out any excess. Set aside.

2. Combine the remaining ¼ cup cocoa powder and the root beer in a small saucepan over medium-high heat. Bring to a boil, then remove from the heat and immediately stir in the chocolate. Continue stirring until the chocolate is melted. Set aside.

3. Beat the cream cheese in a large bowl with an electric mixer or a heavy wooden spoon until creamy. Add the sugar and continue beating until thoroughly incorporated. Slowly mix in the root beer–chocolate mixture and the vanilla, scraping the sides of the bowl as necessary to make sure that the batter stays absolutely smooth. Add the eggs, and beat just until blended. Do not overmix.

4. Pour the batter into the prepared soufflé dish and bake for 6 to 8 hours (it's fine to bake this cake while you sleep), until the top is set and a tester inserted in the center comes out clean.

5. Let the cake cool to room temperature in its pan on a rack. Cover with a sheet of plastic wrap or wax paper, and set a plate upside down over it. Invert, turning the cake out onto the plate. Remove the pan, and refrigerate the cake upside down for at least 1 hour, and for up to 12 hours.

6. Set a serving plate upside down on the cheesecake. Invert, turning the cake right side up onto the serving plate. Remove the top plate and the paper. Cut with a long, sharp knife dipped in warm water to prevent it from sticking. The cake can be stored tightly covered in the refrigerator for up to 5 days.

chocolate cola cake

Leavening cakes with soda pop became popular in the 1950s. Countless recipes appeared in ladies' magazines, local newspapers, and booklets put out by the soda companies. The first pop cakes were from-scratch pound cakes and butter cakes, but by the end of the decade, box-mix cake recipes, in which brand-name soda replaced the milk or water, took over. This is a classic chocolate cake in the original from-scratch tradition. It is baked in a Bundt or tube pan and has a cream cheese cola icing drizzled over the top.

14 tablespoons (1¾ sticks) unsalted butter, cut into pieces

3 ounces unsweetened chocolate, broken into large pieces

1½ cups firmly packed dark brown sugar

1 teaspoon vanilla extract

3 eggs

1 teaspoon baking soda

2¼ cups flour

1 cup Natural Cola (page 104) or purchased cola

Cream Cheese Cola Icing (recipe follows)

12 SERVINGS

1. Preheat the oven to 350°F. Spray a 10-inch nonstick Bundt or tube pan with vegetable cooking spray; set aside.

2. Warm the butter in a large saucepan over medium heat. When it's melted, add the chocolate and remove from the heat. Stir until the chocolate is melted. Mix in the sugar, vanilla, and eggs. Add the baking soda in pinches, stirring well after each addition. Let sit for 1 minute, then add the flour and beat until all of the flour has been well incorporated and the batter is thick. Stir in the cola.

3. Scrape the batter into the prepared pan and bake for 35 to 40 minutes, until a tester inserted into the cake comes out clean.

4. Let the cake cool in its pan on a rack for 10 minutes, then set another rack over it, invert, and turn the cake out of its pan. Let cool to room temperature. Drizzle with the icing.

cream cheese cola icing

¼ cup Natural Cola (page 104) or purchased cola

1 teaspoon vanilla extract

2 tablespoons butter

1 (8-ounce) package cream cheese or light cream cheese, at room temperature

1 cup confectioners' sugar

1. Bring the cola to a boil in a small saucepan. Remove from the heat, add the vanilla and butter, and stir until the butter melts. Set aside to cool to room temperature.

2. Combine the cream cheese and sugar in a bowl and beat until creamy and smooth. Beat in the cooled cola mixture to form a thin, pourable icing. If the icing is too thin, refrigerate it until it achieves the consistency of heavy cream.

soda-pop granita

Granita is a semifrozen dessert popular in Sicily, made by freezing sweetened flavored water. In the States it is usually known as Italian ice. Granita is similar to sorbet but differs by being still-frozen, so that the ice crystals remain big enough to melt separately on the tongue, giving the eater a sensation of intense flavor washed away by ice-cold water. Usually recipes for granitas start with preparing a flavor base, but if you have soda, you're already there. All you have to do is freeze, stir, and eat.

2 cups soda, any type, purchased or homemade

2 tablespoons fruit vinegar, such as apple cider or raspberry

Pinch of salt

4 SERVINGS

Combine the soda, vinegar, and salt in a shallow pan. Stir until the carbonation subsides, then set in the freezer. After 1 hour, stir the ice crystals forming at the edge of the pan into the more liquid portions. Continue to freeze, stirring every 45 minutes, until the whole mixture is a firm slush, about 3 hours. Scrape into dessert dishes or small wine glasses, and serve immediately, with small spoons.

ginger ale gingerbread

There are countless recipes for gingerbread, ranging from confection to cookie to cake. It is my belief that if you are going to make gingerbread, you shouldn't waste your time with the delicate or the mild. You should dive in with all taste buds exposed and go for the spice. In this recipe a triple shot of ginger (from dried ginger, fresh ginger, and ginger ale) is reinforced with an army of aromatics — cinnamon, clove, mustard, and black pepper. The flavor is incendiary and delicious, and the texture of the cake is quite light and so moist that the crumbs will get stuck on your fork.

2½ cups flour

2 teaspoons baking soda

1 teaspoon ground cinnamon

1 teaspoon ground ginger

½ teaspoon ground cloves

½ teaspoon dried mustard

½ teaspoon freshly ground black pepper

½ teaspoon salt

½ cup (1 stick) unsalted butter, cut into pieces, softened

2 tablespoons grated fresh gingerroot

½ cup firmly packed light brown sugar

2 eggs

1 cup light molasses

1¼ cups ginger ale, any type, purchased or homemade

9 SERVINGS

1. Preheat the oven to 375°F. Coat a 9-inch square baking pan with vegetable cooking spray; set aside.

2. Sift the flour, baking soda, cinnamon, ground ginger, cloves, mustard, pepper, and salt into a bowl. Set aside.

3. Beat the butter in a large bowl with an electric mixer until creamy. Add the fresh ginger and the sugar and beat for 1 minute, scraping the bowl as needed to keep the mixture smooth. Add the eggs one at a time, beating well after each addition. Add the molasses, and beat just long enough to mix completely.

4. Heat the ginger ale in a small saucepan over high heat until boiling. Add the sifted flour mixture in three parts and the ginger ale in two parts to the batter, alternating, and beating continuously at low speed.

5. Scrape the batter into the prepared pan and bake for 40 to 45 minutes, until the cake is springy and a tester inserted in the center comes out with just a few crumbs clinging to it.

6. Let the cake cool in its pan on a rack for 10 minutes. Then invert the cake onto the rack, removing the pan. Serve warm or cooled, cut into 3-inch squares.

grapefruit quinine cake with zesty glaze

Grapefruit peel and quinine tonic both have a bitter cast that vibrates relentlessly against the natural sweetness in this cake batter, producing a provocative bitter-sweet sensation. Although any granulated sugar will work in this recipe, I prefer the coarse texture of raw sugar, because it aerates the butter better than conventionally granulated sugar, and gives this cake an exceptional lightness for a pound cake. As with all soda-infused pound cakes, the natural carbonation of the liquid makes chemical leaveners unnecessary — thereby eliminating the need for sifting your dry ingredients.

1½ cups (3 sticks) unsalted butter, softened

2½ cups sugar, preferably raw

1 teaspoon vanilla extract

5 eggs

3 cups flour

¾ cup carbonated Homemade Tonic (page 166) or purchased tonic water

¼ cup grapefruit juice

2 tablespoons finely grated grapefruit zest

½ cup confectioners' sugar (optional)

12 SERVINGS

---

1. Preheat the oven to 325°F. Coat a nonstick 10-inch Bundt or tube pan with vegetable cooking spray; set aside.

---

2. Beat the butter and sugar in a large bowl with an electric mixer until fluffy and smooth. Beat in the vanilla. Add the eggs one at a time, beating well after each addition, scraping the bowl as needed. Gradually beat in the flour. The batter will be very thick. Stir in the tonic and grapefruit juice, and beat just until the batter is smooth. Do not overmix. Stir in the grapefruit zest just until well distributed.

3. Scrape the batter into the prepared pan and bake about 1 hour 15 minutes, until a tester inserted into the cake comes out with just a few moist crumbs clinging to it. If the cake is browning too much, cover it loosely with foil for the last 30 minutes of baking.

4. Let the cake cool in its pan on a rack until the pan is cool enough to handle. Then invert the cake onto the rack, removing the pan. Let cool to room temperature. Dust with confectioners' sugar (if using).

orange soda sorbet

Sorbet and sherbet *are different words for a similar thing: a sweet ice, frozen to minimize the formation of crystals. Sorbet is smooth and creamy, like ice cream, but without the fat. There are several ways to keep ice crystals from forming and ensure creaminess. For this recipe I use beaten egg whites and the carbonation of orange soda to diminish crystallization. Then I let the ice freeze solid and purée it in a food processor to smooth away any iciness. It's simple and delicious, and it doesn't require an ice cream machine.*

2 cups Original Orange Crush (page 66) or purchased orange soda

1 teaspoon freshly squeezed lemon juice

1 egg white

4 SERVINGS

Note: There is a slight risk of salmonella or other food-borne illness when using raw eggs. Exercise caution with people whose immune systems might be compromised.

Combine the orange soda and lemon juice in a shallow pan. Beat the egg white until frothy and then mix it into the soda mixture. Set the pan in the freezer and freeze until solid, 4 hours or longer. Cut into cubes, and purée in a food processor until creamy. This sorbet will keep in a tightly closed container in the freezer for up to 1 week. If the mixture should become solid, purée it again before serving.

brown sugar pecan cake with root beer frosting

This three-layer extravagance is suitable for the most special occasion: the birth of your firstborn, your third and final wedding, your one hundredth birthday. It starts with three big layers of brown sugar chocolate cake enriched with root beer and chopped pecans. The cake layers get stacked with chocolate root beer frosting, and huge peaks of more frosting top the stack. I prefer to leave the sides bare, like you would a German chocolate cake, which this cake resembles in appearance and flavor.

2 cups cake flour

1 teaspoon baking powder

½ teaspoon baking soda

½ teaspoon salt

1 cup (2 sticks) unsalted butter, cut into pieces, softened

2 cups light brown sugar

4 eggs, separated

1 teaspoon vanilla extract

4 ounces semisweet chocolate, broken into pieces and melted

1½ cups root beer, any type, purchased or homemade

2 cups finely chopped pecans

Root Beer Frosting (recipe follows)

12 SERVINGS

1. Preheat the oven to 350°F. Coat three 9-inch round layer pans with vegetable cooking spray; set aside.

2. Combine the cake flour, baking powder, baking soda, and salt in a medium bowl, and stir to blend. Set aside.

3. Cream the butter and sugar in a large bowl with an electric mixer until fluffy. Beat in the egg yolks, followed by the vanilla and the melted chocolate. Add the flour mixture in three parts and the root beer in two parts to the batter, alternating, and mixing well after each addition. Stir in the pecans.

4. Beat the egg whites in a separate bowl until they form firm peaks. Fold the whites into the batter in three parts.

5. Scrape the batter into the prepared pans and bake for about 30 minutes, until a tester inserted into the center comes out with just a moist crumb clinging to it.

6. Let the cakes cool in their pans on a rack for 15 minutes. Then invert the cakes onto the rack, removing the pans. Let cool completely, then assemble the cake, spreading frosting in between the layers and on top.

///

root beer frosting

¾ cup root beer, any type, purchased or homemade

⅓ cup unsweetened cocoa powder

2 teaspoons vanilla

¾ cup (1½ sticks) butter, cut into pieces, slightly softened

5 cups (1½ pounds) confectioners' sugar

Combine the root beer and cocoa in a small saucepan, and stir until the cocoa is thoroughly moistened. Bring to boil over high heat, and let boil until the mixture is reduced by half. Remove from the heat, stir in the vanilla, and let cool for 20 minutes. Add the butter and mix until smooth. Beat the sugar into the frosting until the mixture is smooth and creamy.

///

root beer float double cupcakes

6 SERVINGS

Follow the recipe for Brown Sugar Pecan Cake, baking the batter in two 12-cup cupcake tins for about 20 minutes. To assemble, remove the tops from half the cupcakes. Spread 2 tablespoons Root Beer Frosting on top of each topless cupcake, and layer a whole cupcake on top of it. Dollop a peak of frosting on top of each stacked cupcake. Insert a straw in each cake for decoration. Save the leftover cupcake tops for a snack.

chocolate cola pudding cake

Pudding cakes are a definitively American, decidedly homey dessert, in which a cake batter (in this case rich, fudgy chocolate) is topped with some sort of syrup (in this case one made with cocoa and cola) and then baked. In the alchemy of the oven, the cake rises up through the syrup. Or maybe it's the syrup that sinks down through the cake. At any rate, the exchange produces a moist brownielike cake resting in a pool of chocolate pudding. To serve it, you dish out some cake with its pudding underlayment, and you eat it with a spoon.

1 cup flour

1 cup sugar

½ cup unsweetened cocoa powder

2 teaspoons baking powder

½ teaspoon baking soda

¼ teaspoon salt

   Pinch of ground cinnamon

½ cup milk

¼ cup vegetable oil

1 teaspoon vanilla extract

1 teaspoon rum extract

¾ cup Natural Cola (page 104) or purchased cola

½ cup dark brown sugar

8 SERVINGS

1. Preheat the oven to 350°F. Coat a 9-inch square baking pan with vegetable cooking spray; set aside.

2. Combine the flour, ¾ cup of the sugar, ¼ cup of the cocoa, and the baking powder, baking soda, salt, and cinnamon in a bowl, and mix well. Add the milk, oil, vanilla, and rum extract, and mix into a thick batter. Spread the batter evenly in the prepared pan. Sprinkle the top with the remaining ¼ cup sugar and ¼ cup cocoa.

3. Combine the cola and brown sugar in a small saucepan, and bring to a simmer over medium heat, stirring until the sugar dissolves. Pour the syrup over the cake.

4. Bake the cake for 30 minutes. The cake will be set around the sides, and the top will be very loose and bubbly. Let the cake cool in its pan on a rack for 10 minutes or more. Slice or scoop to serve.

vanilla cream soda bread

Irish soda bread, the world-famous doorstop-size scone, manages to be simultaneously dense and light, a preternatural culinary feat if there ever was one. This rendition emphasizes the light side by using a combination of vanilla soda and yogurt for its liquid. Both are acidic, helping to break down the dough's gluten, a protein that increases toughness/chewiness in baked goods.

2 cups flour

2 teaspoons baking powder

1 teaspoon baking soda

½ teaspoon salt

4 tablespoons (½ stick) cold unsalted butter, cut into small pieces

1 cup golden raisins, coarsely chopped

1 egg, beaten

¼ cup plain lowfat yogurt

¾ cup Plain Delicious Cream Soda (page 216) or purchased cream soda

1 teaspoon vanilla extract

1 tablespoon melted butter

1 tablespoon vanilla sugar or granulated sugar

Butter for serving (optional)

8 SERVINGS

1. Preheat the oven to 375°F. Spray a loaf pan with vegetable cooking spray; set aside.

2. Combine the flour, baking powder, baking soda, and salt in a large bowl, and mix well. Cut in the butter using your fingers, a fork, or a food processor until the mixture has the texture of coarse crumbs. Stir in the raisins.

3. Combine the egg, yogurt, cream soda, and vanilla in a separate small bowl, and mix well. Add the yogurt mixture to the flour mixture and mix just enough to form a soft, cohesive dough; do not overmix. Scrape the dough onto a floured surface and knead lightly into a smooth ball. Ease into the prepared loaf pan and score the top with a sharp knife. Brush the top with melted butter and sprinkle with vanilla sugar. Bake about 45 minutes, until puffed and brown.

4. Let the bread cool in its pan on a rack for 15 minutes. Then remove from the pan and let cool to edible temperature. Serve in slices (preferably while still warm) with butter, if desired.

cola fruit cupcakes
with chocolate cola icing

Fruitcake-phobes take heed: you can stop your sniggering and drop the jokes. I offer these cute, spicy fruit cupcakes peaked with chocolate cola frosting to banish forever the fruitcake's leaden image. Chock-full of nuts and dried fruit (none of those cloying candied citron bits), these cakes are opulent little confections. Make them for a special dessert or to give as little gifts. They freeze excellently before being frosted, and will even stay fresh in the refrigerator for several weeks if well wrapped.

4 tablespoons (½ stick) unsalted butter, cut into pieces

½ cup dark brown sugar

2 teaspoons ground ginger

1 teaspoon ground cinnamon

¼ teaspoon ground cloves

Pinch of salt

1 egg, lightly beaten

1 teaspoon baking soda

1¼ cups flour

⅔ cup Natural Cola (page 104) or Medjool Cola (page 106) or purchased cola or Dr Pepper

2 cups chopped dried fruit (any variety)

1 cup chopped nuts (any type)

Chocolate Cola Icing (recipe follows)

Sprinkles to decorate (optional)

12 SERVINGS

1. Preheat the oven to 350°F. Coat a 12-cup muffin tin with vegetable cooking spray or line with paper liners; set aside.

2. Melt the butter in a large saucepan over medium heat, stirring occasionally. Remove from the heat, pour into a bowl, and stir in the sugar, ginger, cinnamon, cloves, salt, and egg. Add the baking soda in pinches, breaking up any lumps with your fingers. Stir thoroughly. Stir in the flour just until well blended. Stir in the cola, followed by the dried fruit and nuts.

3. Spoon the batter into the prepared muffin tin, filling each cup about three-quarters full. Bake for 20 to 30 minutes, until the cupcakes are springy and fully puffed.

4. Let the cakes cool in their pan on a rack for 5 minutes. Then remove the cupcakes from the pan and let cool to room temperature. Ice the cupcakes with the frosting, decorate with sprinkles (if using), and serve.

chocolate cola icing

½ cup (1 stick) unsalted butter, cut into pieces

⅓ cup Natural Cola (page 104) or Medjool Cola (pge 106) or purchased cola or Dr Pepper

¼ cup unsweetened cocoa powder

1 pound confectioners' sugar

1 teaspoon vanilla extract

1. Melt the butter in a small saucepan. Add the cola and cocoa and stir with a small whisk until smooth. Let the mixture cool until it is thick and creamy.

2. Sift the sugar into a large bowl. Pour the chocolate-cola mixture into the sugar and beat with an electric mixer until the icing is smooth and fluffy. Beat in the vanilla.

ginger cream shortcakes

Shortcakes are a cross between pastry and biscuits, which means they are doughier than pastry and fattier and sweeter than biscuits. The trick is to not overwork the dough, because if you do, the shortcakes will be tough. These are shot through with ginger in four ways: the dry ingredients are infused with ground ginger, the wet ingredients with ginger beer and fresh gingerroot, and the whipped cream with candied ginger.

1¾ cups flour, plus more as needed for cutting out the cakes

3 tablespoons sugar

2 teaspoons baking powder

½ teaspoon baking soda

½ teaspoon ground ginger

¼ teaspoon salt

5 tablespoons cold unsalted butter, cut into small pieces

2 eggs

⅓ cup Szechuan Ginger Beer (page 109) or purchased ginger beer

2 tablespoons finely grated, peeled gingerroot

Ginger Whipped Cream (recipe follows)

2 teaspoons chopped candied ginger

6 SERVINGS

---

1. Preheat the oven to 400°F.

---

2. Combine the flour, 2 tablespoons of the sugar, and the baking powder, baking soda, ground ginger, and salt in a large bowl, and mix well. Cut in the butter with a fork or your fingers until the mixture resembles cornmeal.

---

3. Beat the eggs and ginger beer in a small bowl. Remove 1 tablespoon and reserve. Stir the fresh gingerroot into the egg mixture, and then add the egg mixture to the dry ingredients, mixing just enough to form a soft dough. Do not overmix.

4. Pat the dough out on a floured board with floured hands into a rough ½-inch-thick rectangle, about 6 inches by 9 inches. Punch out six 3-inch-wide biscuits with a biscuit cutter and place them on an ungreased sheet pan, about 2 inches apart from one another. Brush the tops with the reserved egg mixture, and sprinkle the remaining 1 tablespoon sugar on top. Bake about 15 minutes, until puffed and golden brown. Transfer to a rack with a spatula, and let cool to room temperature.

5. Cut each shortcake in half horizontally. Sandwich a big dollop of Ginger Whipped Cream between the two halves, and top each cake with another huge dollop of whipped cream. Sprinkle the chopped candied ginger on top.

ginger whipped cream

1 cup heavy cream, chilled

2 tablespoons honey

1 teaspoon vanilla

2 tablespoons chopped candied ginger

Combine the cream, honey, and vanilla in a chilled bowl. Beat with chilled beaters until soft peaks form. Fold in the candied ginger and beat a few more strokes to firm the cream lightly.

lemon-lime chiffon pie

According to a pamphlet put out by the Gold Medal Flour Company in 1955, chiffon pies were popularized at the turn of the twentieth century as "sissy pies." By the 1940s these egg-white-lightened unbaked mousses, set with gelatin and presented in a prebaked piecrust, were the rage, so much so that they rated their own section in the 1943 edition of Joy of Cooking. *This recipe is in that tradition. It is flavored with lemon and lime juices, and of course lemon-lime soda.*

4 eggs, separated

½ cup sugar

Pinch of salt

2 tablespoons lemon juice

2 tablespoons lime juice

2 teaspoons unflavored powdered gelatin

⅓ cup Four-Citrus Bubbly (page 169) or purchased lemon-lime soda

1 prebaked 9-inch piecrust

Sweetened whipped cream for garnish (optional)

Lemon and lime zest, julienned, for garnish (optional)

8 SERVINGS

Note: There is a slight risk of salmonella or other food-borne illness when using raw eggs. Exercise caution with people whose immune systems might be compromised.

1. Combine the egg yolks, ¼ cup of the sugar, and salt in the top of a double boiler (or a metal mixing bowl that can fit snugly over a pot of simmering water), and beat until fluffy. Mix in the lemon and lime juices and set over simmering water. Cook, mixing with a whisk, until the mixture thickens enough to coat a spoon, about 8 minutes.

2. Meanwhile, sprinkle the gelatin over the lemon-lime soda in a bowl, and set aside until the gelatin dissolves.

3. Remove the pan with the yolk mixture from the double boiler and add the gelatin mixture, stirring until thoroughly incorporated. Set the pan in a large bowl of ice water and stir with a rubber spatula until the mixtures cools to room temperature. Do not allow it to get so cold that the gelatin begins to set.

4. While the yolk mixture is cooling, beat the egg whites in a separate bowl until foamy, using an electric mixer with a whip attachment or by hand with a balloon whisk. Gradually add the remaining ¼ cup sugar, and beat until the whites are thick and glossy.

5. Stir one-third of the beaten whites into the yolk mixture to lighten it, then carefully fold in the remaining whites in two batches. Pour the batter into the prebaked pie shell and smooth the top. Chill until set, at least 2 hours. Serve garnished with whipped cream and zest, if desired.

lemon-lime berries
in rosemary syrup

Dessert doesn't have to be saturated with fat or gilded with sugar to be killer. This one slays with sophistication and surprise. Plus it's so simple — lemon-lime soda is reduced to a concentrated citrus syrup (no added sugar needed) that is brightened with a drop of lemon juice and a fragrant influx of rosemary leaves. I know what you're thinking: rosemary goes with pork, not with berries. But think again. Rosemary shares aromatics with cinnamon, cardamom, and nutmeg, but unlike those spices it has a piney, resinous quality that is wonderful with citrus. That's the surprise. Once the syrup is made, all you do is toss it with the berries and serve it as is, or over ice cream, or with cookies, or with a slice of plain cake, or in a sundae, or on shortcake . . . stop me, please.

2 cups Four-Citrus Bubbly (page 169) or purchased lemon-lime soda

1 teaspoon lemon juice

1 teaspoon finely chopped fresh rosemary leaves

2 pints assorted berries (blackberries, blueberries, raspberries, or quartered hulled strawberries)

4 SERVINGS

1. Bring the lemon-lime soda to a boil in a small saucepan over medium-high heat. Let boil until reduced to ¾ cup, about 15 minutes. Stir in the lemon juice and rosemary leaves, remove from the heat, and let cool for 30 minutes.

2. Toss the syrup with the berries and refrigerate, covered, for at least several hours, and up to 24 hours.

soda-raised pancakes
with root beer sauce

Using carbonated liquid in a pancake batter adds thousands of tiny bubbles to the mix, aerating your flapjacks in the same way as beaten egg whites, except that a splash of soda doesn't require an extra bowl and an extra prep step, and the finished pancakes will be moister and more tender. The pancakes are raised with cream soda, but ginger ale or lemon-lime soda would be equally good options. They are served with syrup made from concentrated root beer.

2 cups flour

1 tablespoon baking powder

Pinch of salt

2 cups Plain Delicious Cream Soda (page 216) or purchased vanilla cream soda

2 eggs, beaten

3 tablespoons butter, melted, plus more for cooking pancakes

Root Beer Sauce (recipe follows)

4 SERVINGS

1. Combine the flour, baking powder, and salt in a large bowl. Add the cream soda and eggs and mix until you have a smooth batter; mix in the melted butter.

2. To cook the pancakes, heat a thin film of butter in a large skillet or on a griddle over medium heat until foamy. For each pancake, pour ¼ cup batter on the hot surface, cook until the top of the cake is covered with bubbles, flip, and cook 1 to 2 minutes longer, until the pancake feels springy. Keep warm while you prepare the rest of the pancakes, greasing the pan with more butter for every batch. Serve with Root Beer Sauce.

//

root beer sauce

1 quart Rooty Toot Root Beer (page 88) or purchased root beer

¼ cup dark brown sugar

Mix the root beer and brown sugar in a small saucepan. Cook over medium-high heat until reduced to 1 cup, stirring frequently near the end of cooking to keep the thickening sauce from scorching.

root beer praline sundaes

Once you get into the groove of whipping up homemade sodas and you have several dozen containers of flavored syrups populating the inner reaches of your fridge, you don't have to use them just for beverages. Here is a recipe for an over-the-top sophisticated sundae. You start by making walnut praline. The praline is broken into pieces and scattered over scoops of ice cream glazed with root beer syrup (cola syrup works too). The sundae is crowned with a peak of whipped cream and droplets of candied orange peel.

½ cup walnuts

½ cup sugar

1 cup Rooty Toot Root Beer Syrup (page 88) or purchased root beer syrup (see Resources)

1 tablespoon butter

Pinch of baking soda

1 quart vanilla or coffee ice cream

½ cup whipped cream

¼ cup candied orange peel

4 SERVINGS

---

1. Preheat the oven to 400°F.

---

2. Scatter the walnuts in a single layer on a small sheet pan and toast in the oven for about 10 minutes, until aromatic and lightly browned.

---

3. Meanwhile, heat the sugar in a medium nonstick skillet over medium-high heat, stirring occasionally with a wooden spoon, until the sugar begins to melt and lump up. Add 2 tablespoons of the root beer syrup. The mixture will start to foam. Stir constantly. The liquid sugar will steadily become thinner and deep amber, and the lumps will start to melt. When almost all the lumps are gone, remove from heat and stir in the butter and baking soda. The liquid will become very foamy for a second. Stir until the foam is no longer streaky, about 10 seconds. Mix in the toasted walnuts and immediately pour the mixture back onto the

sheet pan, scraping as much of the melted sugar from the pan as
possible with your stirring spoon. Allow to set until firm. Torque
the pan and the sheet of caramelized nuts will pop off. Chop into
small pieces.

4. To make sundaes, put a scoop of ice cream into each of four
dessert dishes. Drizzle the remaining root beer syrup (just more
than ¾ cup) over the top, and top with a generous sprinkle of caramelized walnuts. Top each with a dollop of whipped cream and a
spoonful of candied orange peel. Serve immediately.

mocha cappuccino soufflé

Soufflés have a reputation for fragility. True, they are delicate on the palate and watching them wobble vulnerably elicits a mixture of admiration and tenderness, but their reputation for delicacy in the kitchen is profoundly over-stated. Soufflés are thick, sturdy sauces aerated with beaten egg white and then baked. It is possible to mess them up, but highly unlikely. Follow the two rules below and you'll be a master every time.

2–3 tablespoons unsweetened cocoa powder

4 ounces semisweet chocolate, broken into pieces

2 tablespoons butter

3 tablespoons cornstarch

1½ cups coffee soda, any type, purchased or homemade

½ teaspoon vanilla extract

3 eggs, separated

2 egg whites

Pinch of salt

2 tablespoons confectioners' sugar

½ teaspoon ground cinnamon

4 SERVINGS

Soufflé Tips

MAKE YOUR SAUCE REALLY THICK. Thin sauces slip off the network of egg whites as they rise.

DON'T OVERBEAT YOUR EGG WHITES. Stiffly beaten whites are brittle and will collapse. Softly beaten whites that are still moist enough to slump are resilient and stretchy, and therefore less fragile.

1. Preheat the oven to 375°F. Coat the inside of a 6-cup soufflé dish with vegetable cooking spray and dust with cocoa; set aside.

2. Melt the chocolate and butter in the top of a double boiler over simmering water, or in a covered microwave-safe bowl at full power for $1\frac{1}{2}$ minutes. Stir to combine, and set aside.

3. Combine the cornstarch with $\frac{1}{2}$ cup of the coffee soda in a small saucepan, and whisk together. Add the remaining 1 cup soda, stirring until the carbonation subsides and the cornstarch is dispersed in the liquid. Cook over medium heat, stirring constantly, until the mixture thickens and boils. (If it should lump up, remove it from the heat and beat briefly with a whisk.) Remove the syrup from the heat and beat in the chocolate and butter mixture. Stir in the vanilla. Beat in the egg yolks; set aside.

4. Combine the five egg whites and salt in a small bowl, and beat until the whites form soft peaks, using an electric mixer with a whisk attachment or by hand with a balloon whisk. Stir half of the egg whites into the chocolate batter to lighten it, and then fold in the remaining egg whites in two batches.

5. Scrape the batter into the prepared dish, and bake on the middle rack of the oven for about 35 minutes, until puffed at least 1 inch over the rim of the dish.

6. While the soufflé is baking, combine the sugar and cinnamon in a shaker. When the soufflé is puffed, open the oven and quickly sprinkle the top with the cinnamon sugar. Do not remove the soufflé from the oven yet; instead, bake for 10 minutes longer, until the top is brown and a little crispy and the center is still a bit wobbly. Serve immediately.

black cow salted caramels

Salt plus caramel is an innocent ecstasy. The caramel is buttery, bittersweet, and toasty, and the addition of salt heightens everything. Salt and sweet vibrate across the palate, refusing to combine. As soon as you try to pin it down, the sensation changes: salt-sweet-salt-sweet-salt-sweet, setting up a craving that's difficult to stop. These salted caramels have the added flavor dimension of root beer, which contributes its own addictive tang. Fleur de sel is a specialty sea salt that is extremely delicate. If you can't find it (gourmet food stores and high-end supermarkets will have it, as will Internet spice merchants), you can substitute any fine sea salt.

⅓ cup Rooty Toot Root Beer (page 88) or purchased root beer

5 tablespoons unsalted butter, cut into pieces

3 tablespoons heavy cream

1½ cups sugar

¼ cup light molasses

¼ cup water

¾ teaspoon fleur de sel

49 CARAMELS

---

1. Line the bottom and sides of an 8-inch square baking pan with parchment paper or foil, and spray the foil with vegetable cooking spray; set aside.

---

2. Combine the root beer, butter, and cream in a small saucepan. Bring to a simmer over medium heat, then remove from the heat and set aside.

---

3. Combine the sugar, molasses, and water in a heavy saucepan. Bring to a boil over medium-high heat, stirring until the sugar dissolves. Let boil, gently swirling the pan (do not stir), until the syrup is crystal clear, washing any sugar crystals from the inside of the pot with a pastry brush dipped in water.

4. Carefully stir the cream mixture into the boiling syrup; the mixture will bubble vigorously. Let simmer, stirring often, until the liquid reaches 248°F on a candy thermometer, about 12 minutes. At that point the concentration of sugar will be about 87 percent, and a drop of the mixture dribbled into a glass of cold water will form a ball that is firm enough to lift up but flexible enough to flatten between your fingers. Stir in the fleur de sel and immediately pour the mixture into the prepared baking pan. Let cool until the surface is firm, about 30 minutes. Cut into approximate 1-inch squares (a 7×7 grid), and wrap each piece in a 4-inch square of wax paper or cellophane, twisting the ends to close.

sparkling honey ginger gelatin

Gelatin is matter in transition — a solid (gelatin powder) that becomes fluid (dissolved in soda) that becomes solid (chilled in the fridge) that becomes fluid (melts in the mouth), and all for our pleasure. The process seems more like magic than cooking. By making a gelled dessert using unflavored gelatin, you control the amount of sugar, and by using something carbonated for your liquid, you get the added sensual charge of sipping on a carbonated solid.

2 cups Szechuan Ginger Beer (page 109) or purchased ginger beer

2 (1-ounce) envelopes unflavored gelatin

¼ cup honey

4 SERVINGS

1. Pour ½ cup of the ginger beer into a large bowl and sprinkle the gelatin over it. Set aside until the gelatin powder softens; it will not dissolve.

2. Bring 1½ cups ginger beer to a boil. Add the honey, stirring until it dissolves. Pour the honeyed beer into the gelatin mixture; stir gently until the gelatin dissolves and the liquid is clear, about 5 minutes. Divide the mixture among four wine glasses and refrigerate until firm, about 3 hours.

resources

Soda-making equipment, such as reusable bottles, bottle caps, digital thermometers, and electronic scales are available at homebrew stores. My local brew store, Keystone Home Brew, also sells online at http://keystonehomebrew.com. You can buy soda siphons at any cookware store and in the cookware departments of most department stores.

Well-stocked supermarkets and all-purpose online shopping resources, such as Amazon, are the best (and least expensive) sources for unusual sweeteners (turbinado, demerara, and muscovado sugars, agave syrup), fine sea salt or fleur de sel, and nutritional extracts (gingko biloba and vitamin and mineral supplements).

Asian grocery stores or online Asian food sites are the most economical sources for Asian ingredients like coconut milk, coconut cream, lemongrass, star anise, Szechwan peppercorns, and tamarind paste. Many well-stocked supermarkets will also have these ingredients, but usually at higher prices.

There are many aromatherapy sources for essential oils. Most of these products are not recommended for internal consumption, so it is important to look for edible or food-grade oils for soda making. Food-grade oils are mostly sold industrially, but you can find a good selection at Starwest Botanicals (www.starwest-botanicals.com), Atlantic Spice Company (www.atlanticspice.com), or Lorann Oils (www.lorannoils.com).

Dried bark and roots for making root beers are available at homebrew stores. Starwest Botanicals (www.starwest-botanicals.com) and Herbs of Mexico — Herb Emporium (https://herbsofmexico.com) are comprehensive online sources for all sorts of hard-to-find herbs, blossoms, barks, and roots, including lavender and chamomile flowers, cinchona bark, and sumac and hawthorn berries.

Flavoring agents like cola or root beer syrups and citric acid (also called vitamin C powder or sour salt) are sold in many supermarkets, homebrewing stores, and at online grocery sites, such as Natural Foods Inc. (www.bulkfoods.com).

Maltodextrin and gum arabic, used to enhance the mouthfeel of some sodas, are sold at many homebrew stores, and are available online at WillPowder (http://willpowder.net).

Brewing yeast is available at homebrew stores, such as Keystone Home Brew (http://keystonehomebrew.com).

Kombucha starter cultures are available from several online sources, such as Kombucha America (http://kombuchaamerica.com) and Cultures for Health (http://culturesforhealth.com).

index

Page numbers in *italics* indicate photos or illustrations; page numbers in **bold** indicate charts.

Other Storey Titles
You Will Enjoy

✳✳✳

Cookie Craft, by Valerie Peterson & Janice Fryer.
Clear instruction, practical methods, and all the tips and tricks for
beautifully decorated special occasion cookies.
168 pages. Hardcover. ISBN 978-1-58017-694-1.

Cordials from Your Kitchen, by Pattie Vargas & Rich Gulling.
More than 100 easy cordial recipes for delicious, elegant liqueurs for
entertaining or gift giving.
176 pages. Paper. ISBN 978-0-88266-986-1.

The Donut Book, by Sally Levitt Steinberg.
A deliciously engaging book that explores the nostalgia and history of
the donut.
192 pages. Paper. ISBN 978-1-58017-548-7.

Healing Tonics, by Jeanine Pollak.
Tasty, health-promoting recipes for drinks that can help boost mental
clarity, increase stamina, aid digestion, support heart health, and more.
160 pages. Paper. ISBN 978-1-58017-240-0.

Homemade Root Beer, Soda & Pop, by Stephen Cresswell.
More then 60 traditional and modern recipes for fabulous, fizzy
creations.
128 pages. Paper. ISBN 978-1-58017-052-9.

Raw Energy, by Stephanie Tourles.
More than 100 recipes for delicious raw snacks: unprocessed, uncooked,
simple, and pure.
272 pages. Paper. ISBN 978-1-60342-467-7.

A World of Cake, by Krystina Castella.
More than 150 recipes, accompanied by mouthwatering photographs
and fascinating historical and cultural facts.
352 pages. Paper with flaps. ISBN 978-1-60342-576-6.

These and other books from Storey Publishing are available
wherever quality books are sold or by calling 1-800-441-5700.
Visit us at www.storey.com.